DATE DUE

Clinical Geropsychology
(PGPS-127)

Pergamon Titles of Related Interest

Goldstein/Hoyer/Monti POLICE AND THE ELDERLY
Tamir COMMUNICATION AND THE AGING PROCESS:
Interaction Throughout the Life Cycle

Related Journals*

EXPERIMENTAL GERONTOLOGY

*Free specimen copies available upon request.

PERGAMON GENERAL PSYCHOLOGY SERIES
EDITORS
Arnold P. Goldstein, *Syracuse University*
Leonard Krasner, *SUNY at Stony Brook*

Clinical Geropsychology
New Directions in Assessment and Treatment

edited by

Peter M. Lewinsohn
and
Linda Teri
University of Oregon

PERGAMON PRESS
New York   Oxford   Toronto   Sydney   Paris   Frankfurt

Pergamon Press Offices:

U.S.A.   Pergamon Press Inc., Maxwell House, Fairview Park,
                    Elmsford, New York 10523, U.S.A.

U.K.   Pergamon Press Ltd., Headington Hill Hall,
                    Oxford OX3 0BW, England

CANADA   Pergamon Press Canada Ltd., Suite 104, 150 Consumers Road,
                    Willowdale, Ontario M2J 1P9, Canada

AUSTRALIA   Pergamon Press (Aust.) Pty. Ltd., P.O. Box 544,
                    Potts Point, NSW 2011, Australia

FRANCE   Pergamon Press SARL, 24 rue des Ecoles,
                    75240 Paris, Cedex 05, France

FEDERAL REPUBLIC   Pergamon Press GmbH, Hammerweg 6,
OF GERMANY   D-6242 Kronberg-Taunus, Federal Republic of Germany

Library of Congress Cataloging in Publication Data
Main entry under title:

  Clinical geropsychology.

  (Pergamon general psychology series ; 127)
  Bibliography: p.
  1. Aged – Mental health – Evaluation.   2. Aged –
Mental health services.   I. Lewinsohn, Peter M.
II. Teri, Linda.   III. Series.   [DNLM: 1. Mental
disorders – In old age.   WT 150 C6404]
RC451.4.A5C53 1983   618.97′689   83-8340
ISBN 0-08-029413-8

Printed in the United States of America

Contents

Preface

Clinical geropsychology is growing in many diverse and exciting ways. We are witnessing the development of new approaches to the assessment and treatment of psychological problems that are uniquely relevant and important to the elderly. As teachers and clinicians, we are excited to learn about these developments and eager to share them with others.

Acting on our enthusiasm, we organized a conference ("Recent Developments in the Clinical Psychology of Aging," June 11–17, 1982, Eugene, Oregon), to which we invited leaders in these new developments to conduct one-day workshops describing their work in sufficient detail so that practitioners could implement the new approach in their own clinical work. To reach a wider audience than the conference allowed, we also asked workshop leaders to summarize their work in chapters for this book.

We greatly appreciate the willingness of Drs. Richard Bootzin, Dolores Gallagher, Boaz Kahana, Eva Kahana, Roger Patterson, Larry Thompson, Judy Zarit, and Steven Zarit to make the results of their work available to a wide audience of practitioners and professionals-in-training. We wish to extend our appreciation to the authors who have contributed their time and energy in the excellent chapters they prepared and in the interesting and stimulating workshops they conducted.

We also wish to extend a large vote of appreciation to those who helped coordinate the conference. For their help throughout the conference: Mary Hecht for her unfailing sense of commitment and timing which frequently "saved the day"; Alice Lachman for her knowledge of how to get things done and her ability to do them; and Wendy Weicker for her cheery disposition and capacity for hard work. For their help during the conference itself, our appreciation is extended to Elizabeth Bramen, Janice Grounds, Melinda Holman, Susan Taylor, Catherine Turner, and Julie Woods. For their help with the production of this book, our thanks go to Terri Baxter for her consistent and excellent typing, Lisa James for her editorial assistance, and Jerome Frank for his support and enthusiasm throughout the process.

Peter M. Lewinsohn
Linda Teri
Eugene, Oregon
March 17, 1983

Introduction

Peter M. Lewinsohn and Linda Teri

The large discrepancy between the mental-health needs of the elderly and the degree to which these needs are being met by the mental-health delivery system has been amply documented (e.g., Zarit, 1980). Persons over the age of 65 constitute 11 percent of the population, and approximately 25 percent of these are said to have psychological problems severe enough to warrant professional attention (Pfeiffer, 1980). Yet, the elderly constitute only 3 percent of the caseload in mental-health clinics (Kramer, Taube, & Redick, 1973) and an even smaller percentage of the caseload of private practitioners (Gottfredson & Dyer, 1978; Marmor, 1975). While there has been a strong overall trend in the mental-health delivery system toward deinstitutionalization, the elderly have not benefited from this development. Indeed, institutional treatment remains the modal treatment for the elderly even though such treatment is recognized as often custodial and less than optimal (Kahn, 1982).

Several explanations may be offered for the underutilization of community mental-health services by the elderly. Lawton (1978) has suggested that the cohort of people currently labeled as "elderly" (those born before 1920) are reluctant to define their problems in psychological terms. Admitting to having psychological problems is perceived by this age group as a sign of weakness. They are more likely to define their problems in physical terms and to consult physicians who typically have neither the time, the interest, nor the expertise to detect the emotional components of many of the physical complaints shown by the elderly. Another possible reason for the underutilization of mental-health services by the elderly is that most mental-health clinics do not organize their services in ways that would be useful to elderly patients, owing to a lack of staff training or to a lack of interest in attracting such clients (Gatz, Smyer, & Lawton, 1980). There is no question that there is indeed a critical shortage of mental-health professionals with adequate training in gerontology (Birren & Renner, 1981; Santos & VandenBos, 1982), and that the attitude of mental-health professionals toward treating the elderly often is pessimistic (Pfeiffer, 1980; Butler, 1969). It is intellectually provoca-

1

tive but sad to realize that all of these problems have been vocally recognized for at least 10 years, and yet very little change has occurred (Cohen & Cooley, 1983).

Another obstacle to providing mental-health services to the elderly is that the field of clinical gerontology is woefully lacking in the knowledge base necessary for adequate understanding, assessment, and treatment of older patients. In examining recent textbooks (e.g., Hussian, 1981; Storandt, Siegler, & Eliase, 1978; Zarit, 1980), one is struck by the dearth of original, age-relevant material (a fact, of course, also noted by the authors of these books). There has been very little systematic concern with adapting specific assessment and treatment procedures for use with the elderly. The case for relevance is typically made by analogy rather than on the basis of empirical findings. With few exceptions, treatment-outcome studies have largely ignored the needs of the elderly and research on the assessment and treatment of age-specific problems is sparse (Riegel, 1973). It could well be that the elderly are not flocking to mental-health clinics or to mental-health professionals because there is, as yet, very little documented evidence that these mental-health professionals have skills of demonstrated value to offer.

Our underlying assumption in organizing this book is that the core of sound clinical assessment and treatment is constituted by empirically based techniques that have been developed and evaluated for specific use with elderly patients. Each chapter is organized around a specific psychological problem of importance for the elderly.

In this focus on specific problems, we are of course revealing our behavioral orientation within which problematic *behavior* is held as the focal concern. Within this orientation, it is assumed that problematic behavior is controlled by the same principles that control other behaviors and that more adaptive patterns of behavior can be taught to supplant maladaptive ones. Behavioral approaches share a concern with first developing a clear definition of the problematic behavior and then identifying the personal and environmental events that surround it. The behavioral orientation also includes a commitment to the empirical validation of treatments. Without downgrading the potential importance of more open-ended therapeutic approaches, it is our belief that time-limited, pinpointed, and structured behavioral approaches may be especially attractive and effective with the elderly. As numerous writers have suggested (e.g., Richards & Thorpe, 1978; MacDonald & Kerr, 1982; Hussian, 1981), the high degree of therapist activity inherent in behavioral approaches may be preferred by the relatively less active older adult and the emphasis on self-control may be particularly relevant.

We are therefore especially gratified to present the work being done by Drs. Richard Bootzin, Dolores Gallagher, Boaz and Eva Kahana, Roger Patterson, Larry Thompson, Steve and Judy Zarit, and their colleagues. We feel that their work constitutes major contributions to the clinical assessment and treatment of the aged. The specific types of problems being addressed (depression, dementia, insomnia, social and daily living skills, and stress reactions) are among the most prevalent and clinically most significant disorders one encounters in working with elderly patients. These problems are also very important vis-à-vis the older person's ability to maintain his or her independence within the community. Each of the chapters is intended to provide in-depth descriptions and guidelines for the assessment and treatment of *specific* clinical problems. Consequently, it is important to recognize briefly some of the *general* problems inherent in providing high-quality services to elderly patients.

In clinical work with the elderly, it is important to recognize that their problems are usually multiple and typically include psychological, physical, and social-environmental components. Thus, for example, an elderly patient may show symptoms of depression; he or she may also be suffering from a physical illness that limits his or her activities; he or she may have a hearing problem; and he or she may also face financial uncertainties and pressure from relatives to move into a nursing home. Because of the multiplicity of problems presented by elderly patients, assessment should always be comprehensive and systematically include the patient's physical health (including nutrition, exercise, illnesses, and medications), intellectual function, general competencies and coping skills, social network and community-support systems, personality traits, as well as their affective and symptomatic status.

The clinical geropsychologist must be aware of the special difficulties in assessing and treating elderly patients. Sensory deficits (such as hearing loss or visual impairments), mobility problems, and general unfamiliarity with psychological tests and related procedures may make assessment and treatment difficult. The current generation of older people has not undergone the socialization to testing or treatment that the younger generation has (Lawton, Whelihan, & Belsky, 1980). Thus, the older patient may not understand the purpose of the psychological evaluation or intervention and may be understandably fearful about the process and outcome. Finally, the assessment procedures may be biased against the elderly because of such factors as being speed-timed and emphasizing stimuli or activities that are unfamiliar to the elderly person. In addition, age-appropriate norms do not exist for most psychological tests.

In clarifying the multidimensional aspect of assessment and treatment with the elderly, the clinician must also recognize the need to incorporate other services as needed. Rarely does the older person (particularly the frail elderly) present a simple or a single salient problem that belongs neatly to one particular profession or discipline. Rather, the interaction of physical, social, and psychological problems tends to be the rule and presents serious challenges and demands to professionals who must deal with them. While it is possible to focus a service primarily on psychological problems, it is important to recognize that one must have access to many other professions and disciplines such as medicine, audiology, and social work.

Clinicians working with elderly patients must also possess special knowledge, professional skills, and attitudes. They must have a broad understanding of the many diverse physical and psychological changes that affect the elderly. They must be familiar with normal aspects of psycho-social-physical aging and have an overview of the developmental features of later life emphasizing "wellness" and the normal changes that affect older persons in order to be able to understand and differentiate them from and understand psychopathological processes. These clinicians must also be aware of the impact of negative events such as social losses, limited economics, restricted mobility, poor intergenerational relationships, criminal victimization, relocation, terminal illness, and social ageism (Butler, 1969). Just as a child's clinical psychologist has to be very familiar with development norms for psychological functions, so too a clinical geropsychologist should be familiar with developmental norms and changes as a function of increased age in order to differentiate pathological symptoms from normal concomitants of aging with accuracy.

Attitudinal factors are also important for successful work with the elderly (Butler, 1969). It is important for clinicians to be aware of the nature and impact of their attitudes and values toward the elderly. Myths and stereotypes can easily interfere with the conduct of objective and adequate assessment, interpretation, and treatment. It is all too common for the clinician to perceive the elderly as unwilling or unable to change, or as not rewarding to work with (Butler, 1969). In addition, it is important for clinicians to be able to accept different goals as reasonable in different situations, depending on the total context. The clinician needs to be thoroughly familiar with resources in the community available to the elderly. Goals for treatment may include preventing problems by helping patients prepare for expected changes; increasing skills and facilitating successful coping; promoting person-environment fit by reducing environmental disruptions or demands; creating environmental supports; reconciling individual expectations to reality; alleviating or removing pathology and restoring the status quo (Zarit, 1980); and remediating "excess disability" (i.e., dysfunction over and above physiological necessity) (Brody, Kleban, Lawton, & Silverman, 1971). In working with the elderly, the clinician must be aware of the variety of goals obtainable and not limit him or herself unrealistically because of preconceived notions or biases about the elderly. It is all too easy to believe that many of the problems of the elderly are irreversible and progressive. To counter this tendency to be more pessimistic and guarded with elderly clients, it is important for clinicians to set realistic yet positive goals and consciously to maintain positive expectations about their intervention plans. The goal is for the clinician to choose objectively from among viable treatment alternatives and to formulate reasonable and constructive goals in spite of the multiplicity of problems shown by elderly patients. For a more detailed discussion of all of the above-mentioned issues, the reader is referred to Birren and Sloane (1980), Busse and Blazer (1980), Poon (1980), and Schaie and Geiwitz (1982).

REFERENCES

Birren, J., & Renner, V. Concepts and criteria of mental health and aging. *American Journal of Orthopsychiatry*, 1981, **51**, 242–254.

Birren, J. E., & Sloane, R. B. *Handbook of mental health and aging*. Englewood Cliffs, N.J.: Prentice-Hall, 1980.

Brody, E., Kleban, M., Lawton, M., & Silverman, H. Excess disabilities of mentally impaired aged: Impact of individualized treatment. *Gerontologist*, 1971, **11**, 124–133.

Busse, E. W., & Blazer, D. *Handbook of geriatric psychiatry*. New York: Van Nostrand Reinhold, 1980.

Butler, R. N. Age-ism: Another form of bigotry. *Gerontologist*, 1969, **9**, 243–246.

Cohen, L. D., & Cooley, S. G. Psychology training programs for direct services and the aging (Status report, 1980). *Professional Psychology*, 1983, in press.

Gatz, M., Smyer, M., & Lawton, M. P. The mental health system and the older adult. In L. W. Poon (Ed.), *Aging in the 1980's*. Washington, D.C.: American Psychological Association, 1980.

Gottfredson, G. D., & Dyer, S. E. Health service providers in psychology. *American Psychologist*, 1978, **33**, 314–338.

Hussian, R. A. *Geriatric psychology: A behavioral perspective*. New York: Van Nostrand Reinhold, 1981.

Kahana, E. A congruence model of person-environment interaction. In P. G. Windley, T. O. Byerts, & F. G. Ernst (Eds.), *Theory development in environment and aging*. Washington, D.C.: Gerontological Society, 1975.

Kahn, R. L. *Psychology and the older adult: Services and settings*. Washington, D.C.: American Psychological Association, 1982.

Kramer, M., Taube, C. A., & Redick, R. W. Patterns of use of psychiatric facilities by the aged: Past, present, and future. In C. Eisdorfer & M. P. Lawton (Eds.), *The psychology of adult development and aging*. Washington, D.C.: American Psychological Association, 1973.

Lawton, M. P. Clinical geropsychology: Problems and prospects. In *Master lectures on the psychology of aging*. Washington, D.C.: American Psychological Association, 1979. (Originally presented at the meeting of the American Psychological Association, Toronto, August 1978.)

Lawton, M. P., Whelihan, W. M., & Belsky, J. K. *Handbook of mental health and aging*. Englewood Cliffs, N.J.: Prentice-Hall, 1980.

MacDonald, M. L., & Kerr, B. B. *Mental health interventions for the aging. Behavior therapy with the aging*. New York: Praeger, 1982.

Marmor, J. *Psychiatrists and their patients: A national study of private psychiatrists*. Washington, D.C.: American Psychiatric Association, 1975.

Moos, R. Conceptualizations of human environments. *American Psychologist*, 1973, **28**, 652–665.

Pfeiffer, E. Psychopathology and social pathology. In J. E. Birren & K. W. Schaie (Eds.), *Handbook of psychology and aging*. New York: Van Nostrand Reinhold, 1977.

Pfeiffer, E. The psychosocial evaluation of the elderly patient. In E. W. Busse & D. G. Blazer (Eds.), *Handbook of geriatric psychiatry*. New York: Van Nostrand Reinhold, 1980.

Poon, L. W. (Ed.). *Aging in the 1980's: Psychological issues*. Washington, D.C.: American Psychological Association, 1980.

Richards, W. S., & Thorpe, G. L. *The clinical psychology of aging: Behavioral approaches to the problems of later life*. New York: Plenum, 1978.

Riegel, K. F. On the history of psychological gerontology. In C. Eisdorfer & M. P. Lawton (Eds.), *The psychology of adult development and aging*. Washington, D.C.: American Psychological Association, 1973.

Santos, J. F., & VandenBos, R. *Psychology and the older adult*. Washington, D.C.: American Psychological Association, 1982.

Schaie, K. W., & Geiwitz, J. *Adult development and aging*. Boston: Little Brown, 1982.

Storandt, M., Siegler, I. C., & Eliase, M. F. (Eds.). *The clinical psychology of aging*. New York: Plenum, 1978.

Zarit, S. H. *Aging and mental disorders: Psychological approaches to assessment and treatment*. New York: Free Press, 1980.

Chapter 1

Depression*

Dolores Gallagher and Larry W. Thompson

INCIDENCE AND PREVALENCE OF CLINICAL DEPRESSION IN OLDER ADULTS

Depression has been identified as one of the most frequent mental disorders in this country (Blumenthal, Butler & Lewis, 1982). Recent epidemiological studies (Vernon & Roberts, 1982; Weissman & Myers, 1978) have shown that the current point prevalence of major depressive disorders ranges between 2 and 5 percent, while lifetime rates between 15 and 20 percent have been found for general adult populations sampled.

Community surveys (e.g., Gaitz, 1977; Lowenthal & Berkman, 1967) have found that the *majority* of elderly respondents reported depressive symptoms, such as sleep and appetite disturbances, blue mood, and pessimistic views of the future. This does not mean, however, that the majority of older persons are clinically depressed. Since the recent advent of more stringent criteria for the diagnosis of this disorder (see DSM-III, American Psychiatric Association, 1980, and the Research Diagnostic Criteria for depression; RDC: Spitzer, Endicott, & Robins, 1978), several other surveys have estimated the true prevalence rate for the depressive syndrome in older adults to vary between 1 and 7 percent with most studies reporting approximately 4 to 6 percent (Blazer & Williams, 1980; Gerner, 1979; Gurland, 1976; Juel-Nielson, 1961; Kay, Beamish, & Roth, 1964; Parsons, 1965).

There are sex differences in the prevalence of depressive disorders in the general population, but exact figures for elders are difficult to ascertain.

*This work was supported in part by grants MH-37196 from the National Institute of Mental Health and AG-01959 from the National Institute of Aging.

Women show higher rates of depression than men in almost all age decades (Silverman, 1968), though sex differences may become progressively less marked after about age 45 (Gurland, 1976). Blazer and Williams (1980), however, have found a ratio of one-third males to two-thirds females for diagnosable clinical depression. Other factors associated with prevalence include: marital status (Vernon & Roberts, 1982); impairment of social and/or economic resources (Hirschfeld & Cross, 1982); social class (in some studies, high social class was associated with less depression in those over age 60 [see Dovenmuehle & McGough, 1970; Schwab, 1976], but not in others [see Simon, 1970]); and poor physical health (see Salzman & Shader, 1979, for review).

IDENTIFYING DEPRESSION: THE NEED FOR MULTIFACETED ASSESSMENT

Definition of Depression

In 1975, when Akiskal and McKinney reviewed 10 extant etiological models for the depressive syndrome, they clearly illustrated that there was no single model with broad support. Because of this diversity, they concluded that depression is most aptly viewed as a "final common pathway" reflecting simultaneous disturbance in a number of domains (e.g., biological, sociological, and psychological). This notion has been incorporated into current diagnostic thinking, as will become evident in the following paragraphs.

In most instances the primary feature of depression is dysphoria, a feeling of being downhearted and blue. Clinical depression, however, should be viewed as a syndrome or cluster of symptoms, not just a *feeling* of blue mood or sadness. Depression involves changes in behaviors and thoughts about oneself in addition to a negative mood state. Certain physical symptoms, such as sleep and appetite disturbance and low energy level, are also usually present. The following features, abstracted from DSM-III and RDC, define an episode of clinical depression for older, as well as younger, persons (see Dessonville et al., 1982, for empirical support of these criteria as applied to elders).

First, duration of two or more weeks must be established. The individual would need to be experiencing several symptoms of depression on a consistent basis for at least that length of time. This will rule out persons with transitory symptoms that are common in the older age groups.

Second, the primary feeling state during this interval must be established. Clear presence of dysphoria is typical. However, older persons often do not label their "down" feelings as depression; they may prefer to describe their predominant mood state as "pessimistic" or "helpless," or there may be little actual mood disturbance reported (Post, 1965). In the latter instance, the person should be asked if pervasive loss of interest or pleasure was noted for at least two weeks; if that was the case, then they would qualify as having met this criterion.

Third, specific inquiry should be made into the following set of symptoms to determine if they were present more or less continuously for the duration of the episode: increased or decreased appetite; increased or decreased need for sleep; loss of energy, fatigability, or tiredness; loss of interest or pleasure in usual activities (including social contact); feelings of self-reproach or excessive guilt; psychomotor retardation or agitation; and complaints or evidence of diminished ability to think or concentrate. Ideas of suicide or actual suicidal behavior should also be asked about directly. The sustained presence of four or more of these symptoms strongly suggests clinical depression.

Fourth, it is useful to inquire about the impact of all of the above on the person's day-to-day functioning. Have social roles been impaired (e.g., poor work performance or inability to carry out domestic responsibilities)? Has the person been referred for mental-health treatment or sought help from anyone because of the current problem? Is medication being used for relief? A clinical level of depression is more likely to be present if day-to-day functioning has become impaired.

Fifth, it is important to rule out other significant problems that are likely causes of the observed symptoms (e.g., health problems; neurological disturbances; and other types of psychopathology, such as bipolar affective illness or alcoholism). This issue of differential diagnosis is particularly salient with elders and will be discussed in greater detail below.

Information obtained from the elderly patient about these five areas must be evaluated to determine if the majority yield positive findings. If duration is greater than two weeks, several physical and/or psychological symptoms have been present for that time, impairment in daily functioning has occurred, and no physiological causes account for the difficulties, then the primary problem is most likely affective in nature. In such a case, a clinical trial of psychosocial treatment and/or medication is warranted.

It should be noted that the symptoms described in the third point above are very specific. There are eight areas covered; other things that one might think of as part of depression (such as feelings of self-pity, inadequacy, excessive worry and concern, or hypochondriacal features) are *not* included as criteria for classification. This is because these eight symptom areas are best able to distinguish true clinical depression from lower levels of distress, or from other psychological problems (Spitzer, Endicott, & Robins, 1978).

General Aging Issues

Older individuals often are less willing to admit to psychological problems and/or have greater difficulty understanding the meaning of specific questions designed to probe their personal life. Thus, some older persons provide information that may seem deliberately vague or tangential, while at the same time the communication process can be hampered by clinicians who lack the experience or the interest required to elicit the appropriate information. Here is an example of misdiagnosis, illustrating some of these problems.

> Mr. M., an 87-year-old male who had lived alone for 20 years following the death of his wife, was finally forced to give up housekeeping and move to a nursing home. This occurred because of gradually weakening visual and auditory skills, accompanied by increased muscular weakness. His memory and other aspects of cognitive functioning were intact. Because he appeared quite apathetic and withdrawn and did not communicate much with the nursing home staff, he was referred for evaluation and treatment of possible depression. He was first interviewed by an inexperienced staff member who decided that Mr. M. was not currently suffering from any diagnosable psychological problem. Later evaluation by a more experienced clinician revealed that Mr. M. was experiencing a major depressive episode, characterized by intense feelings of self-reproach and death fantasies.

Why were two distinctly different conclusions drawn? The first interviewer indicated that she viewed Mr. M.'s severe psychomotor retardation and somatic concerns as general "frailty" due to aging. Also, because he gave vague answers to questions about his feelings, she concluded that there was little evidence of real dysphoria. She attributed Mr. M.'s lack of communication to his having lived alone for 20 years and assumed that few interpersonal demands had been placed on him during that time. The second interviewer, in contrast, found that Mr. M.'s hearing loss was a significant factor in the interview process. She asked questions in a loud, deep voice and occasionally wrote them out, to be sure that he understood the question's intent. Mr. M. then revealed that he had been unable to hear most of the questions asked in the first interview but felt "too bad" to make an issue of it. He claimed that the first interviewer seemed uninterested in him and provided little direction to assist him in answering difficult questions. In general, he felt frustrated and dissatisfied with that interview, and he appreciated having a second opportunity to express himself more clearly.

In the above situation, the first interviewer discounted many of Mr. M.'s symptoms and attributed them to causes other than depression. She reached this conclusion primarily because no strong evidence of dysphoria was obtained when he was questioned about his feelings. Although Mr. M. did acknowledge pervasive loss of interest and pleasure in his usual activities, the interviewer did not interpret this properly as a significant sign of emotional distress. Yet, as noted earlier, elders often mask depressive feelings (Post, 1965), and so a "depressive equivalent," like pervasive low interest (when present), is regarded as having satisfied the diagnostic criteria for dysphoria.

On the other hand, in situations where patients *do* report psychological distress, the *reverse* may also occur. Complaints that typically accompany the aging process may be erroneously interpreted as depressive symptoms, particularly if no careful questioning has been done to determine if there are alternative explanations. This obviously would lead to "false positives" in the diagnostic process (that is, people who are *not* depressed would be misclassified as depressed). An examination of the DSM-III criteria indicates that many of the signs used to classify patients as depressed routinely occur with advancing age. For example, a universal complaint among the elderly is that they are unable to do things as fast as they used to; they frequently report that they are "slowed down." This complaint is often viewed as evidence of psychomotor retardation. Similarly, many elders report a decrease in strength and a decrease in their overall energy level; they complain of fatigue. Healthy elderly also report problems with their sleep and are often aggravated by an inability to rest comfortably in the prone position (Dement, Miles, & Carskadon, 1982). Finally, appetite changes in the elderly can occur for various reasons, such as a decline in taste sensation or lack of funds to purchase and prepare appealing meals.

These similarities between symptoms of depression and normal changes as a function of age emphasize the need to recognize the role of age-related changes when formulating diagnoses of depression. While this may pose a serious dilemma at times, careful attention to the possibility that symptoms may have multiple causes is helpful in making an accurate diagnosis (see Salzman & Shader, 1979). The clinician working with elders needs to be trained in medical and sociological aspects of aging in order to appreciate this problem. It is also imperative that one keep abreast of the multidisciplinary literature in gerontology and geriatrics in order to stay informed of new discoveries in these fields. The input of a trained geriatric physician may be necessary in complex cases where a nonmedical clinician has serious doubts about the etiology of a particular patient's symptoms. This point is underscored when we examine how abnormal age-related changes (e.g., dementia) can similarly cause some (though not all) of these same symptoms.

Dementia

"Dementia" is a broad term that has classically been misused. With the recent advent of DSM-III, greater precision is now possible. All persons who work with the elderly should be familiar with the prevalence, characteristics, and course of both primary degenerative dementia (called Senile Dementia of the Alzheimer's Type or SDAT by researchers) and multi-infarct dementia (in DSM-III, these are Axis I codes 290.0 and 290.4, respectively). It is also essential to be able to distinguish these chronic conditions from delirium, which is an acute confusional state previously referred to as Acute Brain Syndrome (DSM-III Axis I code 293.00). Papers by Albert (1981) and Roth (1980) review these issues well.

The clinician should also be aware of a classification referred to as "Pseudodementia" that presents a differential diagnostic problem. Several psychogeriatricians (e.g., Post, 1965) have reported that depression can at

Table 1.1   Major Clinical Features Differentiating
Pseudodementia from Dementia.

Clinical Features	Pseudodementia	Dementia
1. Onset of illness	Usually specific.	Determined only within broad limits.
2. Duration	Brief duration before requesting help.	Usually long duration.
3. Progression	Symptoms develop rapidly.	Symptoms develop slowly through course of illness.
4. History	Prior psychiatric problems are common.	Psychiatric dysfunction uncommon.
5. Complaints	Frequent and detailed complaint of cognitive loss. Disability is emphasized; failures are highlighted.	Infrequent and vague complaint of cognitive loss. Disabilities are overlooked or concealed. Satisfaction with accomplishment is frequently noted, however trivial.
6. Efforts	Minimal effort on even simple tasks.	Patients usually struggle to perform tasks.
7. Affect	Change often pervasive with strong sense of distress.	A frequent lack of concern with labile and shallow affect.
8. Social skills	Notable loss, usually early in course of illness.	Often retained in early stages.
9. Nocturnal dysfunction	Uncommon.	Often accentuated.
10. Attention and concentration	Often intact.	Usually faulty.
11. Memory loss	Occurs equally for recent and remote events, but "memory gaps" for specific periods are common.	Loss for recent events usually more severe than remote, but "gaps" for other specific periods are infrequent.
12. Variability in performance	Usually marked.	Consistently poor.

Source: Adapted from Wells, C., American Journal of Psychiatry, by permission of the author.

times impair cognitive functioning so severely that the patient will appear as if he or she is at least moderately demented. Although this does not exist as a category in DSM-III, some discussion of this issue can be found in the DSM-III manual (American Psychiatric Association, 1980, p. 111) and summarized in Table 1.1.

In making a differential assessment between dementia and depression, it is necessary to review the history of the complaint, the patient's physical-health status, current level of cognitive functioning, and recent behavioral changes. Whenever possible, verification of information by a family member or trusted friend should be obtained. Several investigators have reported distinctive patterns of test responses that differentiate demented, depressed, and pseudodemented older persons from normal aged (Raskin & Rae, 1981; Salzman & Shader, 1979; Wells, 1979). On a practical level, it is helpful to remember that clinical depression is primarily a disturbance of *mood*. Although truly depressed persons often complain about memory impairment and difficulty thinking and concentrating, they usually perform adequately when their abilities are tested under standard conditions. Dementia, on the other hand, is primarily a disturbance of intellectual functioning due to brain changes that are not reversible. On formal testing, demented persons are, in contrast to depressives, apt to perform poorly, although they tend to complain less about their functioning.

Thus, evaluating the meaning of complaints about memory loss and other cognitive deficits is a difficult process. Many older persons experience a decrease in their memory; for some, it *is* an early precursor of dementia, but for most it is not of clinical significance. Studies investigating the relationship between memory functioning, complaints about memory, and affective status in older adults generally support the notion that depressed individuals complain of greater deficits than are actually the case when memory performance is objectively evaluated (Kahn, Zarit, Hilbert, & Niederehe, 1975; Popkin, Gallagher, Thompson, & Moore, 1982). These findings emphasize the importance of including a brief objective assessment of memory function, such as immediate and delayed free recall of a word list, recognition of the free recall list items, and recall of a prose passage. This brief battery has been used successfully with elders and is described in Zelinski, Gilewski, and Thompson (1980). Other cognitive processes, such as attentional lapse (Thompson, 1980), should also be evaluated when there is a question about cognitive impairment.

Other Psychopathology

Before concluding that depression is the major problem, it is useful to assess the presence of other kinds of psychopathology that may co-exist or be of greater importance than the depression. For example, paranoid disorders, anxiety disorders, psychosexual problems, and longstanding personality defects have been reported as examples of functional disorders seen in older outpatients (see Zarit, 1980). It is difficult, however, to recommend one omnibus measure for this purpose, since none was developed specifically for use with elders; nor do any have normative data yet available for the aged. Given these limitations, we would recommend the use of two complementary assessment tools: the Brief Psychiatric Rating Scale (Overall & Gorham, 1962) and the Brief Symptom Inventory (short form of the Hopkins Symptom Checklist developed by Derogatis, [1977]). Both provide information about a broad range of psychopathology; the former consists of ratings made by a trained interviewer, and the later is in self-report form.

METHODS FOR EVALUATION OF DEPRESSION

In most clinical settings, the assessment process proceeds along two separate but interrelated paths. The first is descriptive and focuses on obtaining sufficient information to establish an accurate diagnosis. The second is directed toward a better understanding of causal agents in order to pinpoint targets for intervention.

Table 1.2.   Comparison of the Research Diagnostic Criteria (RDC) and DSM-III Criteria for Major Depression.

RDC Criteria for *Major Depressive Disorder (MDD)*	*DSM-III Criteria for* *Major Depressive Episode*
A. Mood Disturbance One or more distinct periods with dysphoric mood or pervasive loss of interest or pleasure.	Dysphoric mood or loss of interest or pleasure in all or almost all usual activities and pastimes.
In both systems, mood disturbance is characterized by descriptors such as: depressed, sad, downhearted and blue, hopeless, down in the dumps, don't care anymore, or irritable. While this disturbance does not need to be dominant, it must be prominent and persistent. Momentary shifts from dysphoric mood to another serious emotional state such as anxiety or anger would preclude a diagnosis of major depression.	
B. Related Symptoms At least five of the following are required as part of the episode and four for probable MDD:	At least four of the following must be present regularly:
1. Poor appetite or weight loss, or increased appetite or weight gain. 2. Sleep difficulty (insomnia) or sleeping too much (hypersomnia).	

Table 1.2.   continued

RDC Criteria for Major Depressive Disorder	DSM-III Criteria for Major Depressive Episode
3. Psychomotor agitation or retardation (but not merely subjective feelings of restlessness or being slowed down).	
4. Loss of energy, fatigability, or tiredness.	
5. Loss of interest or pleasure in usual activities, or decrease in sexual drive not limited to a period of delusion or hallucinating.	
6. Feelings of worthlessness, self-reproach, or excessive or inappropriate guilt.	
7. Complaints or evidence of diminished ability to think or concentrate (e.g., slowed thinking or indecisiveness).	
8. Recurrent thoughts of death or suicide, or any suicidal behavior.	
C. Duration Dysphoric features: 2 weeks for definite; 1–2 weeks for probable. Related symptoms: Not specified but presumed at least 2 weeks.	Dysphoric features: Not specified but presumed at least 2 weeks. Related symptoms: Must be present nearly every day for at least 2 weeks.
D. Exclusionary Criteria 1. None of the following which suggests schizophrenia is present: —Delusions of being controlled, or of thought broadcasting, insertions, or withdrawal. —Nonaffective hallucinations. —Auditory hallucinations. —More than one month of *no* depressive symptoms but delusions or hallucinations. —Preoccupation with a delusion or hallucination to relative exclusion of other symptoms or concerns. —Definite marked, formal thought disorder. 2. Does not meet criteria for schizophrenia, residual type.	1. Preoccupation with a mood-incongruent delusion or hallucination or bizarre behavior cannot be dominant in the clinical picture before or after the occurrence of an affective syndrome. 2. Mood disturbance cannot be superimposed on schizophrenia, schizophreniform disorder, or a paranoid disorder. 3. Organic mental disorder or uncomplicated bereavement is ruled out as a cause of mood disturbance.
E. Impairment of functioning. Sought or was referred for help during the dysphoric period, took medication, or had impairment in functioning with family, at home, at school, at work, or socially.	Not specified.

Descriptive Diagnosis

Classification Procedures. Two sets of operational definitions are available for diagnostic purposes: DSM-III, and the Research Diagnostic Criteria (RDC: Spitzer, Endicott & Robins, 1978). (See Table 1.2.) The latter are more stringent in that greater specificity is present, along with oportunity for finer-grained decisions (e.g., the RDC provides subtypes of major depression, as well as classifications for more chronic kinds of affective disorders). Lewinsohn and Lee (1981) point out a number of important comparisons between the two systems. For example, both distinguish between episodic and chronic conditions, where "episodic" means that there is a period of disorder that is clearly distinguishable from previous functioning. Also, there is a comparability between the specific symptoms used to describe "major depressive disorder" in RDC and "major depressive episode" in DSM-III. (The symptom clusters have been described earlier in this chapter, see pp. 8-9.)

An important difference between the DSM-III and RDC is that the latter contains additional criteria that focus on: (1) evidence that the patient is functionally impaired (e.g., evidences of disturbed daily functioning); *or* (2) evidence that the patient sought or was referred for help during the episode; *or* (3) evidence that the patient took medication for relief of distress. In our opinion, the inclusion of this "extra" qualifier is important when working with elders. As noted above, most of the symptoms used to define unipolar depression are (unfortunately) also normal concomitants of the aging process. By including the notion that either the patient or someone in his environment was *aware* that there was a problem (as is implied in impaired daily functioning, or help seeking, or referral, or ingestion of medication), one is helped to distinguish patients who are experiencing symptomatic distress from those experiencing a full-blown clinical syndrome.

The reader might now ask *how* to go about questioning for the RDC criteria. We recommend use of the Schedule for Affective Disorders and Schizophrenia (SADS: Endicott & Spitzer, 1978). We have found the SADS to be a reliable and valid method of data collection; when used in conjunction with the RDC and certain other assessment tools (described below), the SADS permits careful delineation of major depressive disorders. A recent study has shown that elderly depressed patients have substantially higher scores on all summary scales (and on the individual items comprising these scales) than a normal elderly control group, even when attempts were made to obscure them by maximizing the impact of perceived physical health and age differences (Dessonville et al., 1982). It should be noted that outpatients were used in this study. Further work is needed to determine if the same results would be found with older psychiatric inpatients.

When using the SADS it is essential to assess physical-health status and cognitive functioning independently. Several relatively simple screening methods are available, such as health problem and medication checklists (e.g., as developed by Raskin & Crook at National Institute of Mental Health's (NIMH) Psychopharmacology Research Branch; obtainable from the authors on request) and brief tests of cognitive performance (e.g., the Mini-Mental State Examination of Folstein, Folstein, & McHugh, 1975). As noted above, more comprehensive test batteries should be used when there is a real question as to the presence of dementia.

Measures of Severity or Intensity. Depression level can be determined by both interview and self-report scales. The Hamilton Rating Scale for Depression (HRSD: Hamilton, 1967) is the most frequently used interviewer-administered measure, particularly in clinical research programs. Unfortunately, we find that we cannot strongly recommend this scale because of its sensitivity to somatic concerns (which may reflect normal age-related changes and/or bona fide complaints associated with physical illnesses as well as depression). Unless the interviewer skillfully inquires about health status and uses the information obtained to qualify Hamilton ratings, the scores can be falsely elevated (Gallagher, Slife, & Rose; Waskow).

Common self-report scales include the Minnesota Multiphasic Personality Inventory (MMPI: Hathaway & McKinley, 1943), the Zung Self-rating Depression Scale (SDS: Zung, 1965) and the Beck Depression Inventory (BDI: Beck et al., 1961). Although the MMPI is widely used, its psychometric properties with elderly samples have not been adequately demonstrated (McNair, 1979; Bernal et al., 1977). The Mini-Mult (Kincannon, 1968) has similar problems (see Fillenbaum & Pfeiffer, 1976).

Zung's Self-rating Depression Scale has had more trials with the elderly than any other depression measure (see McNair, 1979, for a review). However, because of its preponderance of somatic items (relative to those tapping psychological distress), and because some items are worded positively while others are worded negatively (necessitating frequent shifts in response sets), both the validity and the reliability of this scale have been called into question (Blumenthal, 1975). McGarvey, Gallagher, Thompson, and Zelinski (1982) reported that the measure's internal consistency was below usual standards when used with the "old-old," and suggested that deletion of somatic items would improve reliability in very old samples (above age 70).

In our experience, the Beck Depression Inventory has been demonstrated to be reliable when used with the elderly (Gallagher, Nies, & Thompson, 1982), and use of traditional cut-off scores for diagnostic classification has good agreement with diagnoses established using the SADS/RDC approach (Gallagher, Breckenridge, Steinmetz, & Thompson, in press). Also, we have observed that the BDI is sensitive to change and thus is a useful tool for assessing treatment progress. Change can be assessed by comparing total BDI scores across time, or by examining patterns of item endorsement. For example, if a patient has had serious sleep difficulties and these have been addressed by teaching relaxation techniques in therapy, that item should be rated differently as treatment progresses.

A relatively new scale that may prove useful in assessing level of depression in the elderly is the Geriatric Depression Scale (Yesavage et al., in press). It contains 30 items rated on a "yes/no" basis for how the person felt over the past week. The authors report reliability and validity indices sufficiently high to consider its use in clinical settings.

Functional Assessment

Functional assessment refers to evaluation of specific personal and environmental factors that are related to an individual patient's depression—what maintains it; what are its behavioral, cognitive, social, and affective concomitants; what coping strengths and social supports are available to assist in recovery; how psychological well-being in general (not just symptoms of depression) can be improved; and so forth. This topic has been comprehensively discussed in a chapter by Lewinsohn and Lee (1981), but not from a gerontological perspective. Nevertheless, that information should be reviewed by all clinicians working with the elderly because the authors detail a number of assessment domains, along with appropriate measurement tools, for conducting a functional analysis of behavior. For example, social behavior, cognitive content, activity level, and the occurrence of both pleasant and aversive events are each viewed as contributors to the origin and maintenance of depression in particular patients. Since their presence and impact vary so greatly from patient to patient, however, the clinician needs to be able to pinpoint the salient factors in a given case. This information results in identification of specific targets for intervention and also facilitates evaluation of the efficacy of one's intervention strategy.

Most of the instruments that will be presented in this chapter have not been widely used with depressed elders; our recommendations therefore must be somewhat tentative. We would suggest that the reader keep abreast of the literature in this regard as there is a great deal of current interest in the development of appropriate measures for use with elders (see Gallagher, Thompson, & Levy, 1980).

The following 10 aspects of the older patient's life warrant inclusion in a functional assessment battery: personality; stressful life events; coping style; social-support network; cognitive distortions; expectancies; attributions of causality and improvement; daily pleasant and unpleasant behaviors/events; social-role functioning; and morale. Despite the length of this list, we have found older patients to be very cooperative in completing all the required questionnaires (although many require assistance because of problems with eyesight or handwriting).

Table 1.3.   Assessment Battery for the Diagnosis and Functional Assessment of Elderly Depressed Patients.

Domain	Instrument	Focus	Format	Reference
1. Physical Health Status	Health History Form Current Medication Form & perceived health rating	Self-report of past & current health status.	Yes/no to presence of symptoms or medication use (from list) severity rating/ health status.	Raskin & Crook, n.d.
2. Mental Status & Cognitive Function	Mini-Mental State Exam	Orientation; immediate & delayed recall; constructional dyspraxia.	Interview questions/ correct or incorrect.	Folstein, Folstein & McHugh, 1975
3. Differential Diagnosis	History	Timeline for symptom presence.	Clinician's judgment.	—
	Schedule for Affective Disorders & Schizophrenia (SADS)	Duration, intensity of mood disturbance & related symptoms.	Interview/rating of items on scale 0–6.	Endicott & Spitzer, 1978
	Brief Symptom Inventory (BSI)	Other psychiatric problems (eg. anxiety).	Indicate how distressing symptoms are; 5-pt. scale.	Derogatis, 1977
	Brief Psychiatric Rating Scale (BPRS)	Presence of other psychopathology.	Interviewer rating of symptom intensity.	Overall & Gorham, 1962
4. Level of Depression	Hamilton Rating Scale for Depression Beck Depression Inventory (BDI)	Associated features, particularly somatic. Mood disturbance and related symptoms.	Interview—17 to 19 items rated 0–3. Self-rating: select 1 of 4 choices for intensity of symptom.	Hamilton, 1960 Hamilton, 1967 Beck, Ward, Mendelson, Mock, & Erbaugh, 1961
	Zung Self-Rating Depression Scale (SDS) Geriatric Depression Scale (GDS)	Same as above. Mood disturbance primarily; designed especially for elders.	Indicate frequency of occurrence of each symptom, presence or absence of each symptom (yes/no format).	Zung, 1965 Yesavage, Brink, Rose, Lum, Huang, Adey, & Leirer, in press
5. Personality	Eysenck Personality Inventory	Introversion/ extraversion; neuroticism.	True/false to whether items apply.	Eysenck & Eysenck, 1968
	Sixteen Personality Factor Questionnaire (16PF)	Separate bipolar factors related to personality traits.	Yes/no/don't know.	Cattell, 1956
6. Occurrence of Stressful Life Events	Health & Daily Living Questionnaire	Frequency of common stresses (e.g., sickness).	Indicate which of a standard list has occurred, when, & how much control.	Moos, Cronkite, Finney & Billings, 1980
7. Coping Styles	Health & Daily Living Questionnaire	How does person cope with stressful event and with depression.	Indicate which of a list of common coping strategies are used and how often.	Moos et al., 1980
8. Social-Support System	Social Support Index and Questionnaire	Perceived support obtainable from others and number in network.	Indicate true/false and describe number in network.	Wilcox, 1981
	Social Network Questionnaire	Amount, frequency, and quality of contact with significant others.	Interview questions and rating scale.	Thompson, Gallagher, & Peterson, 1979

Table 1.3 continued

Domain	Instrument	Focus	Format	Reference
9. Cognitive Distortions	Automatic Thoughts Questionnaire (ATQ)	Occurrence of dysfunctional thoughts.	Frequency and degree of belief in standard list of distorted thoughts.	Hollon & Kendall, 1980
	Young Loneliness Inventory	Perception of social isolation/loneliness.	Select one of four alternatives for each item to reflect intensity.	Young, 1981
10. Expectancies	Hopelessness Scale	Pessimism regarding future and present.	True/false whether items apply.	Beck, Weissman, Lester & Trexler, 1974
	Target Complaints	Current problems (in own words) and goals for therapy.	Interview to obtain number and severity of primary complaints.	Mintz, 1981
	Expected BDI	Expected symptom picture at end of therapy.	Use BDI form; change instructions.	Steinmetz, Lewinsohn, & Antonuccio, in press
11. Attributions	Attributional Style Questionnaire (original)	Degree of internality, globality, and stability re causes of events.	Select cause for vignettes, then rate cause on these three dimensions.	Peterson, Semmel, von Baeyer, Abramson, Metalsky, & Seligman, 1982
	Attribution Index (modified for elders)	Same dimensions.	Vignettes chosen for relevance to elders.	Bisno, Thompson, Breckenridge, & Gallagher, 1982
12. Daily Behaviors	Pleasant and Unpleasant Activities Schedules (PES & UES)	Frequency and impact of number of pleasant and unpleasant everyday activities.	Indicate each dimension on 3-point scales.	PES: MacPhillamy & Lewinsohn, 1982 UES: Lewinsohn & Talkington, 1979
	Older Person's PES and UES: modified versions of above	Events selected for appropriateness for variety of elders.	Same.	Hedlund & Gilewski, In Gallagher et al., 1981
13. Social Adjustment	Social Adjustment Scale self-report (SAS-SR) Katz Adjustment Scales (KAS)	Adjustment to work, leisure, and family life. Frequency and satisfaction with leisure activities and social-role performance.	Respond to specific questions along intensity dimension. Four-point self-rating scales; relatives' form also available.	Weissman, 1980 Weissman & Bothwell, 1976 Katz & Lyerly, 1963
14. Well-being	Morale Scale	Level of well-being and satisfaction.	Indicate agreement with positive and negative statements.	Lawton, 1975
	Life Satisfaction Index	Same.	Agree/disagree with items reflecting outlook on life.	Wood, Wylie, & Shaefor, 1969

We have indexed these domains and the measures we currently use to evaluate them in Table 1.3.

In settings where it is impractical to administer a battery this extensive, we recommend that the clinician at least explore each of these areas in a clinical interview. This will provide a more in-depth understanding of the background factors influencing both the development and maintenance of depression for an individual client. A "tailor-made" treatment plan will then be possible. For example, persons with significant life stresses, few coping strategies and weak social supports, and "neurotic" personality style are likely to need a more intensive and long-term therapy than those patients with few recent stressors who have a variety of coping strategies in their repertoire and who have an adequate (though perhaps underutilized) social-support network. Some severely depressed persons, on the other hand, may be so depleted psychologically (e.g., from multiple stressful life events combined with serious physical problems and relatively few social supports) that provision of an extended supportive relationship may be the most intensive intervention that can be tolerated.

Interventions for the Treatment of Clinical Depression in Elders

Until recently there has been very little substantive information (based on controlled research) to guide the clinician in the treatment of elder depressives. Traditionally, the prevalent view has been that older persons will not respond well to psychological interventions and are therefore poor candidates for any form of psychotherapy (Butler & Lewis, 1982). However, recent clinical and empirical observations argue against this position (see Brink, 1979; Knight, 1978–79; Levy, Derogatis, Gallagher, & Gatz, 1980; Zung, 1980).

Pharmacotherapy has often been regarded as the treatment of choice for elderly depressives (see Gerner, 1979; Gershon & Raskin, 1975). However, few controlled trials have been done specifically with elderly depressives (either inpatients or outpatients). In a recent review of research on pharmacological interventions for depression in the elderly (Strauss & Solomon), it was noted that as of 1980, there were four studies of the effect of tricyclic antidepressants on geriatric depressives, of which only *one* was a controlled double-bind study.

While it appears that tricyclics can be effective in the treatment of some elderly depressed patients (Prusoff, Weissman, & Scholomskas), concomitant medical problems or medications frequently inhibit their use. Problems, such as increased medication side-effects and age-related changes in metabolic processes (as reviewed in Epstein, 1978), have led to the recommendation that alternative forms of treatment be developed and evaluated. Psychological intervention may indeed be safer for many older depressives. When depression has been refractory to many different kinds of interventions, however, then a trial of Electo convulsive shock therapy (ECT) may be justified. Zung (1980) discusses the appropriateness of both drugs and ECT for the treatment of severe depression in the old.

At the present time, there are few controlled studies that compare the efficacy of pharmacotherapy versus psychotherapy for the elderly. Nor are there any published reports on the outcome of combination (drugs *and* psychotherapy) treatment programs of depression in the elderly. Comparisons made in nonelderly samples have yielded equivocal results. Some studies favor pharmacotherapy (e.g., Klerman et al., 1974), while others favor psychotherapy (e.g., Bellack, Hersen, & Himmelhoch, 1981) or some combination of both treatments (e.g., Blackburn et al., 1981). Although no controlled comparisons have been reported for elderly samples, there is little reason to suspect that the results would be any less equivocal. A wide variety of treatments, ranging from jogging and meditation (Niemeyer, Gurman, Klein, & Greist) to behavior therapy with couples (McLean, Ogston, & Grauer, 1973), have been reported to result in short-term relief from depression. Again, persons over 60 have typically been excluded from these investigations.

While it is unfortunate that so little attention has been paid to possible mechanisms of change in the psychological treatment of depressed elders, several approaches have shown promise in providing sustained improvement. These tend to be highly structured techniques that emphasize the importance of developing skills to cope with depression.

Structured Psychotherapies

Most controlled behavioral studies with elders have been carried out using institutionalized samples (for review, see Richards & Thorpe, 1978). A few case studies that describe the use of behavioral contracting and self-reinforcement to mitigate elders' grief reactions have been reported with depressed outpatients (see Flannery, 1974; Gauthier & Marshall, 1977). One of the first controlled experimental studies with depressed outpatients was done by Gallagher (1981). Elders were randomly assigned to either behavioral or supportive group psychotherapy and were treated for ten sessions in groups led by experienced therapists. Results indicated that depression improved significantly over time for patients treated with either modality, and that gains were maintained after a five-week, no-treatment follow-up period.

Another study evaluated the usefulness of individual behavior therapy with older depressed outpatients (Gallagher & Thompson, 1982). Similar to the earlier study, comparable improvement in level of depression from pre- to posttreatment was found for patients treated with behavior therapy, cognitive therapy, or an insight-oriented relational control condition. During the one-year follow-up period, however, significantly more patients in the relational control condition relapsed (56 percent) compared to patients treated with either behavioral or cognitive therapy (11 percent).

These two studies support recent arguments (Mintz, Steuer, & Jarvik, 1981; Knight, 1978–79) that psychotherapy can be an effective tool for treating depression in the elderly. From the existing studies, it appears that gains made in treatment are maintained when therapy is highly structured and focuses on acquisition of skills to control negative mood swings. In addition, elders appear more able to *maintain* clinical improvement when they have participated in treatment programs that provide a cogent rationale for the development of depression and also teach specific skills for coping with future depressogenic events (see Gallagher & Thompson).

At present it appears that both cognitive and behaviorally oriented therapies meet these criteria, so it is not surprising that both appear to have similar impact. While group effects for behavioral and cognitive therapies are comparable, they may be differentially effective for different patients. Although research evidence is not yet available to support this position, several trends have emerged from individual case studies conducted in our clinic. In general, patients with marked negative thinking patterns and a capacity for self-reflection have responded more quickly to cognitive therapy, particularly if their daily activity levels were in the normal range. In contrast, patients engaging in few pleasant activities each day (or those with diminished capacity to enjoy daily events) have responded more quickly to behavioral therapy, particularly if their thought patterns were relatively undistorted. There are numerous exceptions to these "rules of thumb," and, more often than not, patients do not fit neatly into these categories. We hope that greater specificity will emerge as more extensive research findings on these issues become available.

Individual Behavioral Therapy. The original impetus for this work came from collaboration with Peter Lewinsohn, who kindly made available the various treatment manuals being used at the University of Oregon Depression Research Unit (Lewinsohn & Grosscup, 1978) with younger and middle-aged depressed persons. We soon learned that modifications of Lewinsohn's procedures improved the effectiveness of his approach with elders. For example, changes in how material was presented, timing, and therapeutic pacing made it easier for elders to learn the desired skills. A recent manual from our work presents, in a session-by-session format, the basic knowledge necessary to conduct individual behavior therapy with depressed elderly persons (Gallagher et al., 1981). We will highlight the main aspects of this approach here.

We begin by orienting the patient fully to the nature of this therapy, the expectancies we have for his or her participation in the treatment process, and the various paper-and-pencil tools that are used. We then stress the importance of increasing pleasant events and decreasing unpleasant events in order to minimize depression. Information about specific positive and negative events in the patient's environment is obtained through completion of two self-report scales: the Older Person's Pleasant and Unpleasant Events Schedules (OPPES and OPUES: Gallagher et al., 1981).

Patients are first taught to monitor mood and behavior on a daily basis and then to graph the relationship between them, in order to learn what kinds of events are most related to their mood. As understanding is achieved, problem solving begins, so that pleasant activities can be systematically increased and unpleasant activities decreased. This results in the development of a self-change plan in which skill acquisition becomes an important focus (e.g., relaxation training to decrease the aversiveness of unpleasant interpersonal encounters, followed by development of communication skills so that more positive interactions with people can occur). With older depressives, the therapist usually has to work fairly hard to obtain cooperation at this point because they lack conviction that learning skills will resolve the problems that required them to come for therapy.

Older patients tend to frame their problems globally. For example, "I feel bad; I don't know what to do with my time because there is nothing to really enjoy anymore." If skill training is to be successful, the patient has to be helped to see his or her problem in small, definable units for which a specific behavioral skill will have relevance. We have found it helpful to present skill acquisition as an experiment; this usually enables the client to get started and have some success, which is in itself reinforcing. In addition, many patients do not perceive their own power or control in common everyday situations; extensive support and encouragement are needed to keep patients "on target" with their self-change plan and accompanying homework.

Final therapy sessions are spent reviewing what has been learned and developing an explicit "maintenance" plan to be used after therapy has ended. There are also relationship issues to resolve, since many older adults find it difficult to accept therapy termination. Having found an empathic helpful person, older patients often wish to continue the relationship on a social level and are hurt when the therapist declines such invitations. It is important to be prepared for such issues so that they can be handled tactfully and without defensiveness.

We also regularly schedule "booster sessions" approximately 6 and 12 weeks after termination. At these times, specific problems encountered during these intervals are discussed, and the therapist reinforces the continued use of those behavioral skills that were most helpful. This procedure makes termination a less abrupt process; since older persons seem to have difficulty with termination of therapy, it seems considerate to taper appointments rather than to terminate them with finality.

Behavior Therapy Case Illustration. Mr. B. is a 73-year-old who has been a widower for 10 years. Three years ago neighbors found him collapsed in his apartment and called our office for assistance. Mr. B. was unkempt, unshaven, confused, and disoriented as to place and time. His only response to questions was, "I just want to die." The little food in the apartment had apparently not been touched for days. There was no evidence of alcohol consumption or drug use, and neighbors reported that they had never observed him to drink.

Mr. B. was taken to the emergency service of a local hospital where he was diagnosed as having an acute brain disorder. Lab tests revealed a kidney infection and dehydration. He was hospitalized, and within a few days his thought processes were clear and oriented and the kidney infection had subsided. At this time, his depression stood out clearly. He refused to eat and complained that he was miserable. He viewed treatment as worthless because it was "only" extending his life. His speech and thinking were markedly slowed, his affect was blunt, and he saw no hope for the future. Mr. B. received a series of 10 ECT treatments over a six-week period and was released from the hospital as markedly improved. He functioned reasonably well for about eight weeks, when he again began to experience severe mood shifts. The neighbors, who were now alert to his problem, insisted that he contact our clinic for assistance.

At intake Mr. B. was diagnosed as having a major depressive disorder. Functional assessment indicated that problems with negative thoughts about himself and the future were only marginally elevated at this time. Analysis of Mr. B.'s response to individual items on the Beck Depression Inventory also revealed a minimal focus on negative self-evaluation. In contrast, his score on the Loneliness Inventory was comparatively high (see Young, 1981, for scoring information on this scale). This was consistent with the interviewer's impression that Mr. B. was experiencing intense loneliness and feelings of social isolation. His scores on the Older Person's Pleasant and Unpleasant Events Schedules indicated that he was engaging in very few pleasant activities, although he was not having any more than the usual number of unpleasant activities for a person of his age and economic condition (see Teri & Lewinsohn, 1982 and Gallagher et al., 1981, for normative aging information on inventories of this type).

Mr. B.'s social history indicated that he had had no meaningful interpersonal relationships since the death of his wife. His few old friends and relatives lived in the Midwest (Mr. B. lived on the West Coast) and he had not been in contact with them since his wife's funeral. Since his major problems were decreased pleasant activities and intense loneliness, with only minimal evidence of negative thinking, it was decided that therapy would focus on enhancing his pleasant life events and increasing his meaningful interpersonal relationships.

Mr. B. was seen twice weekly in individual behavioral therapy for a total of 16 sessions. During the first month, therapy was supplemented by weekly visits to Mr. B.'s home by several volunteers, at which time he was encouraged to leave his apartment to have lunch and then visit the park or visit his neighbors. By the end of this time, he had increased his activities and a clear relationship between his mood and his activities was evident from his daily tracking log. His energy level had increased and his depression was already somewhat improved.

Mr. B. and his therapist then decided to work on improving his ability to relate to people. The goal was to help him to feel more comfortable in interpersonal relationships, thus setting the stage for decreasing his loneliness. His positive response to social-skills training was remarkable. As therapy progressed, Mr. B. took the initiative to plan activities that involved repeated social contacts. For example, he started to attend the local senior center, joined a card club, and scheduled coffee dates with both men and women.

During the remainder of therapy, several negative events occurred that resulted in transient dysphoria for Mr. B. However, his earlier successes had impressed him with the value of using a problem-solving approach. As he felt his mood declining, he immediately initiated some type of self-change plan. With the help of his therapist, he gradually became quite skillful in aborting potentially harmful mood swings. The final therapy sessions were spent reviewing his progress, highlighting the particular behavioral skills that had been most helpful to him, and developing a maintenance plan for the next three months. At his last session, Mr. B.'s BDI was 8 (which is in the "normal" range and much better than his initial score of 32). He expressed confidence in his capabilities. By the end of therapy, he had increased his social relations and was making a good adjustment. This was maintained throughout the one-year follow-up with only minor disruptions in his mood.

Individual Cognitive Therapy. This approach follows the description of cognitive therapy in Beck, Rush, Shaw and Emery (1979) with modifications to make the procedures more useful for older depressed patients (discussed further in Emery, 1981; Emery, Gallagher, & Thompson).

The first session orients the patient to therapy by providing a pamphlet entitled "Coping with Depression" (Beck & Greenberg, 1974) that illustrates the relationship between negative thoughts and mood changes; it also provides information concerning various processes involved in thought distortion. The questions that arise from reading this pamphlet are helpful to clarify the rationale and techniques of cognitive therapy.

It has been our experience that at the beginning of treatment some patients are too depressed to use those cognitive strategies intended to demonstrate that thoughts affect mood. In such instances patients are asked to record their daily activities and rate them according to experienced mastery and pleasure (see Beck et al., 1979; Burns, 1980, for examples of this technique). This exercise directs the patient to thoughts that interfere with activities and thus paves the way for a more concentrated cognitive approach. These early steps also bring some symptomatic relief and motivate the patient to continue.

As soon as possible, patients are asked to identify their negative automatic thoughts through daily recordings on the Dysfunctional Thought Record (DTR: copies are obtainable from the Center for Cognitive Therapy in Philadelphia, Pennsylvania). This completed form is brought to each therapy session. After patients achieve some skill with the DTR, they are encouraged to become increasingly aware of the frequency of negative thoughts in daily life. Older persons seem to have more difficulty with this than younger patients; thoughts are so "automatic" that it takes time and practice to become aware of them as negative thoughts. Yet this is a critical aspect of cognitive therapy. To obtain optimal benefit from treatment, patients must develop a level of skill in monitoring their thoughts that becomes nearly as automatic as the thoughts themselves.

As the relationship between thoughts and mood fluctuations becomes more salient to the patient, the next step is to identify the particular cognitive distortions involved in these negative thoughts. It is important to help the client recognize the label distortions properly so that the focus of therapy can shift to correcting these errors in thinking.

To accomplish these goals, therapists make use of a number of specific cognitive techniques, including: reattribution, examining the evidence, listing pros and cons of maintaining an idea, and examining the consequences that follow from that idea. These techniques help the patient to develop greater perceptual and cognitive flexibility. To facilitate this process, patients are asked temporarily to suspend their belief in troublesome ideas so that they can "try out" different ways of thinking about their experience. Older patients often require more time and encouragement to do this effectively; they easily become defensive when their ideas and beliefs are challenged. It is important to point out repeatedly that the ideas are not "right" or "wrong," but are just more or less adaptive and influential on mood. Homework is always assigned and its faithful completion is critical for successful therapy.

Once these skills have been mastered, the focus of therapy shifts to modifying the more basic underlying themes responsible for the negative thoughts. Ideally, the final treatment sessions consist of relating themes (from the patient's dysfunctional thought records) to longstanding personal assumptions (e.g., "I have been a failure all my life," or "No one ever really loved me"). If these can be identified and modified (in light of the person's life history and his or her new-found knowledge about how to correct errors in thinking), then the patient will be less vulnerable to future episodes of depression. According to Beck et al. (1979), although the identification and modification of underlying themes does not always occur in short-term therapy, it is a desirable goal. We have observed that it is a difficult goal to achieve with older patients; often they are well defended about such underlying beliefs and do not really wish to explore them. Despite this, however, they are able to maintain the gains made in cognitive therapy, especially when they continue to use cognitive strategies on their own after therapy has ended.

Cognitive Psychotherapy Case Illustration. Mrs. H. is a 64-year-old retired travel agent who sold her business four years ago in order to be able to spend more time at home with her husband. The couple has two sons who live in another section of the country and who only contact them when they need financial assistance. Both the patient and her husband had been active in community affairs and social clubs, had traveled extensively, and, in general, had led well-organized lives with many exciting and pleasant activities. Mrs. H., however, believed she had been a failure in life and that she had not treated her husband or her sons properly. Further, she had become obsessed with the idea that were she to kill herself, her family would draw closer together. Her physical health was excellent; she had an active social-support network; there were no unusual life stresses; and there was no other co-existing psychopathology. Mrs. H. appeared to have a strong tendency for negative thinking about herself despite the fact that she participated in a variety of potentially pleasant experiences in a friendly, supportive environment. In view of this, cognitive therapy was selected as the treatment of choice.

Since Mrs. H.'s activity level was already high, there was no need to use the activity-scheduling technique. Therapy focused immediately on highlighting her cognitive distortions and the role these played in her depression. Mrs. H. was taught to use the DTR and therapy focused on examining these records sessions. Mrs. H. recorded a voluminous number of negative thoughts. Two examples were: anger towards her husband for forgetting to pick up clothes from the cleaners; and intense sadness at night when she thought about her estrangement from her sons. She quickly picked up the connection between her thoughts and her mood changes. The most useful technique was challenging the "all-or-none" thinking that pervaded her appraisal of herself and her life. She also learned to "catch" herself making negative predictions and making "should have" and "if only I had" statements to herself. By trying out other ways of evaluating her thoughts, Mrs. H. was able to obtain marked relief from her depression and to become more flexible in her attitudes.

By the 12th session, Mrs. H.'s BDI was within normal range (a score of 10 as compared to an initial score of 28) and continued that way for the remaining four appointments. During these sessions, the therapist linked Mrs. H.'s current negative thoughts with her earlier marital history in order to identify her underlying assumptions about self-worth that had plagued her for many years. Mrs. H. was able to tolerate this kind of exploration, saying that it was important to her to understand herself and to locate the roots of her discomfort. The main issue that surfaced was guilt. Because she had been a working mother long before that was socially acceptable, Mrs. H. was convinced that she had neglected her children and husband and that she had sacrificed their well-being for her own success in business.

During the first four months of follow-up, Mrs. H. continued to record negative thoughts when they occurred and was able to maintain her social activities satisfactorily. Her husband then had had a major attack and bypass surgery. This caused many changes in their lifestyle and Mrs. H. complained that trying to "think differently" did not help her cope with the new problems she was encountering. After considerable encouragement from her therapist, she agreed to resume daily use of the DTR.

At a six-month booster session, the therapist focused on the belief, "I can't be happy unless things are the way they used to be," which was readily identified in Mrs. H.'s DTR themes. Once this belief was identified, Mrs. H. quickly grasped its maladaptive nature and began to re-assess her present situation from a more realistic perspective. She generated new thoughts, such as, "Things change in life all the time," and "Sometime what appears to be a major trauma can in fact open new doors of understanding and satisfaction if approached properly." This provided an opportunity for both Mr. and Mrs. H. to redefine what they meant by happiness—does happiness consist primarily of being active and traveling or can other sources of happiness be identified? At the one-year follow-up, Mrs. H. reported that she had successfully reframed her perception of her husband's illness and that both she and her husband felt less stress; they had, in fact, initiated some positive changes that brought them closer together.

Psychoeducational Approaches. Recently Lewinsohn and his colleagues have developed a psychoeducational model for the treatment of depression (Lewinsohn, Steinmetz, Antonuccio, & Teri, 1982). Traditional behavioral strategies used have been adapted into a classroom framework for a course on "Coping with Depression." A modification of this course has been successfully used to treat elderly depressed outpatients in a major depressive episode (Hedlund & Thompson). It has also been used successfully on elderly community volunteers with mild to moderate negative mood swings (Thompson, Gallagher, Nies, & Epstein, in press). This approach is particularly appealing to older adults, since it minimizes the stigma often attached to deliberately seeking mental-health services. Older individuals experiencing psychological distress, who are reluctant to see a psychotherapist, seem more inclined to enroll for a course on "Coping with Depression." This course also assists persons with mild current distress to develop skills to prevent the onset of more serious depression in the future.

We have offered these "Coping with Depression" courses extensively in our clinic and in various community settings (e.g., senior centers, senior housing facilities, day health-care programs). Participant and leader workbooks are available that present material in a nonthreatening, humorous manner. Classes meet for six weeks; each session lasts about two hours; and two instructors are used. Maximum enrollment is six to eight persons, depending on the setting and the functional capabilities of those enrolled.

The first hour of each class begins with a general discussion of what the past week was like, followed by setting the agenda and briefly reviewing past homework. Then a workshop session is held with instructors rotating among participants to individually review principles embedded in the homework and to problem-solve related issues (e.g., factors interfering with scheduling daily pleasant events). Then a coffee break is held. The second hour begins with a brief lecture on the principles of upcoming homework for the next class, followed by a second workshop session to determine that participants understand and feel that they are able to complete the new assignments. Usually participants anticipate several obstacles, and again individualized plans and strategies are worked out jointly with class leaders.

One new behavioral skill is taught at each meeting. Skills include: mood monitoring, learning to do daily tracking on tailor-made lists of pleasant and unpleasant events, and learning how to graph relationships between mood changes and activity levels. Even more essential, however, is that participants learn to develop their own plans for self-change and learn how to follow through on these plans.

After the basic course is finished, members can enroll in more advanced classes that presuppose a rudimentary grasp of the self-change process. Currently these include: techniques of overt and covert relaxation; strengthening coping strategies to prepare for stressful life events in the future; or participating in discussions about the impact of society's changing values on the meaning one constructs for one's own life.

The basic "Coping with Depression" course has had a positive impact on the majority of elders who participated (Thompson et al.), despite the fact that they came from diverse educational and socioeconomic backgrounds. Certain characteristics, however, are highly predictive of negative outcome. Older persons with severe levels of depression, alone or in combination with any of the dementias, do not do well in this course. Those who do not consistently complete homework assignments also do not do well, although they tend to report positive benefits from the socialization aspects of the class. Finally, elders who tend to become obsessed with, and repeatedly focus on, negative thoughts are also unlikely to do well (i.e., in common parlance, they have a "one-track mind"). They relate all events in the class to these focal thoughts and never quite seem to become involved in the class, or really allow themselves to comprehend the concepts and techniques presented.

Thompson et al. (in press) further investigated whether or not these courses could be successfully taught by non-mental-health professionals in the aging service-delivery system (such as recreation aides at senior centers). Thirty-two leaders (16 professionals and 16 nonprofessionals) were trained and subsequently rated by independent observers to evaluate their skill as instructors. In the 16 different class series taught by these leaders, it was found that non-mental-health professionals were as effective as professionals when their respective participants were compared for improvement in negative thinking, depression, and quality of life. Also, dropout rates did not differ significantly by leader status. When instructors were rated for their overall teaching competence, however, significant differences occurred between classes taught by highly competent versus relatively noncompetent leaders (regardless of background). No meaningful improvement was detected on any of the outcome measures for individuals in classes taught by trainers who were evaluated as functioning poorly (e.g., disorganized; relatively inflexible; uncomfortable with behavioral material and methods, etc.).

This finding has obvious implications for future use of psychoeducational approaches with elders. Leaders need to be willing and able to adhere to the principles and techniques of the course. They should be assessed as adequately trained *prior* to conducting the course, and they should be able to apply behavioral methods flexibly to the broad spectrum of problems that emerge in a heterogeneous classroom situation such as we have been describing. Yet, despite this need for careful screening and training of leaders, we believe that there is great practical utility in modifying both content and method so that the "coping class" approach can be made relevant to elders experiencing other kinds of psychological distress. For example, we have since developed classes for caregivers who are responsible for the care of frail elderly relatives and have also developed a class series for recently widowed older persons. It seems to us that there are many other creative variations yet to be developed on this theme; further work along these lines should increase the number of elders who can be served with good results outside the traditional mental-health delivery system. The positive benefits of coping class participation can perhaps best be illustrated with a final brief case report.

Mrs. R. is a 70-year-old married woman who recently completed a "Coping with Depression" class series at a local senior center. She participated in the class in a warm, self-disclosing manner, although she was moderately depressed at the start (BDI = 20), apparently in response to internal feelings of boredom with her life and negative self-appraisal at her inability to change things. She quickly understood the rationale of the course (realized she was doing many things she did not enjoy and few things that would give her pleasure) and committed herself to making conscious choices that would increase her daily sense of self-satisfaction. By the end of the six class meetings, her BDI had dropped to 10 and she had organized her daily life in a much more satisfactory manner. Shortly thereafter, however, her husband became critically ill with emphysema and the subsequent burdens of caregiving and stress during this time were extremely difficult. Yet she came through this period without increased depression (as reported at a two-month reunion of the class). Mrs. R. attributed her ability to weather the stress and uncertainty of that time to her continued practice of daily pleasant-event scheduling (despite the formidable obstacles of her situation). She said that she knew she could keep her mood and energy level up (and thereby be strong enough to do all the things she had to do for her husband) by scheduling in a minimum of two pleasant activities each day. At the reunion she gave the instructors a note expressing her feelings: "I can never thank you enough for the help this course has given me. . . . I would not have weathered all this stress without the knowledge I gained from your class."

REFERENCES

Akiskal, H., & McKinney, W. Overview of recent research in depression. *Archives of General Psychiatry*, 1975, **32**, 285–304.

Albert, M. Geriatric neuropsychology. *Journal of Consulting and Clinical Psychology*, 1981, **49**, 835–850.

American Psychiatric Association. DSM-III. Washington, D.C.: APA, 1980.

Beck, A. T., & Greenberg, R. *Coping with depression*. Philadelphia: Center for Cognitive Therapy, 1974.

Beck, A., Rush, J., Shaw, B., & Emery, G. *Cognitive therapy of depression*. New York: Guilford, 1979.

Beck, A. T., Ward, C. H., Mendelson, M., Mock, J. E., & Erbaugh, J. An inventory for measuring depression. *Archives of General Psychiatry*, 1961, **4**, 561-571.

Beck, A., Weissman, A., Lester, D., & Trexler, L. The measurement of pessimism: The Hopelessness Scale. *Journal of Consulting and Clinical Psychology*, 1974, **42**, 861-865.

Bellack, A., Hersen, M., & Himmelhoch, J. Social skills training compared with pharmacotherapy and psychotherapy in the treatment of unipolar depression. *American Journal of Psychiatry*, 1981, **12**, 1562-1567.

Bernal, G. A., Brannon, L. J., Belar, C., Lavigne, J., & Cameron, R. Psychodiagnostics of the elderly. In W. G. Gentry (Ed.), *Geropsychology: A model of training and clinical service*. Cambridge, Mass.: Ballinger, 1977.

Bisno, B., Thompson, L. W., Breckenridge, J., & Gallagher, D. *Cognitive predictors of outcome for older adults participating in psychoeducational program for the treatment of depression*. Paper presented at the meeting of the Western Psychological Association, Sacramento, Calif., April 1982.

Blackburn, I. M., Bishop, S., Glen, A., Whalley, L., & Christie, J. The efficacy of cognitive therapy in depression: A treatment trial using cognitive therapy and pharmacotherapy, each alone and in combination. *British Journal of Psychiatry*, 1981, **139**, 181-189.

Blazer, D., & Williams, C. D. Epidemiology of dysphoria and depression in an elderly population. *American Journal of Psychiatry*, 1980, **137**, 439-444.

Blumenthal, M. Measuring depressive symptomatology in a general population. *Archives of General Psychiatry*, 1975, **32**, 971-978.

Blumenthal, M. *Research problems in mental health and illness of the elderly*. Report to the research task force of the President's Commission on Mental Health, 1978.

Brink, T. L. *Geriatric psychotherapy*. New York: Human Sciences Press, 1979.

Burns, D. D. *Feeling good*. New York: New American Library, 1980.

Butler, T., & Lewis, M. *Aging and mental health* (3rd ed.). St. Louis: Mosby, 1982.

Cattell, R. B. A shortened "basic English" version (form C) of the 16 PF questionnaire. *Journal of Social Psychology*, 1956, **44**, 257-278.

Covi, L., Lipman, R., Derogatis, L. R., Smith, J., & Pattison, J. Drugs and group psychotherapy in neurotic depression. *American Journal of Psychiatry*, 1974, **131**, 191-198.

Dement, W. C., Miles, L. E., & Carskadon, M. A. The white paper on sleep and aging. *Journal of American Geriatric Society*, 1982, **30**, 26-50.

Derogatis, L. *Brief Symposium Inventory (BSI)*. Baltimore: Johns Hopkins Univ., 1977.

Derogatis, L., & Spencer, P. M. *Brief Symptom Inventory (BSI) Manual I: Scoring and procedures for the BSI*. Baltimore: Clinical Psychometrics Research, 1983.

Dessonville, C., Gallagher, D., Thompson, L., Finnell, K., & Lewinsohn, P. M. Relation of age and health status to depressive symptoms in normal and depressed older adults. *Essence*, 1982, **5**, 90-117.

DiMascio, A., Weissman, M., Prusoff, B., Neu, C., Zwilling, M., & Klerman, G. Differential symptom reduction by drugs and psychotherapy in actue depression. *Archives of General Psychiatry*, 1979, **36**, 1450-1456.

Dovenmuehle, R., & McGough, W. Aging, culture and affect: Predisposing factors. In E. Palmore (Ed.), *Normal aging*. Durham, N.C.: Duke University Press, 1970.

Emery, G. Cognitive therapy with the elderly. In G. Emery, S. Hollon, & R. Bedrosian (Eds.), *New directions in cognitive therapy*. New York: Guilford, 1981.

Emery, G., Gallagher, D., & Thompson, L. *Cognitive therapy for depression in the elderly*. New York: Guilford, in press.

Endicott, J., & Spitzer, R. L. A diagnostic interview for affective disorders and schizophrenia. *Archives of General Psychiatry*, 1978, **35**, 837-844.

Epstein, L. J. Anxiolytics, antidepressants, and neuroleptics in the treatment of geriatric patients. In M. Lipton, A. DiMascio, & K. Killman (Eds.), *Psychopharmacology: A generation of progress.* New York: Raven Press, 1978.

Essen-Moller, E., & Hagnell, O. The frequency and risk of depression within a rural population group in Scandinavia. *Acta Psychiatrica Scandinavica*, 1961, **Suppl. 162**, 28–32.

Eysenck, H. J., & Eysenck, S. B. *Manual for the Eysenck Personality Inventory.* San Diego: Educational & Industrial Testing Service, 1968.

Fillenbaum, G., & Pfeiffer, E. The Mini-Mult: A cautionary note. *Journal of Consulting and Clinical Psychology*, 1976, **44**, 698–703.

Flannery, R. B. Behavior modification of geriatric grief: A transactional perspective. *International Journal of Aging and Human Development*, 1974, **5**, 197–203.

Folstein, M., Folstein, S., & McHugh, P. "Mini-Mental State"—A practical method for grading the cognitive state of patients for the clinician. *Journal of Psychiatric Research*, 1975, **12**, 189–198.

Friedman, A. S. Interaction of drug therapy with marital therapy in depressive patients. *Archives of General Psychiatry*, 1975, **32**, 619–637.

Gaitz, C. M. Depression in the elderly. In W. Fann, I. Karacan, A. Pokorny, & R. Williams (Eds.), *Phenomenology and treatment of depression.* New York: Spectrum, 1977.

Gallagher, D. Behavioral group therapy with elderly depressives: An experimental study. In D. Upper & S. Ross (Eds.), *Behavioral group therapy* Vol. 3. Champaign, Ill.: Research Press, 1981.

Gallagher, D., Breckenridge, J., Steinmetz, J., & Thompson, L. W. The Beck Depression Inventory and Research Diagnostic Criteria: Congruence in an older population. *Journal of Consulting and Clinical Psychology*, in press.

Gallagher, D., Nies, G., & Thompson, L. Reliability of the Beck Depression Inventory with older adults. *Journal of Consulting and Clinical Psychology*, 1982, **50**, 152–153.

Gallagher, D., Slife, B., & Rose, T. *Psychological correlates of immunologic disease in older adults.* Paper presented at Western Psychological Association annual meeting, Sacramento, Calif., April 1982.

Gallagher, D., & Thompson, L. W. Differential effectiveness of psychotherapies for the treatment of major depressive disorder in older adult patients. *Psychotherapy, Theory, Research and Practice*, in press, 1982.

Gallagher, D., & Thompson, L. W. *Stressful events, coping, and relapse rates in depressed elderly.* Paper presented at the American Psychological Association meetings, Washington, D.C., August 1982.

Gallagher, D., Thompson, L., Baffa, G., Piatt, C., Ringering, L., & Stone, V. *Depression in the elderly: A behavioral treatment manual.* Los Angeles: University of Southern California Press, 1981.

Gallagher, D., Thompson, L. W., & Levy, S. Clinical psychological assessment of older adults. In L. Poon (Ed.), *Aging in the 1980's.* Washington, D.C.: American Psychological Association, 1980.

Gauthier, J., & Marshall, W. Grief: A cognitive-behavioral analysis. *Cognitive Therapy and Research*, 1977, **1**, 39–44.

Gerner, R. Depression in the elderly. In O. Kaplan (Ed.), *Psychopathology of aging.* New York: Academic Press, 1979.

Gershon, S., & Raskin, A. *Genesis and treatment of psychologic disorders in the elderly.* New York: Raven Press, 1975.

Gurland, B. The comparative frequency of depression in various adult age groups. *Journal of Gerontology*, 1976, **31**, 283–292.

Hamilton, M. A rating scale for depression. *Journal of Neurology, Neurosurgery, and Psychiatry*, 1960, **23**, 56–62.

Hamilton, M. Development of a rating scale for primary depressive illness. *British Journal of Social and Clinical Psychology,* 1967, **6,** 278-296.

Hathaway, S. R., & McKinley, J. C. *The Minnesota Multiphasic Personality Schedule.* Minneapolis: University of Minnesota Press, 1943.

Hedlung, B., & Gilewski, M. *Development of pleasant and unpleasant events schedules for older adults: a validation study of short forms for use with elderly individuals.* Unpublished mimeo, Univ. of Southern California, Los Angeles, 1980.

Hedlund, B., & Thompson, L. W. *Teaching the elderly to control depression using an educational format.* Paper presented at the meeting of the American Psychological Association, Montreal, August 1980.

Hirschfeld, R. M. A., & Cross, C. K. Epidemiology of affective disorders. *Archives of General Psychiatry,* 1982, **39,** 35-46.

Hollon, S., & Kendall, P. Cognitive self-statements in depression: Development of an Automatic Thoughts Questionnaire. *Cognitive Therapy and Research,* 1980, **4,** 383-395.

Juel-Nielson, N. Frequency of depressive states within geographically delimited population groups. 3. Incidence (The Aarhus County Investigation). *Acta Psychiatrica Scandinavica,* 1961, **Suppl. 162,** 69-80.

Kahn, R., Zarit, S., Hilbert, N., & Niederehe, G. Memory complaints and impairment in the aged. *Archives of General Psychiatry,* 1975, **32,** 1569-1573.

Katz, M. M., & Lyerly, S. B. Methods of measuring adjustment and social behavior in the community: I. Rationale description, discriminative validity and scale development. *Psychological Reports,* 1963, **13,** 503-535.

Kay, D. W., Beamish, P., & Roth, M. Old age mental disorders in New-Castle-upon-Tyne: A study of prevalence. *British Journal of Psychiatry,* 1964, **110,** 146-159.

Kincannon, J. C. Prediction of the standard MMPI scale scores from 71 items: The Mini-Mult. *Journal of Consulting and Clinical Psychology,* 1968, **32,** 319-325.

Klerman, G., DiMascio, A., Weissman, M., Prusoff, B., & Paykel, E. Treatment of depression by drugs and psychotherapy. *American Journal of Psychiatry,* 1974, **131,** 186-191.

Knight, B. Psychotherapy and behavior change with the non-institutionalized aged. *International Journal of Aging and Human Development,* 1978-79, **9,** 221-236.

Kovacs, M., Rush, A. J., Beck, A. T., & Hollon, S. D. Depressed outpatients treated with cognitive therapy or pharmacotherapy: A one year follow-up. *Archives of General Psychiatry,* 1981, **38,** 33-39.

Lawton, M. P. The Philadelphia Geriatric Center Morale Scale: A revision. *Journal of Gerontology,* 1975, **30,** 85-89.

Levy, S., Derogatis, L., Gallagher, D., & Gatz, M. Intervention with older adults. In L. Poon (Ed.), *Aging in the 1980's: Psychological issues.* Washington, D.C.: American Psychological Association, 1980.

Lewinsohn, P. M., & Grosscup, S. *Decreasing unpleasant events and increasing pleasant events: A treatment manual for depression.* Unpublished mimeograph, University of Oregon, 1978.

Lewinsohn, P. M., & Lee, W. M. L. Assessment of affective disorders. In D. H. Barlow (Ed.), *Behavioral assessment of adult disorders.* New York: Guilford, 1981.

Lewinsohn, P. M., Munoz, R. F., Youngren, M. A., & Zeiss, A. M. *Control your depression.* Englewood Cliffs, N.J.: Prentice-Hall, 1978.

Lewinsohn, P. M., Steinmetz, J. L., Antonuccio, D. O., & Teri, L. *The coping with depression course: A psychoeducational intervention for unipolar depression.* Unpublished mimeograph, University of Oregon, 1982.

Lewinsohn, P. M., & Talkington, J. The measurement of aversive events and relations to depression. *Applied Psychological Measurement,* 1979, **3,** 83-101.

Lowenthal, M. F., Berkman, R. L., & Associates. *Aging and mental disorder.* San Francisco: Jossey-Bass, 1967.

MacPhillamy, D. J., & Lewinsohn, P. M. The Pleasant Events Schedule: Studies on reliability, validity, and scale intercorrelation. *Journal of Consulting and Clinical Psychology*, 1982, **50**, 363–380.

McGarvey, B., Gallagher, D., Thompson, L. W., & Zelinski, E. Reliability and factor structure of the Zung Self-Rating Depression Scale in three age groups. *Essence*, 1982, **5**, 141–153.

McLean, P., & Hakstian, A. R. Clinical depression: Comparative efficacy of outpatient treatments. *Journal of Consulting and Clinical Psychology*, 1979, **47**, 818–836.

McLean, P. D., Ogston, K., & Grauer, L. A behavioral approach to the treatment of depression. *Journal of Behavioral Therapy and Experimental Psychiatry*, 1973, **4**, 323–330.

McNair, D. M. Self-rating scales for assessing psychopathology in the elderly. In A. Raskin & L. S. Jarvik (Eds.), *Psychiatric symptoms and cognitive loss in the elderly*. Washington, D.C.: Hemisphere, 1979.

Mintz, J. *Target complaints questionnaire and scoring manual*. Unpublished manuscript, 1981. Available from the author at VA Medical Center, Brentwood, West Los Angeles, Calif.

Mintz, J., Steuer, J., & Jarvik, L. Psychotherapy with depressed elderly patients: Research considerations. *Journal of Consulting and Clinical Psychology*, 1981, **49**, 542–548.

Moos, R., Cronkite, R., Billings, A., & Finney, J. *Health and Daily Living Form manual*. Unpublished manuscript, 1980. Available from authors at Social Ecology Laboratory, Stanford University and VA Medical Center, Palo Alto, Calif.

Niemeyer, R. A., Gurman, A. S., Klein, M. H., & Greist, J. H. *Cognitive change during noncognitive therapies: A comparison of three treatments for depression*. Paper presented at the meeting of the Society for Psychotherapy Research, Jeffersonville, Vermont, June 1982.

Overall, J. E., & Gorham, D. R. The Brief Psychiatric Rating Scale. *Psychological Reports*, 1962, **10**, 799–812.

Parsons, P. L. Mental health of Swansea's old folk. *British Journal of Preventative Social Medicine*, 1965, **19**, 43–47.

Peterson, C., Semmel, A., von Baeyer, C., Abramson, L., Metalsky, G., & Seligman, M. E. P. The Attributional Style Questionnaire. *Cognitive Therapy and Research*, 1982, **6**, 287–299.

Popkin, S., Gallagher, D., Thompson, L. W., & Moore, M. Memory complaint and performance in normal and depressed older adults. *Experimental Aging Research*, 1982, **8**(3), 141–145.

Post, F. *The clinical psychiatry of late life*. Oxford: Pergamon, 1965.

Prusoff, B., Weissman, M. M., Klerman, G., & Rounsaville, B. Research diagnostic criteria subtypes of depression. *Archives of General Psychiatry*, 1980, **37**, 796–801.

Prusoff, B., Weissman, M. M., & Scholomskas, A. *Pharmacotherapy and psychotherapy in the treatment of depressed elderly patients*. Paper presented at the meeting of the American Psychological Association, Washington, D.C., August 1982.

Raskin, A., & Crook, T. NIMH Psychobiology of Depression Health and Medical History forms. N.d. Available from the authors upon request.

Raskin, A., & Rae, D. S. Psychiatric symptoms in the elderly. *Psychopharmacology Bulletin*, 1981, **17**, 96–99.

Richards, W. S., & Thorpe, G. L. Behavioral approaches to the problems of later life. In M. Storandt, I. Siegler, & M. F. Elias (Eds.), *The clinical psychology of aging*. New York: Plenum, 1978.

Roth, M. Senile dementia and its borderlands. In J. Cole & E. Barrett (Eds.), *Psychopathology in the aged*. New York: Raven, 1980.

Rush, A. J., Beck, A., Kovacs, M., & Hollon, S. Comparative efficacy of cognitive therapy and imipramine in the treatment of depressed outpatients. *Cognitive Therapy and Research*, 1977, **1**, 17–37.

Salzman, C., & Shader, R. I. Clinical evaluation of depression in the elderly. In A. Raskin & L. F. Jarvik (Eds.), *Psychiatric symptoms and cognitive loss in the elderly*. Washington, D.C.: Hemisphere, 1979.

Schwab, J. J. Depression among the aged. *Southern Medical Journal,* 1976, **69**, 1039-1041.

Silverman, C. *The epidemiology of depression.* Baltimore: Johns Hopkins University Press, 1968.

Simon, A. Physical and socio-psychologic stress in the geriatric mentally ill. *Comprehensive Psychiatry,* 1970, **11**, 242-247.

Spitzer, R. L., Endicott, J., & Robins, E. Research Diagnostic Criteria: Rationale and reliability. *Archives of General Psychiatry,* 1978, **35**, 773-782.

Steinmetz, J. L., Lewinsohn, P. M., & Antonuccio, D. O. Prediction of individual outcome in a group intervention for depression. *Journal of Consulting and Clinical Psychology,* in press.

Strauss, D., & Solomon, K. *Psychopharmacologic intervention for depression in the elderly.* Paper presented at the meeting of the Gerontological Society of America, San Diego, Calif., November 1980.

Steuer, J., Jarvik, L. F., Gerner, R., Hammen, C. L., McCarley, T., Rosen, R., Cochran, S., & Motoike, P. *Group psychotherapy versus medication in treatment of depressed elderly.* Paper presented at the meeting of the Gerontological Society of America, Toronto, November 1981.

Teri, L., & Lewinsohn, P. M. Modification of the Pleasant and Unpleasant Events Schedules for use with the elderly. *Journal of Consulting and Clinical Psychology,* 1982, **50**, 444-445.

Thompson, L. W. Periodic "lapses" in attentional processes: A possible correlate of memory impairment in the elderly. In L. W. Poon, J. Fozard, L. S. Cermack, D. Arenberg, & L. W. Thompson (Eds.), *New directions in memory and aging.* Hillsdale, N.J.: Erlbaum, 1980.

Thompson, L. W., Gallagher, D., Nies, G., & Epstein, D. *Psychoeducational approaches for treatment of depression in elders.* Paper presented at the American Psychological Association meetings, Washington, D.C., August 1982.

Thompson, L. W., Gallagher, D., Nies, G., & Epstein, D. Evaluation of the effectiveness of professionals and nonprofessionals as instructors of "Coping with Depression" classes for elders. *Gerontologist,* in press.

Thompson, L. W., Gallagher, D., & Peterson, J. *Social support questionnaire.* Unpublished questionnaire, 1979. Available from authors at Bereavement Longitudinal Research Project, University of Southern California, Los Angeles, Calif.

Vernon, S. W., & Roberts, R. E. Use of the SADS-RDC in a tri-ethnic community survey. *Archives of General Psychiatry,* 1982, **39**, 47-52.

Waskow, I. E. (Chair) *The psychotherapy of depression collaborative research program: The first year experience.* Symposium presented at the meeting of the Society for Psychotherapy Research, Aspen, Colorado, June 1981.

Weissman, M. M. *Social adjustment scale—self report (SAS-SR).* Unpublished manuscript, 1980. Available from the author at Yale University School of Medicine, New Haven, Connecticut.

Weissman, M. M., & Bothwell, S. Assessment of social adjustment by patient self-report. *Archives of General Psychiatry,* 1976, **33**, 1111-1115.

Weissman, M. M., Klerman, G., Prusoff, B., Scholomskas, D., & Padian, N. Depressed outpatients: Results one year after treatment with drugs and/or interpersonal psychotherapy. *Archives of General Psychiatry,* 1981, **38**, 51-55.

Weissman, M. M., & Myers, J. K. Affective disorders in a US urban community: The use of Research Diagnostic Criteria in an epidemiological survey. *Archives of General Psychiatry,* 1978, **35**, 1304-1311.

Weissman, M. M., Prusoff, B., DiMascio, A., Neu, C., Goklaney, M., & Klerman, G. The efficacy of drugs and psychotherapy in the treatment of acute depressive episodes. *American Journal of Psychiatry,* 1979, **136**, **4B**, 555-558.

Wells, C. E. Pseudodementia. *American Journal of Psychiatry,* 1979, **136**, 895-900.

Wilcox, B. L. Social support, life stress, and psychological adjustment: A test of the buffering hypothesis. *American Journal of Community Psychology,* 1981, **9**, 371-386.

Wood, V., Wylie, M. L., & Shaefor, B. An analysis of a short self-report measure of life satisfaction: Correlation with rater judgments. *Journal of Gerontology,* 1969, **24,** 465–469.

Yesavage, J., Brink, T., Rose, T., Lum, O., Huang, O., Adey, V., & Leirer, V. Development and validation of a geriatric depression screening scale: A preliminary report. *Journal of Psychiatric Research,* in press.

Young, J. E. Cognitive therapy and loneliness. In G. Emery, S. D. Hollon, & R. C. Bedrosian (Eds.), *New directions in cognitive therapy.* New York: Guilford, 1981.

Zarit, S. *Aging and mental disorders.* New York: Free Press, 1980.

Zelinski, E., Gilewski, M., & Thompson, L. W. Do laboratory tests relate to self-assessment of memory ability in the young and old? In L. W. Poon, J. Fozard, L. S. Cermack, D. Arenberg, & L. W. Thompson (Eds.), *New directions in memory and aging.* Hillsdale, N.J.: Erlbaum, 1980.

Zung, W. A self-rating depression scale. *Archives of General Psychiatry,* 1965, **12,** 63–70.

Zung, W. Affective disorders. In E. W. Busse & D. G. Blazer (Eds.), *Handbook of geriatric psychiatry.* New York: Van Nostrand Reinhold, 1980.

Zung, W., Gianturco, D., Pfeiffer, E., Wang, H., & Potkins, S. Pharmacology of depression in the aged: Evaluation of Gerovital H-3 as an antidepressant drug. *Psychosomatics,* 1974, **15,** 127–131.

Chapter 2
Cognitive Impairment
Steven H. Zarit and Judy M. Zarit

DESCRIPTION OF PROBLEM

Cognitive impairments, especially decrements of memory and intellect, are one of the most common expectations people have about aging. The aging process is often conceptualized as a gradual downward trajectory, with ever-increasing levels of impairment, until the person is helpless, doddering, and incompetent. This model of aging, however, has not been supported by empirical studies. While there are notable differences in cognitive performance between older and younger persons, the vast majority of individuals over age 65 are able to live independently and to manage their daily lives in a competent way. Furthermore, estimates of the effects of aging on cognitive performance have been exaggerated by a number of factors, including generational differences and older persons' lack of familiarity with testing procedures (Schaie & Labouvie-Vief, 1974; Schaie & Schaie, 1977; Schonfield, 1974). Individual differences among older persons are also considerable. Even on those abilities that are reported to have the most age-related decline, such as reaction time, some older persons perform at or near levels typical of the young (Schonfield, 1974). Overall, the cognitive changes that most people experience as they grow older are relatively benign.

Some older persons, however, do suffer major cognitive losses. A serious disruption of memory and intellect is extremely disabling for the afflicted individual, and can place tremendous burdens on relatives and friends. Cognitive loss may be one of the major factors leading to nursing home placement, with an estimated 50 percent of nursing home patients having significant cognitive impairments (*National Nursing Home Survey*, 1977).

In the past, all the cognitive problems of aging were blamed on "hardening of the arteries" (Roth, 1955). As research has generated better understanding of the causes of severe cognitive loss, there has been more forward impetus differentiating between different kinds of senile dementia, such as Alzheimer's Disease. In some instances, however, this has led to assuming the presence of a dementia without sufficient supporting evidence and cases where the cognitive impairment is caused by a potentially treatable condition have been overlooked. (In our clinical experience, two common errors until quite recently have been lack of careful diagnosis of cognitive symptoms and indiscriminant attribution of such problems to "old age." More recently there has been a shift toward diagnosing many problems as Alzheimer's Disease, often erroneously.)

The task for clinicians working with older adults is to distinguish the relatively mild and benign cognitive changes of normal aging from the more severe disruptions of function and to differentiate between treatable and untreatable causes of cognitive impairment. Proper identification of potentially reversible problems will reduce the numbers of older people suffering from cognitive impairments. A second major task is to develop strategies for working with cognitively impaired older persons and their families. Even when the impairment has been caused by an irreversible condition, it is still possible to identify treatable aspects of cognitive impairment in order to develop interventions to improve some areas of functioning and to assist family members in caring for these individuals.

Causes of Cognitive Impairment

While many diverse problems can cause cognitive impairment in later life, most fall into four broad categories: senile dementia, delirium and reversible dementia, focal brain damage, and depression. Other possible causes, such as chronic alcoholism or Huntington's Chorea, which may have their onset earlier in life, will not be discussed in this chapter.

Senile Dementia. Senile dementia refers to a global and progressive impairment of intellect. Once considered synonymous with aging, senile dementia is now recognized as the result of degenerative brain disorders that affect only a minority of the aged. The earliest symptom is an increase in forgetfulness, which is difficult to distinguish from normal fluctuations in memory. As the disease progresses, these lapses in memory increase in frequency and begin to affect other abilities, such as work, hobbies, and household chores. In time, more extensive impairments develop, and the afflicted person may not be able to perform even the most basic tasks, for instance, dressing.

Community surveys have found the overall prevalence of senile dementia to be relatively low (Gurland, 1980; Kay, Beamish, & Roth, 1964; Larsson, Sjogren, & Jacobson, 1963); approximately 4 percent of people over age 65 have definite symptoms of dementia (Mortimer, Schuman, & French, 1981). The prevalence of dementia rises substantially with advancing age to a rate of almost 20 percent among people over age 80 (Gurland, Dean, Craw, & Golden, 1980; Kay, 1972). There are more women with dementia than men

(Gurland et al., 1980), although this difference is probably related to women's greater longevity rather than to higher susceptibility.

Morphological studies have identified several major subtypes of dementia and their characteristic pathologies (Blessed, Tomlinson, & Roth, 1968; Terry, 1978; Terry & Wisniewski, 1977). The most common type of dementia has been termed "Senile Dementia of the Alzheimer's Type" (SDAT). Alzheimer's Disease was originally described as a pre-senile dementia, affecting people before age 55, but the pathological changes characteristic of it are found in approximately 60 percent of cases of dementia in people over age 65. These changes include the appearance of abnormal structures in the brain peculiar to this disease: senile plaques, neurofibrillary tangles, and granulovascular structures.

The other major type is multi-infarct dementia, which has been estimated to account for 10 to 20 percent of cases (Gurland et al., 1980; Roth, 1980; Terry, 1978). This type of dementia occurs when the person suffers a series of small strokes, presumably caused by pieces of plaque on artery walls breaking off and traveling to the brain (Hachinski, Lassen, & Marshall, 1974). Both types of dementia are progressive, but multi-infarct is characterized by a stepwise course, while SDAT usually involves gradual deterioration.

The remaining cases of dementia are either of the mixed type, with both Multiinfarct and Alzheimer's features, or are caused by rarer illnesses such as Pick's Diseases or Creutzfeldt-Jacob's Disease.

There are various theories about the etiologies of these illnesses. Alzheimer's type has been linked to genetic, viral, and biochemical factors (Miller & Cohen, 1981; Roth, 1980). Genetic theories have been stimulated by findings of slight familial tendencies, especially when the onset of the disease is before age 55 (Mortimer, Schuman, & French, 1981). The possibility that a slow-acting virus is the cause of the brain changes in Alzheimer's dementia is based in part on observations of viral transmission in Creutzfeldt-Jacob's Disease and in kuru, a rare, degenerative illness found in New Guinea. Biochemical theories have been spurred by recent findings of deficits in the cholinergic system in the brain of Alzheimer's patients (Perry, Perry, Blessed, & Tomlinson, 1977; Roth, 1980). Aluminum and zinc poisoning have also been the subject of speculation as possible causes. Multi-infarct dementia seems to be related to the same risk factors as stroke and heart disease, although why these disorders lead to a dementia in one person and not another is not known (Roth, 1980).

At present, accurate medical diagnosis of Alzheimer's Disease is difficult and depends on morphological findings at postmortem. There are no tests that provide a definitive diagnosis (Libow, 1977; National Institute of Aging Task Force, 1980). For this reason, DSM-III uses the category, "primary neuronal degeneration," rather than Alzheimer's Disease. Nevertheless, behavioral and cognitive manifestations of dementia are reliably related to brain pathology and can be used to determine that a disease is present. In a major study of the relation of brain changes and behavior, Blessed, Tomlinson, and Roth (1968) found that evidence of widespread presence of senile plaques characterized dementia patients, while patients with other psychiatric disorders (such as depression), and controls with no psychiatric history, had few or none of these brain abnormalities. Within the dementia group, severity of behavioral and cognitive symptoms before death was generally associated with the extent of plaques. Similar findings have been reported for patients with multi-infarct dementia (Roth, 1980).

Various medical treatments for dementia have been tried, thus far unsuccessfully. Among the approaches used have been tranquilizing and stimulating medications, vasodilators, vitamins, and hyperbaric oxygen (Funkenstein, Hicks, Dysken, & Davis, 1981; Thompson, Davis, Obrist, & Heyman, 1976). In follow-ups on recent findings of an acetylcholine deficit in SDAT, ingestion of large amounts of choline, usually in the form of lecithin, has also been attempted; again without success. It has also been suggested by Roth (1980) that treatment of the causes of infarcts in the early stages of multi-infarct dementia may reduce the likelihood of further decline.

Delirium and Reversible Dementia.   The terms "delirium" and "reversible dementia" (sometimes called "pseudodementia") are less clearly defined than "senile dementia," and have heterogeneous etiologies. Nevertheless, patients with these disorders share an important characteristic: they manifest cognitive impairments that resemble those of the senile dementias, but the causes of these impairments stem from treatable (i.e., reversible) conditions.

Delirium refers to a syndrome of disturbed mental functioning that has been described since the earliest medical writings. Clinical features are: impaired awareness of self and surroundings; attention deficits; a tendency for hallucinations and delusions; disorientation; increased or decreased alertness; disturbed sleep patterns; and rapid fluctuations in symptoms and their severity (Lipowski, 1980). Memory is usually impaired, although the deficit can be selective (Kahn & Miller, 1978). The common underlying factor is presumed to be a disruption of cerebral metabolism (Lipowski, 1980). Reversible dementia has been described as virtually indistinguishable from senile dementia on the basis of presenting symptoms (Libow, 1977; National Institute of Aging [NIA] Task Force, 1980).

There are few estimates of the incidence or prevalence of delirium or reversible dementia. Delirium among older persons following surgery appears high (Linn et al., 1953). Symptoms include disorientation, hallucinations, and paranoid ideation, and usually subside within a week after surgery, except in cases where there are other medical complications. Simon and Cahan (1963) reported that over half of the patients admitted to an acute geriatric screening ward had evidence of possible delirium. The number of untreated cases in nursing homes may be considerable, although precise figures are unavailable (Zarit, 1980).

(An important consideration related to prevalence is that a delirium can also be present in someone with dementia. In fact, brain damage of any sort may make the person more susceptible to delirium [Lipowski, 1980].)

A recent report by a task force of the National Institute of Aging (1980) emphasizes that virtually any internal disturbance can lead to cognitive symptoms in an older person. Common causes include toxic effects of medications or interactions between drugs, infections, electrolyte imbalances, malnutrition, and potassium deficits. Cognitive symptoms may also occur following surgeries, fractures, head injuries, or environmental changes, including relocation or the death of a spouse. Unless there is also an underlying dementia, or the cause of the symptoms cannot be treated, complete recovery is possible. A list of medical factors that can cause reversible cognitive impairments appears in Table 2.1.

Table 2.1.   Reversible Causes of Dementia Symptoms and Delirium.*

	Dementia	Delirium	Either or Both
Therapeutic drug intoxication			Yes
Depression	Yes		
Metabolic			
a. Azotemia or renal failure (dehydration, diuretics, obstruction, hypokalemia)			Yes
b. Hyponatremia (diuretics, excess antidiuretic hormone, salt wasting, intravenous fluids)			Yes
c. Hypernatremia (dehydration, intravenous saline)		Yes	
d. Volume depletion (diuretics, bleeding, inadequate fluids)			Yes
e. Acid-base disturbance		Yes	
f. Hypoglycemia (insulin, oral hypoglycemics, starvation)			Yes
g. Hyperglycemia (diabetic ketoacidosis, or hyperosmolar coma)		Yes	
h. Hepatic failure			Yes
i. Hypothyroidism			Yes
j. Hyperthyroidism (especially apathetic)			Yes
k. Hypercalcemia			Yes
l. Cushing's syndrome	Yes		
m. Hypopituitarism			Yes
Infection, fever, or both			
a. Viral			Yes
b. Bacterial			
Pneumonia		Yes	
Pyelonephritis		Yes	
Cholecystitis		Yes	
Diverticulitis		Yes	
Tuberculosis			Yes
Endocarditis			Yes
Cardiovascular			
a. Acute myocardial infarct		Yes	
b. Congestive heart failure			Yes
c. Arrhythmia			Yes

Table 2.1 continued

	Dementia	Delirium	Either or Both
d. Vascular occlusion			Yes
e. Pulmonary embolus		Yes	
Brain disorders			
a. Vascular insufficiency			
Transient ischemia		Yes	
Stroke			Yes
b. Trauma			
Subdural hematoma			Yes
Concussion/confusion		Yes	
Intracerebral hemorrhage		Yes	
Epidural hematoma		Yes	
c. Infection			
Acute meningitis (pyogenic, viral)		Yes	
Chronic meningitis (tuberculous, fungal)			Yes
Neurosyphilis			Yes
Subdural empyema			Yes
Brain abscess			Yes
d. Tumors			
Metastatic to brain			Yes
Primary in brain			Yes
e. Normal pressure hydrocephalus	Yes		
Pain			
a. Fecal impaction			Yes
b. Urinary retention		Yes	
c. Fracture		Yes	
d. Surgical abdomen		Yes	
Sensory deprivation states such as blindness or deafness			Yes
Hospitalization			
a. Anesthesia or surgery			Yes
b. Environmental change and isolation			Yes
Alcohol toxic reactions			
a. Lifelong alcoholism	Yes		
b. Alcoholism new in old age			Yes
c. Decreased tolerance with age producing increasing intoxication			Yes
d. Acute hallucinosis		Yes	
e. Delirium tremens		Yes	
Anemia			Yes
Tumor—systemic effects of nonmetastatic malignant neoplasm			Yes
Chronic lung disease with hypoxia or hypercepnia			Yes
Deficiencies of nutrients such as vitamin B_{12}, folic acid, or niacin	Yes		
Accidental hypothermia		Yes	
Chemical intoxications			
a. Heavy metals such as arsenic, lead, or mercury			Yes
b. Consciousness-altering agents			Yes
c. Carbon monoxide			Yes

*Source: NIA Task Force. Senility reconsidered. *Journal of the American Medical Association,* October 1980.

The implication for diagnosis and treatment is that any cognitive disturbance, including new changes in someone with a preexisting dementia, needs
to be vigorously investigated. The first hypothesis to account for any cognitive deficit should be that there is some treatable component, and this must be
ruled out before the changes can be ascribed to dementia (NIA Task Force,
1980). If the cause of the disturbance can be ameliorated with treatment,
cognitive symptoms may be substantially or totally reversed.

Focal Brain Damage.   A less common source of cognitive impairment in the
elderly is focal brain damage. Focal damage is associated with selective,
rather than global, impairment of abilities and is not necessarily progressive.
While localization of brain damage is typically the first consideration for
younger patients, this possibility is frequently overlooked in the old. Common causes of focal brain damage are head trauma, strokes, and brain
tumors.

In contrast to the dementias, the onset of symptoms in cases of focal
damage is usually abrupt. It is, of course, also possible for focal and diffuse
brain damage to co-exist in the same patient. For example, one patient seen in
our clinic had symptoms of both SDAT and brain tumor. In cases of multi-
infarct dementia, early strokes might result in selective impairment, but over
time more global and generalized impairment becomes evident.

The distinction between focal damage and dementia has implications for
treatment and prognosis. When the cause is a tumor or a stroke, medical
interventions can sometimes prevent further damage. The prognosis is good
when the cause of the damage can be arrested or in cases of traumatic head
injury where the deficits remain static. The key to planning interventions is a
careful delineation of the affected functions.

Depression.   Depression among older people is often difficult to distinguish
from dementia. Common symptoms such as psychomotor retardation and
withdrawal from activities can create the impression of dementia. Moreover,
many depressed people complain of memory loss. Some studies have found
that complaints of poor memory are not associated with the severe type of
memory impairment typical of senile dementia but are more likely to reflect
the exaggerated ways depressed people evaluate themselves (Gurland, et al.,
1976; Kahn, Zarit, Hilbert, & Niederehe, 1975). Among dementia patients,
the extent of memory complaints is inversely related to severity of symptoms,
and the person in the later stages of the illness may have no awareness at all of
memory loss (Kahn et al., 1975).

On the other hand, cases have been reported (in the literature) in which
depression was accompanied by severe cognitive impairment typical of dementia and where cognitive symptoms diminished with appropriate treatment
(Kiloh, 1961). Unfortunately, the exact nature of the cognitive impairments
observed in these cases has not been well documented.

Another consideration is that dementia and depression are not actually exclusive conditions. Depression is often present in early stages of a dementia (Epstein, 1976; Kahn et al., 1975). In these cases the cognitive impairment will presumably get worse, whereas when dementia is not present, cognitive symptoms that are due to the depression will lessen as mood improves.

The prevalence and treatment of depression among the elderly are considered elsewhere in this volume. However, the possibility that depression can be responsible for cognitive change is important. As is the case with medical conditions that can cause cognitive symptoms, depression must be ruled out before dementia can be diagnosed. Whenever mild cognitive loss and depressed affect are found, treatment for depression should be considered. Even with more definite evidence of dementia, treatment for the depression may result in some improvement of the patient's current functioning (Epstein, 1976).

ASSESSMENT

Assessment of cognitive impairment has several important goals. First, it is crucial to distinguish the relatively benign changes that occur with aging from the more profound impairments that indicate brain dysfunction. Second, when clinically significant cognitive impairments are identified, there needs to be a determination of the type of impairment: whether it is dementia, or a reversible condition. And third, when a dementia is confirmed, assessments should provide accurate information about the difficulties that the cognitive impairment causes in the person's everyday life. This latter type of information is especially useful in planning psychosocial interventions.

The first two assessment goals are more typical of medical diagnosis than the behavioral analysis that has had a prominent role in evaluations of functional psychological disorders. The objective is to determine if there is an underlying disease and of what sort. There are certain risks involved in this type of diagnostic process. One possible outcome is the failure to detect that an illness is present or what is termed a Type I error. On the other hand, one could make a Type II error of diagnosing an illness when none is present.

Kahn and Miller (1978) provide a cogent analysis of the consequences of these two types of diagnostic errors. Pointing out that there currently are no effective medical treatments for dementia, they suggest that a Type I error does not result in denying the patient appropriate therapies. Therefore, the consequences are minimal. The Type II error of incorrectly labeling an older person as demented can have important consequences by generating a sense of therapeutic nihilism about the patient. Because of the different risks involved in these errors, Kahn and Miller suggest that conservative criteria be used for assessing dementia and that such a diagnosis be made only when the evidence is very compelling.

Table 2.2.   A Summary of Assessment Procedures

	Dementia	Delirium	Reversible Dementia	Focal Brain Damage	Depression	Normal Aging
1. Current Symptoms						
a. Complaints of Memory Problems	Reported by others; patient often unaware	Patient often denies problems	Reported by others; patient often unaware	Patient may complain of memory loss	Patient usually complains of memory problems	Patient may complain of memory loss
b. Types of Memory Problems Reported	Major—interfere with activities of daily living	May be selective and variable; major activities disrupted	Major—interfere with activities of daily living	Specific functions more affected (e.g., spatial but not verbal abilities or vice versa)	Mild, mostly due to inattention	Mild increase in normal forgetting (e.g., names)
c. Hallucinations and Delusions	Paranoid accusations sometimes present with mild memory loss; illusions in severe cases	Sometimes vivid hallucinations and well-developed delusions are present	Not described well in the literature	Absent	Absent, except in extremely severe cases	Absent
2. History						
a. Onset	SDAT: insidious multi-infarct: sometimes sudden	Usually sudden	Not described well in the literature	Sudden; associated with brain trauma	Coincides with life changes; onset often abrupt	Reactions to normal life changes; no specific aging pattern
b. Duration	Months or years	A few days or weeks	Not described well in the literature	Dates from incident	At least 2 weeks; can be several months or years	
c. Progression	SDAT: gradual multi-infarct: stepwise	Prodromal symptoms become severe in a few days	Not described well in the literature	Not progressive	Not progressive	Minimal change over long periods of time
d. Fluctuations	SDAT: little multi-infarct: some daily fluctuation, usually worse in evening	Can be extreme, even from hour to hour	Not described well in the literature	Little	Typically worse in the morning	Mild situational fluctuations
3. Tests						
a. Mental Status Questionnaire (MSQ)	2 or more errors	Connotative errors may be present	2 or more errors	Usually 0 or 1 error, unless damage is severe	Usually 0 or 1 error	Usually 0 or 1 error
b. Face-Hand	Errors after 4th trial	May make errors after 4th trial	Errors after 4th trial	No, or unilateral, errors	No errors after 4th trial	No errors after 4th trial
c. Neuropsychological	Severe global deficit	Selective impairment, especially attention	Not described well in the literature	Only certain abilities affected, depending on site of damage	Normal aging pattern; speeded tests may be lower	Normal aging pattern

Table 2.2 continued

	Dementia	Delirium	Reversible Dementia	Focal Brain Damage	Depression	Normal Aging
d. Memory & Behavior Problems Checklist	Mild to extensive impairment	Mild to extensive impairment	Not described well in the literature	Usually only a few problems present	No, or a few, problems	No, or a few, problems
e. Caregiver's Burden	Mild to severe	Not determined	Mild to severe	Absent or mild	Mild to severe	If present, related to long-standing relationship problems or physical disability

With respect to delirium and reversible dementia, the costs associated with diagnostic errors are reversed. Failure to diagnose a delirium or a reversible dementia means that the underlying condition will be untreated, with potentially serious negative consequences for the individual. Therefore, errors should be in the direction of overdiagnosis. An appropriate medical evaluation should be recommended whenever there are reasonable grounds for suspecting that cognitive symptoms are due to a reversible condition.

There have been few systematic studies of diagnostic errors, although the general impression is that dementia is frequently misdiagnosed. One of the most interesting examples of overdiagnosis of dementia comes from the United States–United Kingdom Cross-National Study (Cowan et al., 1975). Older patients in New York and London were evaluated, respectively, by American and British psychiatrists. By comparing differences in rates of diagnosis, it was found that British psychiatrists diagnosed depression more frequently, while the Americans made more diagnoses of dementia. Apparently, these differences were due to a tendency on the part of the American psychiatrists to view depressive symptoms in an older person as signs of dementia.

Because there is no single medical or psychological test that unequivocally proves the presence of dementia, one must always evaluate evidence from several sources. From the pattern of findings it is possible to determine whether or not a disorder is likely to be present.

A useful approach for evaluating cognitive impairment is to begin with the designated patient and relevant family members or friends. The purpose of the interview is to determine current problems and their history. The interview is then followed by testing of cognitive functioning to confirm the presence of an impairment and to generate hypotheses about probable cause. A third step is to obtain an appropriate medical evaluation. Finally, a functional assessment of the patient is useful for planning interventions. A summary of diagnostic steps is provided in Table 2.2.

Current Symptoms and Complaints

When a patient comes or is brought to a clinic by relatives with complaints about memory or other cognitive problems, the first step in the assessment process is to obtain specific information about the types of problems that are occurring, their frequency, and possible antecedents or consequences. It is recommended to begin by obtaining as much of this information as possible from the patient. Someone with a cognitive impairment, however, may be unable to provide accurate information or may deny any problems with memory or other functions.

When the patient complains of memory loss, it often suggests that memory may be within normal ranges or only mildly impaired. As noted earlier, complaints of poor memory are commonly made by depressed older persons, even though they do not have the severe impairments typical of dementia (Kahn et al., 1975). A person worried about his or her own aging and the possibility of diminishing abilities may also show an excessive concern with memory. Since a certain amount of forgetting is normal at any age, the depressed person seems to focus on these common incidents and attributes them to an age-related decline. Their frequency, however, is generally low, and no major problems such as getting lost or forgetting how to perform well-learned activities are reported.

There are instances, however, when the complaints reflect cognitive loss due to brain pathology. Persons with early and mild dementia may be aware of their memory loss to some degree, and some individuals with more severe dementia also have occasional awareness of these problems. A patient with a delirium usually denies problems, although awareness can also be noted on occasions (Weinstein & Kahn, 1955). Another possibility is that the person complaining of poor memory may have focal brain damage, such as from a head trauma or other injury. Memory may indeed be impaired, but the overall cognitive deficits would be neither global nor progressive. The presence of memory complaints generates hypotheses about current functioning. Other evidence must then be obtained to differentiate between these various problems, including history and test results.

When the patient cannot give much information, other informants should be interviewed. The person who spends the most time with the patient can usually provide the best information. Here, it is important to get specific behavioral descriptions of problems rather than to rely on catchwords, such as "memory loss," "confusion," or "disorientation." These terms can be used in very different ways. Memory loss, for instance, may refer to occasionally forgetting a name or to being unable to remember how to dress oneself, but these examples have very different implications. Similarly, the term "confusion" is sometimes used to refer to behaviors typical of dementia, such as being unable to follow directions, but often also describe the fluctuating awareness seen in delirium. A healthy person who gets frustrated over some problem might also be described as "confused."

Another important presenting symptom is the presence of hallucinations or delusions. In the early stages of dementia, paranoid ideation may be present (Berger & Zarit, 1978; Post, 1966). The person appears to be accounting for lapses of memory by blaming family members, mysterious intruders, or others. As an example, when having difficulty finding something, the person might say it has been stolen. Sometimes it is difficult to distinguish these types of complaints from those made by older persons with paranoid delusions but no dementia (Post, 1966). Paranoid symptoms in dementia patients tend to diminish as the disease progresses. In more severe dementias, "illusions" are more likely to be observed than either hallucinations or delusions. Typical illusions such as reporting seeing a cat or other small animal (which is not present) appear related to deficiencies in processing incoming visual stimuli.

While psychotic symptoms may be part of the dementia, more frequently hallucinations and delusions are manifestations of delirium. (The presence of these symptoms in a dementia patient suggests the need for an evaluation for possible delirium.) Because of the dementia patient's lower tolerance of drugs, especially psychoactive medications, these are frequent causes of psychotic symptoms (Kapnick, 1978; Lipowski, 1980).

The presense of hallucinations and delusions raises one other diagnostic question—the possibility of the longstanding psychosis. This can usually be determined from history, although persons with chronic mental disorders can also develop dementia and delirium.

Agitation and restlessness are common complaints in dementia, and can be present in delirium as well. Major tranquilizers are usually prescribed for patients with agitation and restlessness. While some therapeutic gain is possible, the opposite effect may also be observed. A typical course is for the patient to have an initially positive response, but as the drug builds up to toxic levels, symptoms may actually increase.

The following is an example of how medications can produce problems that are mistakenly viewed as symptoms of dementia:

The husband of a 77-year-old woman with a 10-year history of progressive impairment complained that his wife's symptoms had recently changed for the worse. She was now having angry outbursts and hallucinatory experiences, especially in the evening. She had been taking a stimulant, Ritalin (Methylphenidate) for some time. When these new symptoms were first manifested, the prescribing physician recommended doubling the dose. Her symptoms increased markedly after that. Because she was on a medication that can become toxic, and since her symptoms worsened after the drug dosage was increased, the first hypothesis was that problems were related to the drug. Taking her off the medication resulted in total cessation of the hallucinations and outbursts within one week. Six-month follow-up indicated no recurrence, although cognitive functioning continued to be severely impaired.

This example illustrates a medication reaction in someone who had a dementia, but similar reactions have been observed in patients with no dementia. In addition to drugs, these problems can be caused by many of the acute medical problems shown in Table 2.1 above, and in some instances, by emotional stress. It is critical to assume that agitation, restlessness, or hallucinations are due to dementia unless other causes are indicated.

History

The history of symptoms and complaints of the patient's current symptoms provide the most reliable indicators for distinguishing dementia from other conditions (Gurland, 1980). Dementia generally has an insidious onset (that is, developing so gradually as to be well established before becoming apparent), with gradual deterioration thereafter. In contrast, changes associated with normal aging are usually not perceptible from one year to the next. In cases of dementia, families typically report that they first noticed occasional lapses of memory; these did not appear much different from normal, nor were they associated with any particular event or change in the person's life. Gradually, over a period of time from one to two years, the symptoms became more pronounced and memory loss began to interfere with well-learned activities, such as work, household chores, or leisure activities. Over time, the person is able to perform fewer and fewer activities.

Occasionally, the onset of symptoms is relatively sudden, but the progression after that point is gradual. Multi-infarct dementia can first be noticed following a small stroke, or "transient ischemic attack" (TIA). Sometimes the patient or family recalls definite evidence of a TIA, including momentary loss of consciousness, temporary weakness or paralysis of limbs, or aphasia. In other cases, no clear episode will be reported. Symptoms may also begin following a trauma, especially head injury or surgery involving a general anesthetic. Dementia is suggested by the relatively slow progression of symptoms after the initial episode.

Families sometimes link the onset of symptoms to retirement. While the possible contributory role of social stressors such as retirement cannot be ruled out, our clinical observations suggest that in most instances the cognitive symptoms were present before retirement and may actually have influenced the decision to retire.

In contrast to the gradual course of dementia, delirium has a sudden onset, with symptoms developing over the course of a few days or weeks. Recent events may sometimes provide clues as to the causes. For instance, symptoms may begin after the person started a new medication, following a fracture, or after a long period of not eating adequately. Onset can occasionally be gradual, as in cases of pernicious anemia (Libow, 1977; NIA Task Force,

1980). Reversible dementia has not been adequately described, so it is not clear whether onset is gradual, as in dementia, or relatively sudden. In general, however, the more sudden and recent the onset, the more likely that there is some problem other than dementia. As in the example given earlier, sudden changes in dementia may indicate a delirium.

Histories of depression in older persons follow at least two temporal patterns. One is episodic, with relatively recent development of symptoms. Such episodes of depression usually follow losses or other changes in the person's life (Post, 1962). In contrast to delirium, depressive complaints are prominent. The other pattern is a relatively longstanding and chronic unhappiness, which can date back several years. This latter type of depression is distinguishable from dementia because there is no gradual worsening of cognitive functioning.

History and types of symptoms also permit classification of dementia patients according to the probable cause of the cognitive impairment. Hachinski, Lassen, and Marshall (1974) propose empirical criteria for distinguishing Alzheimer's from multi-infarct dementia. They assign patients an "ischemic" score based on the presence of characteristic features of multi-infarct dementias which include relatively sudden onset, nocturnal fluctuations, focal neurological signs and symptoms, and histories of stroke, hypertension, and heart disease. Eisdorfer, Cohen, and Veith (1981) have developed a modification of the ischemic scoring system, which is generally believed to reflect the status of current research and clinical findings. Scores of 4 or less are suggestive of SDAT, while above 6 is more typical of multi-infarct dementia. This scale appears in Table 2.3.

Table 2.3.   Ischemic Score.

Clinical Feature	Score* (if present)
1. Abrupt onset	2
2. Stepwise deterioration	1
3. Fluctuating course	2
4. Nocturnal confusion	1
5. Emotional lability	1
6. History of hypertension	1
7. History of strokes	2
8. Evidence of associated atherosclerosis	1
9. Focal neurological symptoms	2
10. Focal neurological signs	2

Source: Modified from Eisdorfer, Cohen and Veith, 1981.

*Scores of 4 or less suggest Senile Dementia of the Alzheimer's Type. Seven and above indicate possible multi-infarct dementia. Between 4 and 7 are mixed or indeterminant cases.

Preliminary findings indicate good validity for the ischemic score using various criteria, including cerebral blood flow (Hachinski et al., 1974), and findings from biopsies and autopsies (Rosen et al., 1980; Simard et al., 1971). Both types of dementia, however, have been found to have similar impact on family members, and patients classified as SDAT or multi-infarct differ little from each other in functional behavior (Hassinger, Zarit, & Zarit, 1982).

Cognitive Testing

Cognitive testing is essential for confirming or disconfirming the presence of deficits typical of dementia. There are two traditions in the literature on assessment of dementia. The first is drawn from clinical practice and emphasizes the use of the mental status examination. The second stems from the field of neuropsychology, which stresses the use of test batteries. Each approach has different strengths and weaknesses. The two approaches can be applied in conjunction to improve the overall reliability of assessment.

Mental Status Tests. The most widely used clinical procedure for assessment of dementia is the brief mental status test. Several standardized mental status examinations have been developed, with considerable overlap in test items (Folstein, Folstein, & McHugh, 1975; Jacobs, Bernhard, Delgado, & Strain, 1977; Kahn, Goldfarb, Pollack, & Peck, 1960; Pfeiffer, 1975). Questions typically include orientation ("Where are you?"; "What is today's date?"), personal information ("How old are you?"; "When is your birthday?"), and current events ("Who is the president of the United States?"). Some tests also include calculations, figure drawings, naming objects, spelling backwards, and recall tests. Kahn and his associates supplement their mental status questions with a test of perception of double, simultaneous stimulation, the Face-Hand test (Fink, Green, & Bender, 1952).

Because mental status tests tap relatively overlearned and straightforward information, errors indicate obvious cognitive impairments. On the Mental Status Questionnaire (MSQ) of Kahn et al. (1960), shown in Table 2.4, two or more errors indicate significant cognitive impairment (Zarit, Miller, & Kahn, 1978). Errors on the Face-Hand test after the fourth trial also are related to significant cognitive impairment. Hypotheses about the causes of the impairment are developed by considering the patterns of errors as well as history and medical status.

Clinical differences exist in mental status responses between depression, delirium, and dementia. Dementia patients will try to answer mental status questions but will get them wrong. Occasionally, someone will refuse to answer or will make a socially appropriate evasion, such as "I didn't look at the calendar today." With prompting, the person either does not guess the

Table 2.4.   The Mental Status Questionnaire (MSQ)

1. Where are you now? (If necessary, ask: What place is this? What is the name of this place? What kind of place is it?)
2. Where is it located? (Approximate address)
3. What is the date today?—Day of the month? (Correct if within 3 days.)
4. Month?
5. Year?
6. How old are you? (Correct if within one year.)
7. When is your birthday? Month.
8. Year of birth.
9. Who is president of the United States?
10. Who was president before him?

Additional questions:

—Have you ever been in another (place with same name)?
—Who am I?
—What do I do? What's my job called?
—Have you ever seen me before?
—Where were you last night?

date or guesses incorrectly. In contrast, delirium patients sometimes respond to connotative aspects of questions (Kahn, & Miller, 1978; Weinstein & Kahn, 1955). For instance, when asked, "Where are you?" someone with a delirium may state, "In a hotel," or "In a restaurant." Patients may say they were in a hospital with the same name located in a different part of town or may say they were somewhere else the night before. These responses have in common a tendency to minimize illness and stimuli associated with it (Weinstein & Kahn, 1955).

Depressed older persons, on the other hand, rarely make errors on mental status examinations, despite their complaints of poor memory. In the event that someone with prominent depressive symptoms scored in the impaired range on a mental status test, two possibilities should be considered. One is that the person has a dementia as well as being depressed. The other alternative is that the individual is not attending to the questions as a result of altered mood. History and future course will clarify the role of depression in these cases.

The brain-injured person with a focal brain injury will not generally make errors on a mental status examination. When someone with a history of head trauma does score in the impaired range, evaluating the course of symptoms can clarify the situation. If there has been little or no progression of symptoms since the injury, then the condition is probably stable and interventions can be planned accordingly. On the other hand, someone whose symptoms are worsening may have some other problem secondary, or in addition, to the original injury. This person should have a medical evaluation to determine if the problem has treatable aspects. One cautionary note is that complaints of worsening should be verified by testing, whenever possible. The brain-injured person who is depressed may magnify episodes of memory impairment or other cognitive symptoms, even though actual functioning has not changed. During the recovery period from an acute trauma, complaints may even increase as the person's functioning improves. As has been stressed throughout, evaluating complaints of cognitive dysfunction is an important part of the clinical picture, but complaints are not a reliable indicator of cognitive abilities.

The major advantage of mental status tests is that the items represent overlearned material, which is not generally confounded by education, motivation, or other transitory factors (Zarit, Miller, & Kahn, 1978). Because the test items are relatively easy, they differentiate persons with definite cognitive impairment from the rest of the population. Hence, mental status testing meets the criterion proposed by Kahn and Miller (1978) of a conservative test and yields few false-positive errors.

The drawback of these tests is that they are not sensitive to early, mild dementia symptoms. They are also not useful for measuring subtle changes. These problems are directly related to the advantages of these tests. By being uncomplicated, they are useful in identifying obvious cases of impairment but cannot measure subtle differences.

Neuropsychological Assessment. The advantages and drawbacks of neuropsychological approaches mirror those of the mental status tests except that there is more potential for identifying early cases of dementia, but more risk of confounding factors such as education, motivation, and fatigue (Kahn & Miller, 1978).

The Wechsler Adult Intelligence Scale (WAIS) (Wechsler, 1958) has been used extensively with older adults, and the literature on it illustrates how persons with normal functioning are sometimes erroneously labeled as brain-damaged. (The typical age pattern on the WAIS is for scores on performance subtests to be lower than scores on verbal subtests.) Cross-sectional comparisons between young and old subjects have confirmed that age differences are larger for performance subtests (Botwinick, 1977; 1978). Because the performance subtests are sometimes considered to reflect functioning in the non-dominant hemisphere of the brain, it has been presumed that aging results in a differential impact on that hemisphere, and many clinicians have regarded all elderly as brain damaged, without making the distinctions between normal aging and a more devastating decline. This aging pattern, however, does not appear to be a forerunner of dementia. In fact, subscales most likely to be affected by dementia are verbal ones, with Information and Vocabulary, the two subtests that hold up best with age, apparently the most clearly altered by dementia (Birren, 1952; Botwinick & Birren, 1951).

The normal age pattern may also not be a reliable indicator of selective right-hemisphere impairment. Studies of neuronal loss with age indicate the greatest change in the frontal cortex and in the superior temporal gyrus. Selective lateralized hemispheric change is not apparent (Bondareff, 1977). An alternative explanation of the verbal-performance differential in normal elderly is that these subtests differ in the demands they place on the older person's cognitive functioning. The items on the verbal subtests involve highly overlearned information which is being probed for in a familiar and unambiguous manner. Performance subtests, on the other hand, often employ novel material that must be manipulated in unfamiliar ways. (It is possible that good performance on one task requires more "resources" of a particular neural subsystem than does another [Norman & Bobrow, 1975; Zarit & Eiler, in press].) The verbal-performance differences typical of healthy older people may thus reflect qualitative differences in the demands of verbal and performance subtests, rather than indicating lateralized neuronal loss. The tendency for normal older persons to score poorly on the more complex batteries such as the Halstead-Indiana (Reitan & Davison, 1974) can perhaps be explained in similar ways.

The WAIS and the Halstead-Indiana battery represent broad-band approaches to neuropsychological assessment, in which complex tasks are used that depend on the integration of several cognitive abilities (Boll, 1981). In contrast, narrow-band tests use tasks that measure discrete and relatively independent constructs. Procedures tend to be simpler and may therefore be less likely to overload the resources of the older patient.

As an illustration of this narrow-band approach, Albert (1981) recommends that evaluation of dementia involve tests of attention, initiation and perseveration, conceptualization, construction, and memory. She also offers specific suggestions for procedures to be used for testing the severely impaired patient, who typically "bottoms out" on most tests. These include a continuous recognition paradigm consisting of a target stimulus followed by a choice between the correct item and a distractor and the use of concrete stimuli. The Luria-Nebraska Neuropsychological Battery (Golden, Hammeke, & Purisch, 1978; 1979), which uses a narrow-band approach, may also be useful in the assessment of senile dementia (Boutselis, 1982).

Although these approaches have the potential for identifying early cases of dementia, some caution is advisable. There are no studies that differentiate reliable signs of dementia from fluctuations in performance that are due to other factors, such as prior levels of achievement, education, motivation, and mood. Since confirming a diagnosis of dementia depends on the ultimate course of cognitive symptoms, longitudinal studies are needed to determine which patterns of performance indicate early dementia.

A major clinical application of neuropsychological tests may, in fact, be to affirm normal functioning. Adequate performance on a neuropsychological battery provides strong evidence that a dementing process is not present. Testing is especially helpful in cases where symptoms or complaints suggest possible dementia, although mental status findings are negative. Under those circumstances, good performance would suggest that current problems are not due to dementia. Poor performance, while not confirming dementia, can be useful for generating hypotheses about the causes of symptoms. The most important consideration is to diagnose dementia only when there is unequivocable evidence.

The following example indicates how a neuropsychological battery can establish a normal functioning. The key feature in this case was repeated testing at a six-month interval to determine the course of symptoms.

Mr. H. is a 66-year-old retired engineer. His wife and daughter reported a gradual onset of memory problems for the past few years, including not remembering events. For instance, he would do some repair work at his daughter's house and then not remember that he had done so. Mr. H. confirmed these and other memory problems. He also had a tremor and had been treated for Parkinson's Disease. When he had severe side-effects from the anti-Parkinson's medications, he sought another medical opinion. The neurologist he saw said he did not have Parkinson's and discontinued the medication but could not determine the cause of his problems.

During the initial interview, Mr. H. raised one other crucial issue. He asked the interviewer if mercury poisoning could be contributing to his problem. He had been using a topical application for several years which contains mercury and had recently read that prolonged use could be harmful.

Mental status testing was normal, and because of the severity of his presenting problems, it was decided to do the Luria-Nebraska battery to provide additional data. While his performance on the Luria-Nebraska was also within normal limits, there were some weak areas, including tasks involving attention (which could account for his memory failures) and recognizing tones. Because Mr. H. had an exceptional educational and work history, one would have expected better performance and the test results were interpreted as indicating possible mild cerebral impairment. Coupled with his tremor, the test scores suggested the possibility of mercury poisoning or some other cerebral disorder.

As a next step, Mr. H. was referred to a psychiatrist for further evaluation. When tests for mercury poisoning proved negative, the psychiatrist diagnosed Mr. H. as having early Alzheimer's Disease. Our assessment was that neither the history nor testing provided clear-cut evidence of dementia, and it was decided to retest him in six months. If a dementia was present, it would be more apparent by that time.

Retesting on the Luria-Nebraska revealed improved functioning, including on those subtests that had initially been low. Mr. H. and his family also reported improved functioning. Mr. H. clearly did not have a dementia. While definitive evidence of mercury poisoning was never obtained, he had stopped the medicine at the time of the initial testing and had not used it since.

Another important use of a neuropsychological assessment is to differentiate cognitive changes due to dementia from focal brain damage, such as that caused by a head injury or stroke. With focal damage, performance will be more selectively impaired. Differences in prognosis between dementia and a focal problem are, of course, substantial. The following example illustrates the use of neuropsychological testing for this purpose.

Mr. B. is a 74-year-old man who had been experiencing memory problems for the past 5 years, following a head injury. Both he and his wife confirmed problems such as forgetting where he parked his car. In addition, his wife complained of personality changes, mainly that he sometimes yelled at her, and of major lapses in judgment during the past year, which led him to lose their life's savings on an investment scheme. Besides these judgment problems, his wife was unable to provide a clear history that indicated whether or not symptoms were progressive. Mental status testing revealed no obvious impairment. He was then given the Luria-Nebraska Neuropsychological Battery. Results indicated specific, rather than global, impairments, with judgment, abstraction, following directions, visual-spatial performance, and memory the most affected abilities. Calculations, reading and writing, and motor and tactile functions were relatively intact. The pattern of performance is consistent with frontal-lobe and right-hemisphere damage, perhaps in the parietal and temporal regions. Further medical tests were negative and did not indicate the presence of a tumor, which might cause the observed cognitive symptoms. In the absence of further worsening of problems, it would appear that his errors in judgment and memory are related to the earlier head trauma, and not to dementia.

Medical Assessment

As noted earlier, there are no definitive medical tests for dementia, and the function of medical assessment is to rule out other possible causes of cognitive impairment. Persons should be referred for a medical evaluation under the following circumstances: (1) if someone with cognitive symptoms has not previously been assessed for potentially reversible causes; (2) when symptoms or history suggest a delirium; or (3) when there is a sudden worsening in a patient with a preexisting dementia. In our experience, the type of medical specialty is not as important as finding a physician who is knowledgeable about the medical aspects of dementia.

The types of problems causing reversible impairments are listed in Table 2.1, and the components of a comprehensive evaluation appear in Table 2.5. Determination of current medications, including over-the-counter drugs, should also be done because of the possibility that medication is contributing to the cognitive symptoms.

The CAT scan (computerized axial tomography) is a frequent part of the medical workup for dementia, and initially appeared to be a promising tool for diagnosis. Cortical atrophy and, correspondingly, enlargement of the ventricles and sulci, as determined through CAT scans, have been found to

Table 2.5.   Medical Evaluation for Senile Dementia.

1. Basic tests
    a. Complete blood count
    b. Erythrocyte sedimentation rate
    c. Serum Na+, K+, Cl−, BUN, Sugar (SMA-6)
    d. Serum Ca^{2+}, PO_4, liver function tests (SMA-12)
    e. Serum B_{12} and foliate
    f. Serologic test for syphilis (VDRL, etc.)
    g. Thyroid function test (i.e., total serum T_4 concentration, T_3 resin uptake, serum-free T_4 and T_3, or PBI)
    h. Chest X-ray
    i. Electrocardiogram
2. Elective tests: Where specifically indicated
    a. Skull X-ray
    b. Spinal tap with examination of cerebro-spinal fluid (CSF) (in the absence of papilledema or other evidence of increased intracranial pressure, such as erosion of the dorsum sellae, etc.)
    c. Brain scan
    d. Electroencephalogram (EEG)
    e. Computerized axial transverse tomography (CAT; EMI scanner, etc.)
    f. Isotope eistemography
    g. Cerebral angiography[a]

[a]The pneumoencephalogram is intentionally omitted because of its morbidity, especially in the elderly, and because the CAT scan has essentially excluded its need.

Source: L. S. Libow. "Senile Dementia and 'Pseudosenility': Clinical Diagnosis," in C. Eisdorfer and R. O. Friedel, (Eds.) *Cognitive and Emotional Disturbances in the Elderly.* Chicago: 1977. Year Book Medical Publishers.

correlate with measures of cognitive impairment in dementia patients (Caird, 1977; Fox, Topel, & Huckman, 1975; Kasniak, Garron, & Fox, 1975). Some degree of atrophy, however, may be normal in middle-aged and older adults, so that findings of atrophy without other evidence of dementia does not have diagnostic significance (Caird, 1977; NIA Task Force, 1980; Wells & Duncan, 1977). Conversely, there are instances of dementia symptoms without positive findings on the CAT scan. This combination of findings may suggest a reversible cause, such as a metabolic disorder, pernicious anemia, or some other factor (Caird, 1977). A major use of the CAT scan is to rule out a tumor as a cause of cognitive symptoms.

The following is an example of how relying solely on the CAT scan can lead to an incorrect diagnosis.

Mr. B., a 74-year-old man with an eighth-grade education, had retired from his job as a greengrocer two years earlier. Shortly after his retirement he had developed spurs on his heels and had seen an orthopedist who prescribed lifts for his shoes. He had difficulty walking with the lifts, and when the pain from the spurs subsided, he stopped wearing the lifts. He continued to have problems walking, dragging his feet and moving slowly. His family was also concerned because he was so inactive, even discontinuing activities he had enjoyed in the past, such as reading. Their physician recommended a neurological examination. The neurologist did a thorough evaluation, including a CAT scan, and found evidence of cortical atrophy. This diagnosis was disturbing to Mr. B. and to his family and they sought another opinion.

An evaluation was done, consisting of an interview and psychological testing. Mr. B. was cooperative during the assessment but responded slowly and appeared depressed. Mental status testing revealed only one error. Further neuropsychological testing was done, but the results were ambiguous. His scores were low, but because of his limited education, it was not clear whether they indicated impairment or reflected his low level of prior academic achievement. In the process of testing, Mr. B. was given feedback that he was performing within normal limits (which was the case on many of the tests), and that there was no reason to presume that he should limit his activities. Consequently, he started increasing his activities, and when an opportunity to return to work part-time arose, he did so. His family reported that his mood and even his walking improved. Follow-ups at six months, one year, and two years indicated he was still improved and working. Whatever the significance of the findings of atrophy, it did not indicate a progressive dementia. It is more useful to view Mr. B.'s problems as due to inactivity and depression, rather than dementia. As in the previous examples, this case illustrates the importance of not diagnosing dementia without unequivocal evidence.

Functional Assessment

Once it is determined that a patient has dementia, a functional assessment paves the way for effective interventions by identifying the problems and resources present in that particular case. Many clinicians assume that the diagnosis of dementia tells them enough about the patient's functioning and course of symptoms. There is even a notion of "stages" of dementia. But the patient's level of functioning cannot be inferred just on the basis of the diagnosis of dementia; nor can it be determined from cognitive tests, which only indirectly measure the skills involved in activities of daily living. Individual differences in the course and types of functional problems are considerable. Some patients will maintain well-established habits, while others experience a more rapid decline. Some patients may never have problems thought to be typical of dementia, such as wandering, agitation, or incontinence, while others will have these problems relatively early in the disease. Similarly, personality changes are prominent in some cases but not in others. Social skills are sometimes well maintained, and this can mask the dementia from casual observers, even when the extent of cognitive impairment is severe. Families also differ considerably in their response to the dementia and in the personal and financial resources they can bring to bear on the problem. All these factors should be included in a functional assessment.

Table 2.6.   Memory and Behavior Problems Checklist.

INSTRUCTIONS TO INTERVIEWER: This checklist is administered in two parts. In part A, the frequency with which problems occur is determined. In Part B, it is determined to what degree the behavior upsets the caregiver. When you find out that a problem occurs, then ask if it is upsetting.

INSTRUCTIONS TO CAREGIVER: "I am going to read you a list of common problems. Tell me if any of these problems have occurred during the past week. If so, how often have they occurred? If not, has this problem ever occurred? (Probe for a response that matches the frequency choices below)."
(For part B): "How much does this problem bother you?" (Probe for a response that matches the choices below. Hand the subject the card on which these choices are written.)

FREQUENCY RATINGS

REACTION RATINGS: How much does this bother or upset you when it happens?

0 = never occurred
1 = has occurred, but not in the past week
2 = has occurred 1 or 2 times in the past week
3 = has occurred 3 to 6 times in past week
4 = occurs daily or more often
7 = would occur, if not supervised by caregiver (e.g., wandering except door is locked).
8 = patient never performed this activity

0 = not at all
1 = a little
2 = moderately
3 = very much
4 = extremely

BEHAVIORS	FREQUENCY	REACTION
1. Wandering or getting lost	0 1 2 3 4 7	0 1 2 3 4
2. Asking repetitive questions	0 1 2 3 4	0 1 2 3 4
3. Hiding things (money, jewelry, etc.)	0 1 2 3 4	0 1 2 3 4
4. Being suspicious or accusative	0 1 2 3 4	0 1 2 3 4
5. Losing or misplacing things	0 1 2 3 4	0 1 2 3 4
6. Not recognizing familiar people	0 1 2 3 4	0 1 2 3 4
7. Forgetting what day it is	0 1 2 3 4	0 1 2 3 4
8. Not completing tasks	0 1 2 3 4	0 1 2 3 4
9. Destroying property	0 1 2 3 4	0 1 2 3 4
10. Doing things that embarrass you	0 1 2 3 4	0 1 2 3 4
11. Waking you up at night	0 1 2 3 4	0 1 2 3 4
12. Being constantly restless	0 1 2 3 4	0 1 2 3 4
13. Being constantly talkative	0 1 2 3 4	0 1 2 3 4
14. Engaging in behavior that is potentially dangerous to others or self (interviewer's judgment for whether behavior is dangerous or merely troublesome)	0 1 2 3 4 7	0 1 2 3 4
15. Reliving situations from the past	0 1 2 3 4	0 1 2 3 4
16. Seeing or hearing things that are not there (hallucinations or illusions)	0 1 2 3 4	0 1 2 3 4
17. Unable to dress self (partly or totally)	0 1 2 3 4 7	0 1 2 3 4

Table 2.6 continued

BEHAVIORS	FREQUENCY							REACTION				
18. Unable to feed self	0	1	2	3	4	7		0	1	2	3	4
19. Unable to bathe or shower by self	0	1	2	3	4	7		0	1	2	3	4
20. Unable to put on make-up or shave by self	0	1	2	3	4	7		0	1	2	3	4
21. Incontinent of bowel or bladder	0	1	2	3	4	7		0	1	2	3	4
22. Unable to prepare meals	0	1	2	3	4	7	8	0	1	2	3	4
23. Unable to use phone	0	1	2	3	4	7		0	1	2	3	4
24. Unable to handle money	0	1	2	3	4	7		0	1	2	3	4
25. Unable to clean the house	0	1	2	3	4	7	8	0	1	2	3	4
26. Unable to shop	0	1	2	3	4	7	8	0	1	2	3	4
27. Unable to do other simple tasks—specify (e.g., put groceries away, simple repairs)	0	1	2	3	4	7		0	1	2	3	4
28. Unable to stay alone by self	0	1	2	3	4	7		0	1	2	3	4
29. Other (specify)	0	1	2	3	4	7		0	1	2	3	4

The most frequently reported functional problems associated with dementia have been compiled into an assessment tool, the Memory and Behavior Problems Checklist (Zarit, Reever, & Bach-Peterson, 1981; Zarit, 1982). It consists of 29 items and is designed to be completed by an informant. A revised version of this measure appears in Table 2.6. As can be seen, several items are concerned with everyday manifestations of cognitive loss. These include: asking the same question over and over again, wandering and getting lost, and failing to recognize familiar people. Another group of items measures changes in the ability to carry out daily tasks. Following Lawton (1971), both instrumental daily activities (e.g., cooking and cleaning) and personal activities (e.g., dressing and bathing) have been included. Finally, some items measure disruptive behavior, such as incontinence or being constantly restless.

The caregiver is asked to indicate how often each of these problems occurred during the past week. When a problem is present, the caregiver is also asked how much that behavior bothers or upsets him. While it is often assumed that behavioral deficits have a similar impact on caregivers, they actually show a range of reactions. Some caregivers even cope with severe problems, such as incontinence, without reporting being troubled or upset. The cross-product of how frequently problems occur and how disturbing they are predicts the impact of the dementia on the family better than the frequency ratings alone (Zarit, 1982).

The idiosyncratic reactions of caregivers to behavioral deficits can be illustrated by the following example.

A man caring for his wife who had a dementia with early onset (in her 50s) had considerble trouble in the early stages of the disease when it became necessary for him to take over the financial management of their household. This problem was more upsetting to him than his wife's incontinence, when it occurred later in the illness.

Table 2.7.   Burden Interview.

INSTRUCTIONS: I am going to read you a list of statements, which reflect "how people sometimes feel when taking care of another person. After each question, tell me how often you feel that way, never, rarely, sometimes, quite frequently, or nearly always." (Show subject card.)

SCORING: 0 = never
          1 = rarely
          2 = sometimes
          3 = quite frequently
          4 = nearly always

1. Do you feel that N asks for more help than he or she needs?
2. Do you feel that because of the time you spend with N you don't have enough time for yourself?
3. Do you feel stressed between caring for N and trying to meet other responsibilities (e.g., family, job)?
4. Do 'you feel embarrassed over N's behavior?
5. Do you feel angry when you are around N?
6. Do you feel that N currently affects your relationships with other family members or friends in a negative way?
7. Are you afraid of what the future holds for N?
8. Do you feel that N is dependent upon you?
9. Do you feel strained when you are around N?
10. Do you feel that your health has suffered because of your involvement with N?
11. Do you feel that you don't have as much privacy as you would like?
12. Do you feel that your social life has suffered because you are caring for N?
13. Do you feel uncomfortable about having friends over? (If subject says, "No one comes over," ask, "Would you be uncomfortable . . .".)
14. Do you feel that N seems to expect you to take care of him or her as if you were the only one he or she could depend on?
15. Do you feel that you don't have enough money to care for N in addition to the rest of your expenses?
16. Do you feel that you can't take care of N much longer?
17. Do you feel that you have lost control of your life since N's illness?
18. Do you wish that you could just leave the care of N to someone else?
19. Do you feel uncertain as to what to do about N?
20. Do you feel you should be doing more for N?
21. Do you feel you could do a better job in caring for N?

Clinical norms have not been established for the Memory and Behavioral Problems Checklist. The best application of the instrument is to use it to identify current problem areas, as defined by their frequency and the caregiver's reactions. The problems that are most troubling to caregivers can be focused on in the intervention.

Because of the dependence of the dementia patient on others for supervision and assistance with daily tasks, assessment of the support system is important. There is usually a particular family member who functions as the primary caregiver for community-residing patients. This person is typically the spouse of the patient, or a daughter when there is no spouse. Occasionally, siblings, other relatives, or friends take on this role.

Assessment should include how stressful the caregiving activities are for this person. Caregiving places physical, emotional, and financial demands on family members (Adams, Caston, & Danis, 1979; Lowenthal, Berkman, & associates, 1967; Sainsbury & Grad, 1963) and the stress on the primary caregiver can be determined from clinical interviews. A research instrument, the Burden Interview, has also been developed to measure the impact on caregivers (Zarit, Reever, & Bach-Peterson, 1981; Zarit, 1982). This instrument assesses the extent to which caregivers perceive caregiving activities to have affected their health, emotional adjustment, social life, and financial status. A revised version of this measure appears in Table 2.7.

An assessment can also determine the extent to which the primary caregiver receives help in managing the dementia patient either from paid sources or from other family members. The attitudes of these family members are also important, particularly their support, criticism, or involvement with the primary caregiver.

INTERVENTIONS WITH DEMENTIA PATIENTS AND THEIR FAMILIES

Custodial Care

The prevailing approach to the treatment of patients with dementia is custodial. Families are often advised by physicians, other professionals, and by friends and relatives to place the dementia patient in a nursing home. They are told that they will face insurmountable problems if they try to keep the person at home. As they have already had some experience with difficulties in caring for a dementia patient, this advice carries a lot of weight. But nursing homes are sometimes a poor alternative, both for the patient and, ultimately, for the family.

Relocation from community to nursing home is a traumatic event for many older people, and it may even be catastrophic for dementia patients (Borup, Gallego, & Hefferman, 1979; 1980). Effects include losses in functioning, as well as increased risk of mortality, when compared to persons who are not relocated (Blenkner, 1967). Because of their cognitive deficits, dementia patients will have considerable difficulty learning routines in a new environment. Moreover, because they have problems adjusting to their new surroundings, they are frequently tranquilized, and the drugs most commonly used—the phenothiazines—sometimes exacerbate rather than alleviate behavioral problems.

Relocation also does not necessarily relieve the burden of family members. Rather, it changes the type of burden they experience (Sainsbury & Grad de Alarcon, 1970). Instead of providing primary care, family members now visit their relative in the nursing home, often interacting with staff in order to ensure better quality of care. Seeing their relative in an institution is often in itself stressful, especially when the dementia patient is placed on a locked ward with severely disturbed psychiatric patients. Since there is only limited third-party payment for nursing home care, it is likely to be a major financial strain as well.

Alternatives to Institutionalization

An alternative to placement in a nursing home is to find ways of relieving some of the burden on family caregivers so that they can continue to provide assistance to the patient at home. It is often assumed that because there are no medical treatments for senile dementia, the problem is completely intractable and the only solution is nursing home care. But if senile dementia is viewed as a problem with many components, some of which can be treated, then it becomes reasonable to work with families in order to identify ways of lowering the strain on them. Kahn (1975) has proposed that dementia be viewed as a "bio-psycho-social" phenomenon; while its biological aspects may not currently be modifiable, some of the psychological and social problems often improve with treatment.

The burden that family members experience is only partly related to the severity of the illness. Some caregivers experience a high amount of burden with only minimal changes in the afflicted person, while other caregivers report little or no subjective burden, even when they are providing considerable assistance (Zarit, Gatz, & Zarit, 1981; Zarit, Reever, & Bach-Peterson, 1981). Community surveys have found that there are more dementia patients living at home than in institutions, and the impairments of the former are often as great as those of the latter (Kay, Beamish, & Roth, 1964; Lowenthal, Berkman, & associates, 1967). Placement in a nursing home often occurs when the family has become physically or emotionally exhausted in providing care.

There are some preliminary findings on factors that are related to caregivers' burden. In a study of 30 subjects comprised of husbands, wives, and daughters who were each primary caregivers for a dementia patient, burden was inversely related to the number of visits by other relatives to the household (Zarit, Reever, & Bach-Peterson, 1981). Where there were more visits, caregivers reported less burden. Severity of cognitive and behavioral symptoms was only minimally related to burden. A subsequent study compared husbands and wives who were caregivers (Zarit, 1982). Wives reported more burden as a group, although their spouses' symptoms were not greater than those of the husbands in the sample. Furthermore, different factors were found to predict burden for husbands and for wives. Husbands who perceived they were getting enough help from other people reported less burden. In contrast, wives reporting more burden were those who became more upset when behavioral problems occurred, as indicated by the cross-product score on the Memory and Behavior Problems Checklist. The frequency of problems was not necessarily greater. Rather, it was how wives reacted to problems that made a difference. Another factor related to burden for wives was the quality of their prior relationship with their husband. When the quality was better, current burden was less.

Clinical observations have suggested two other factors that may be important in determining burden. These are the ability of caregivers to accept help from outside sources and the judicious use of medications. Overall, burden appears to be a complex interaction of several variables, some of which can be modified.

Intervention Procedures

A program of intervention that we have used successfully aims at helping caregivers provide home care for dementia patients. This will now be described. The goal of this program is to reduce the burden on the primary caregiver, thereby delaying or preventing institutionalization of the dementia patient. The focus is primarily on the caregiver and, to a lesser extent, on the dementia patient. Patients themselves may, on occasion, benefit from brief counseling sessions, especially when they have some awareness of their problems. But too much focus on trying to change the patient will be frustrating to both the caregiver and the professional. The more productive approach is to help caregivers identify practical changes they can make that will lower the burden.

The treatment program is comprised of three treatment techniques and three treatment modalities. The techniques are information, problem solving, and support. The three modalities are one-to-one counseling with the primary caregiver, family meetings, and support groups. The three treatment techniques are usually used in each of the treatment modalities.

As determined by the specific needs of caregivers and other family members, the techniques and modalities can be combined in a flexible way. The amount of time spent on each technique depends upon its relevance to the caregiver's problems. Sometimes it is sufficient to provide accurate information to primary caregivers or their relatives, who are then able to use their own problem-solving skills with little further assistance from the professional. In other cases, the caregiver or family may need more assistance in problem solving, or emotional support may be the prominent issue. Similarly, treatment modalities can be used differently depending on the case. The usual order of treatment is one-to-one counseling with the primary caregiver, a family meeting, and then participation in a support group; but the order and time spent in each modality can vary. Some caregivers may receive only a few sessions of one-to-one counseling, followed by a family meeting. Others may need the intensive attention of one-to-one counseling for a longer period of time. Sometimes there are reasons to make greater use of support group or family meetings because these modalities are potentially more effective for handling certain problems. The implementation of these strategies and modalities is described below.

Controlled evaluations of this program have not been done as yet. Our impression of the program, however, is that it is effective in alleviating some of the burden caregivers are feeling, and that it often results in delaying or preventing institutionalization. While treatment does not alter the course of the dementing illness, it can improve the quality of life both for the patient, who can stay longer in familiar surroundings, and for the caregiver, who learns ways of managing day-to-day problems without excessive burden.

Treatment Techniques

1. Providing Information about Senile Dementia. Families often have little or no information about senile dementia. They sometimes report that physicians have told them very little, calling the problem "old age" or "arteriosclerosis" and not giving any explanations about etiology, course, or management. Even when prior explanations have been more detailed, caregivers may still have many questions about these issues. It is important to take some time to answer these questions to create an information base for approaching current problems. Since each caregiver will have a different set of questions and will possess varying amounts of information, it is important to respond to their questions, rather than lecture about senile dementia.

Questions about causes and cures can be handled by providing current information about dementia in lay terms. In addition, some useful booklets that can be given to caregivers are available. These are: "Questions and Answers about Alzheimer's Disease" (National Institute on Aging, National Institutes of Health Publication No. 80-1646) and "The Dementias: Hope through Research" (National Institutes of Health Publication No. 81-2252). Copies can be ordered from the National Institute on Aging Information Office, National Institutes of Health, Bethesda, Maryland 20205.

Families will naturally be concerned with the possibility of a cure for dementia. The therapist must face the difficult tasks of dissuading the caregiver from seeking ineffective cures while also providing the hope that changes can occur. Treatments about which caregivers commonly inquire are various drug and vitamin regimens, hyperbaric oxygen, and lecithin. Other "miracle" cures are sometimes mentioned, such as nose sprays to improve memory and Gero-vital. No matter how preposterous the treatment may be, the counselor should be sensitive to the caregiver's concerns about finding a cure. If the caregiver wants to go ahead and try something anyway, he can be encouraged to view that treatment as an experiment and to report the results back to the counselor.

Another difficult task is answering the family's questions about whether or not dementia is hereditary. Using the information presented earlier in this chapter, the professional can say that heredity is one theory, but the degree of inheritability has not been determined. Based on current knowledge, even if inheritance plays a part, the increased risk to children of parents with dementia is small.

Among the most useful interventions is to explain and relabel for caregivers troubling behavior caused by the illness, which they may misinterpret. For instance, many caregivers are upset by the repetitive questions that the patient asks and complain that the patient should be more aware that he asked the question earlier. This problem occurs because the caregiver does not understand the effects of dementia. The therapist can explain that someone with severe memory loss cannot remember that he cannot remember. It is important, at the same time, to acknowledge the caregiver's frustration over this problem. Similarly, caregivers may believe that the dementia patient could remember better if only the patient tried harder. Again, it can be pointed out that the patient is probably able to sustain only limited efforts. Sometimes attempts by caregivers to stimulate memory by providing cues are useful. Research has suggested that recognition tasks are easier for dementia patients (Miller, 1975; Zarit, Zarit, & Reever, 1982) than free recall tasks. These cues, however, should be viewed as an experiment since some dementia patients may find memory tasks too frustrating. The limited gains that are possible with memory training (such as using mnemonics or other strategies to learn word lists) have also proven to be frustrating to the caregivers (Zarit, Zarit, & Reever, 1982). One other useful intervention is to break requests or instructions into simple steps. Our clinical observations have indicated that dementia patients with severe cognitive impairment can respond to one command at a time but will be unable to complete a task when asked to do two or more things at the same time.

Caregivers also have questions about whether the dementia patient should continue certain activities and how much assistance they should provide. If the dementia patient has begun to have trouble with a particular activity, such as dressing, the counselor should explore if there is some minimal intervention that could be made to help the patient continue doing what he or she can of that activity, such as having the dementia patient dress himself, with the caregiver providing step-by-step instructions how. In general, it is best to advise caregivers to allow dementia patients to do as much for themselves as possible. Because the degree of impairment increases over time, taking away activities before it is necessary to do so means that there are fewer ways to keep the dementia patient busy. On the other hand, caregivers *do* need to intervene when there is an obvious danger, such as leaving the stove on or driving dangerously. Some dementia patients, however, can perform even these complex tasks, and the decision must be based on the total assessment of each particular situation and not on preconceived notions of what dementia patients are or are not supposed to be able to do.

Caregivers will also ask about the course of the dementia illness. While acknowledging that the disease will get worse with time, the counselor should emphasize that each patient is different, and that it is difficult to predict what will happen next. The rate of change varies considerably, and some afflicted persons will show little or no decrement over long periods of time.

2. Problem Solving. Problem solving involves identifying possible strategies for modifying the dementia patient's behavior and the reactions of caregivers. The Memory and Behavior Problems Checklist (Table 2.6) is useful for identifying specific problems that are upsetting to caregivers. A first step is to obtain baseline information of problems caregivers have identified as upsetting, including when and how often they occur. Record keeping sometimes helps identify antecedents and consequences of problems, which, in turn, suggest possible interventions. A common problem is a patient who is up all night, keeping the caregiver awake. Record keeping might reveal that the patient has spent the day taking naps. This observation suggests that the person should be kept awake and active during the day. Cases of sleeplessness at night are usually due to napping or a lack of activity during the day, and an increase of activity reduces the problem. Often, however, sleeplessness is viewed as part of the disease, and patients are given sleeping or tranquilizing medications. Drugs may work for a while, but then they typically have paradoxical effects (that is, causing more agitation and sleeplessness).

When record keeping does not suggest an obvious intervention, a trial-and-error approach by the caregiver sometimes reveals solutions. This involves changing the caregiver's characteristic approach to the patient and recording its effects. Some caregivers, for example, find that they can deal with repetitive behaviors, such as asking the same question over and over again or restless motor activity, with affection, rather than by trying to reason with the patient. They have reported that touching and hugging appear to have a calming effect. Sometimes behavioral record keeping suggests that the caregiver's thoughts or beliefs are contributing to the problem. A cognitive problem-solving approach, which helps caregivers identify and examine their thoughts, is often useful (Beck, Rush, Shaw, & Emery, 1979). As an example, one caregiver tended to become upset over small problems, which she readily saw as having no important consequences. Each incident, however, reminded her of her husband's illness. With her counselor, she worked out a plan to consider more carefully how she evaluated each problem or incident. A few nights later, she saw her husband staring off into space. When she asked him what he was doing, he said he was watching TV. At first, she began to get upset as in the past, but she caught herself and thought instead, "At least he's happy." Rather than becoming emotionally drained by these trivial incidents, she was now better able to conserve her energies and work toward her goal of keeping him at home.

Finally, if caregivers are helped to observe the pattern of the dementia patient's behavior, they will also begin to see that they get upset at certain times and not at others. They sometimes will note that it is the accumulation of stress, and not any one particular thing, that upsets them. At that point, the counselor can encourage the development of a plan for the caregiver to get some relief before tension builds up too high. Solutions have included: relaxation exercise, going into a room alone, going for a walk, or getting someone into the house to stay with the patient while the caregiver goes out. Finding ways for caregivers to lower the stress on themselves is critical and is discussed more in the section on support below.

An important aspect of problem solving is the recognition that there is no "right" solution for a particular problem, and that strategies for dealing with the same behavior, such as asking repetitive questions, can vary considerably from case to case. The solution depends on the caregiver's values and resources, as well as on the habits and personality of the patient. One caregiver may find that affection works to control repetitive questions, while another caregiver does not, and another caregiver is too angry to try. Similarly, patients vary in what they can do. For instance, notes and other reminders work as memory aids for some patients and not for others. The response of patients to notes or other interventions often depends on habits they had before the onset of the illness. In our experience, the best use of written reminders was by a man with a moderately severe dementia. His wife was the primary caregiver, but when she broke her hip, there was no one to stay with him while she recuperated in the hospital. Faced with having to take care of himself, he made extensive use of a notebook to remind himself to eat and to take care of various household chores. While many patients have not been able to use similar memory aids, the key in this case was that he was a writer and had always depended on a notebook for reminders.

Because solutions are unique, the counselor should be concerned with the problem-solving process and not with reaching a particular solution. That process involves finding out what a caregiver has tried, what did not work, and what he or she is willing to try because it might work. As much as possible, solutions should build on the patient's habits, rather than involving new learning.

A particularly discouraging event is when a strategy that had been effective for a while no longer works. This can create a sense of hopelessness for both the caregiver and the counselor. Before concluding that the patient has worsened and requires institutionalization, the counselor should look at what has led up to the change. One man, for instance, had been able to leave notes on the door when he went out, telling his wife where he went, and that kept her from wandering. When he reported that leaving notes no longer worked, inquiries by his counselor revealed that, instead of destroying old notes, he saved them so that he could reuse them. He then realized that his wife was probably reading those old notes, did not know which one to believe, and then wandered out to look for him. After he destroyed those old notes and left only the current message on the door, the wandering stopped.

In other instances, it appears than an old strategy no longer works because the patient's condition has worsened. Some problems can certainly become unmanageable but when an old strategy no longer works, caregivers can find something new that does.

3. Support. Problem solving is one way of relieving some of the burden of care. Caregivers also report feeling isolated and alone, and so the understanding provided by the counselor can be important. A nonjudgmental attitude is particularly helpful since caregivers are likely to have received all sorts of advice about what they should do.

There is another way in which the counselor's support can be very important. Caregivers often fall into the role of trying to provide around-the-clock care. Most people, however, need some relief from being continually in the caregiving role. Part of the problem is beliefs caregivers hold about their responsibilities. Many express the thought that they cannot turn the care of their relative over to anyone else. Some say that no one else could care for the patient as well. Others think it would be too much of an imposition on someone else, or that they should be able to do all that is needed by themselves. Wives particularly feel that they ought to be able to handle all the household responsibilities, as well as supervising their husbands.

A first step in helping caregivers obtain more support is to identify assumptions like these, which may be preventing them from asking for help, and to use a cognitive problem-solving approach for generating alternatives. For instance, caregivers who feel guilty about leaving a spouse in someone else's care may recognize that if they do not get some relief, they are more likely to be unable to continue providing care. They may also realize that some of their fears of what might happen when they are away are exaggerated. They may then respond to the suggestion that it is appropriate to accept some help as a way of taking care of themselves, so they can continue assisting their spouse.

Sometimes the belief that accepting help is "wrong" is held very strongly. One woman was able to place her husband in a day-care program so she could continue working, but when she came home, she had no time to herself because of the amount of supervision her husband required. She recognized that she was becoming emotionally drained but could not see any solution. After some inquiries by her counselor, the woman indicated that her daughter was willing to stay in the house, so she could go away for a weekend. She felt, however, that it would be "wrong" to do so. The counselor worked with her to identify the beliefs she had about accepting help. At one point she thought that if she went away, she would not come back; but after considering that idea, she saw that was not what kept her from accepting her daughter's help. Eventually she was able to recognize her feeling that accepting help meant that she was weak. The counselor then helped her explore that belief, and she was able to reframe accepting help as a positive step.

It is also important to present alternative ways of getting help. Assistance may come from social-service agencies or from within the family. The counselor needs to have a good knowledge about the kinds of community services available. Such things as housekeepers, someone to sit up with the dementia patient, day care, and respite care can make the caregiver's task a lot easier. Unfortunately, such services are not consistently available, or they may be quite expensive. Some service programs for the elderly who overtly or covertly refuse to assist dementia patients. Because of these problems, the counselor may sometimes want to be an advocate for the caregiver in seeking help.

Treatment Modalities

1. One-to-one Counseling. There are good reasons for providing one-to-one counseling for the primary caregiver as the first step of an intervention. Many caregivers initially have a lot of questions about the causes and possible treatments for senile dementia that are best dealt with in individual sessions. Furthermore, they often ask for help at a point when they are feeling quite isolated and stressed. The individual sessions establish the basis for problem solving and serve to identify potential help from family members or from social agencies.

The course of the counseling will be influenced by the behavioral and cognitive skills of the caregiver. Some caregivers are effective problem solvers and readily see how they can reduce the stress on themselves, as well as provide better care for the dementia patient. Other caregivers are more typical of patients who come for psychotherapy in that they have difficulty making changes in how they act or think about a situation. The most frequently used techniques are problem solving (Haley, 1976), behavioral analysis of problems and increasing pleasant events (Lewinsohn, Munoz, Youngren, & Zeiss, 1977), relaxation training (Goldfried & Davison, 1976), and cognitive restructuring (Beck et al., 1979).

2. Family Meetings. In our experience, the most impressive changes have occurred in family meetings. In some instances, individual counseling goes quite well for a while and then reaches an impasse when the next goal in treatment is to obtain more support from family and friends. The timely calling of a family meeting may make the difference between termination with only moderate gains and terminating with more substantial success in alleviating the burden on the primary caregiver.

Because caregivers feel less burdened when there is more support from family and friends, the family meeting is a natural way to proceed. The goals of the meeting are: (1) to bring the family's level of information about the illness up to that of the caregiver; (2) to identify the caregiver's most pressing needs; and (3) to problem-solve for the family to provide more support. It has generally been helpful to have two counselors chair the family meeting. Initially, counselors need to be more active answering questions about dementia. Later in the meeting, counselors should encourage the family to use their own problem-solving skills to help the primary caregiver.

The people invited to the family meeting can include relatives, friends, or anyone else who visits or calls the caregiver. Often these people are willing and able to help but have no idea how to do so, and caregivers are hesitant or embarrassed to ask. Sometimes all the caregiver wants or needs is a phone call. In one case, a husband was the caregiver for his wife and provided around-the-clock supervision. Most of his family did not realize how difficult that was for him. Discussion of her problems at the family meeting made them aware of how much he did. Family members then readily volunteered to take turns sitting with their mother so that their father could have some time away from her. Whether it is a phone call or actually sitting with the impaired person, the caregiver needs to know that his or her family understands the problem and that their sympathy and support are there when it is really needed.

Families, like individuals, will vary in the extent to which they can respond, but even families troubled by longstanding conflicts have been able to pull together on the specific problem of helping a parent. In one case involving a large family, there was a longstanding feud that divided them into two factions. The family meeting had to be arranged at the house of the one person who spoke to both groups. The two feuding factions came to the meeting and sat on opposite sides of the room. During the meeting, however, they recognized how serious the changes in their mother were and, despite their feud, were able to work out a plan to assist their father, the primary caregiver.

3. Support Groups. Support groups for caregivers are currently a popular intervention and are available in many communities. These groups create the opportunity for caregivers to share information with one another and to understand their own experience better. For instance, caregivers have said that they felt they were going crazy, until they learned that there were other people facing the same situation and experiencing similar frustrations.

The problem-solving process takes on new dimensions in the support group. Caregivers make suggestions to one another based on their own experience of what has been successful. The group leaders find that participants' problem-solving alternatives are sometimes quite creative. Caregivers will often try something new if it is proposed by another caregiver when they might not follow a counselor's suggestion. Caregivers also learn new strategies of responding to the dementia patient by observing what the other participants did. This is an important source of new learning, especially in areas where caregivers previously had trouble making changes. In one group, some of the women caregivers had been reluctant to bring help into the household to care for their husbands. They felt that they should be able to do everything their husbands needed, despite being overwhelmed by the demands for constant attention. The example set by the men in the group who felt very comfortable about using household help was instrumental in overcoming the women's belief that they should be able to manage by themselves.

The support from other caregivers can have a profound effect. In one instance, a caregiver who was experiencing chest pains was reluctant to keep his doctor's appointment and only went after the urging of others in the group. His condition was serious, and required bypass surgery. During the recovery period, he received calls and visits from group members, and he later said that their intervention helped save his life.

Caregivers often enter support groups without any preparation or screening. As stated earlier, it is better to begin with one-to-one counseling, to answer some of the initial questions and to reduce some of the stress. These initial interactions may also reveal if a caregiver is inappropriate for a group, for instance, if he or she demands too much attention or is too insensitive to others.

Support groups are sometimes led by nonprofessionals, and while there are advantages to using "peer" leaders, serious problems can result. A major reason to have a trained leader is to ensure that group norms and group processes do not become destructive. Some untherapeutic behaviors are: giving advice; allowing one person to dominate the conversation; ignoring quieter members; changing the subject when someone is talking about a troubling issue; putting someone down for holding a particular belief or having certain feelings; and not supporting members who cry or become upset. In one ongoing group comprised of husbands and wives who were caregivers, two women spent the first hour discussing their problem of taking time for themselves away from their husbands. They were making good progress on what had been a difficult issue for them when another woman, who was younger and more outgoing that the others, joined the group.

Immediately the men in the group focused their attention on her, leaving the other two women unable to complete the work they had started. When the leader became aware of what happened, she talked to this woman privately about the importance of coming on time and made sure in future sessions that she did not dominate or sidetrack the group.

Sometimes the gentle intervention of the leader can ensure that important issues are discussed. In a group of spouses, a relative newcomer asked what other people thought about going out occasionally with someone of the opposite sex. The others went on to something else, as if he had not asked the question, but when the leader pointed this out, they were able to laugh at themselves and then had a very constructive discussion of their needs for social interaction.

Relocation of the Dementia Patient. Although the goal of intervention is to prevent relocation, it must be recognized that families vary in their ability to provide home care. Just as families should not be told to institutionalize their relatives, they should also not be told *not* to do so. When families decide, after having considered various alternatives, to institutionalize the patient, their decision should be supported.

A major advantage of a program that helps families to consider alternatives is that when they do make the decision to institutionalize, they know that they have done everything possible to prevent it. There will be times when it seems to the counselor that a patient is being inappropriately rushed into a nursing home; and there will be times when caregivers hold out against institutionalization at considerable cost to themselves. It is important to accept the caregiver's preferences, rather than imposing the counselor's own values or beliefs. In this very personal and difficult decision, there is ultimately no right or wrong, only the recognition that caregivers must decide for themselves.

Final Case History. The final case history is intended to illustrate some of the problems encountered in working with patients with dementia to emphasize the need for a flexible approach in implementing interventions to meet the needs of an individual case.

> *Presenting Problems.* Mrs. H. was 55 years old when she first came to the clinic. Her husband was then 61 years old. He had been diagnosed as having Alzheimer's Disease 13 years earlier. Her initial request was for counseling to help her decide whether or not she should divorce him. She was caring for him at home with limited assistance from their youngest son, who was then 19. Two other children lived a considerable distance away.
> *History and Assessment.* Mr. H. was not present at the initial interview, but his wife described the course of his illness as gradual, with the first memory lapses occurring during his mid-40s. Mr. H. had been an attorney who specialized,

ironically, in probate law, and one of his memory errors had been to forget to renew their health insurance. Mr. H. had a very efficient secretary, who managed to compensate for his increasing memory problems for several years. However, the income from his practice was declining each year to the dismay of his wife. Mr. H. had undergone a personality change at home as well. Formerly patient and easygoing, he had become prone to angry outbursts for no apparent reason. These outbursts created discord between him and his family.

When the problems could no longer be ignored, Mrs. H. prevailed upon him to see a doctor. He was referred to a neurologist who performed the first of many extensive evaluations, all of which arrived at the same conclusion; that he had Alzheimer's Disease. When the diagnosis was made, Mrs. H.'s physician recommended that she divorce Mr. H. to protect her half of their community property. She could then place him in a nursing home without losing all their assets.

Mrs. H. decided that the time for placement was nowhere near, and that the many good years of their relationship could not be discounted so easily. They were fairly comfortable financially, and she chose to care for him at home. She protected their children from Mr. H.'s disordered behavior as much as possible.

During the years that intervened between the first diagnosis and Mrs. H.'s seeking help at the clinic, Mr. H.'s illness had been steadily progressive. Mrs. H. had gone to work for a few years to help out financially, but had finally had to quit her job when Mr. H. had deteriorated too much to be left at home alone.

Because Mr. H. had been thoroughly tested on numerous previous occasions, no further testing was felt to be necessary. Mr. H.'s memory and behavior problems at the time of the intake interview included the tendency to wander, very poor recent memory, repetitive questions, restlessness, and he required assistance in all activities of daily living. Mrs. H. felt that she could handle all of these problems if she only knew how much longer it would go on.

Treatment. Mrs. H. was an articulate and intelligent woman. She had been advised on many occasions by her family and her physicians to institutionalize Mr. H. While she did not want to take this step, she was feeling increasingly burdened and stressed after 13 years of providing for him. Thus, her presenting question, that of divorce, was her way of saying she did not know how much longer she could physically and emotionally bear the burden of his care.

Mrs. H. had been extremely competent in her handling of her husband's problems. When he first started wandering, she secured the house in such a way that he could not manipulate the locks without her knowledge. When he started losing bladder control, she began taking him to the bathroom at regular intervals. When he could no longer manage the fastenings of his clothing, she assisted him. Her problem-solving skills were impressive.

Mrs. H. had not been as successful at maintaining social support for herself. Their friends no longer visited and she continued to protect her children from knowing the full extent of the burden she bore. During the course of five sessions of one-to-one counseling, she explored alternative means of obtaining support. Once she accepted the necessity of getting away from the situation for short periods of time, she located a retired nurse to care for Mr. H. three mornings a week. At the conclusion of the five sessions, she joined an ongoing support group. There, for the first time, she encountered others facing the same situation. She derived comfort from realizing she was not alone in her decision to provide care at home, and she became a valued member of the group for her problem-solving skills and empathy.

Approximately one year later Mrs. H. contacted her counselor again. She reported that Mr. H. had deteriorated to the point where she no longer felt she could manage him. At this time the counselor arranged to visit the home. Mr. H. could no longer formulate words, could not initiate any activity, nor could he coordinate swallowing. Consequently, Mrs. H. spent hours each day helping him take small sips of liquified food and otherwise caring for him.

Mrs. H. now felt ready to place Mr. H. in some sort of institution. Her physicians felt that he should be in a locked facility because of his tendency to try to wander. The counselor could not find another suitable alternative in their community. She discussed with Mrs. H. the possible consequences of relocation, including that her husband would not receive the kind of nurturance that he was receiving at home. Mrs. H. understood the possibility that he would deteriorate further and felt ready to proceed with institutionalizing Mr. H. She did so, and within a week, the family was in crisis.

The daughter and son who lived in another town were outraged that their mother had "heartlessly put their father away." They had no comprehension of the amount of care she had provided for so many years. The counselor recommended a family meeting in which the children could be acquainted with the magnitude of the problem and their mother's role in caring for Mr. H. It was scheduled for a Saturday morning, but on Friday night Mr. H. suffered what was thought to be a heart attack and was transferred to a medical center. Mrs. H. broke down under the stress and was able to describe to her children what she had done all these years and to tell them that she could no longer do it. Once the children understood, they supported her completely, thus obviating the need for the counselor to intervene. Mr. H. died a week later, officially of pneumonia. Mrs. H. continued to be active in a local support group for some time after her husband's death.

Mrs. H. is typical of many caregivers who have been urged to institutionalize their relative, but who make the decision not to. Because of her good problem-solving skills, she initially needed only support with her decision to care for her husband at home. One year later his condition had deteriorated so much that she chose to institutionalize him. Despite his extreme problems, she had been able to maintain him at home almost to the end of the disease. While many people feel that it is impossible to keep dementia patients at home, it is important not to proceed with preconceived ideas about what can and what cannot be done. Mrs. H. was able to decide for herself how long she wanted to provide care and to institutionalize her husband when she was satisfied that there was nothing more that she could do.

REFERENCES

Adams, M., Caston, M. A., & Danis, B. C. *A neglected dimension in home care of elderly disabled persons: Effects on responsible family members.* Paper presented at the meetings of the Gerontological Society, Washington, D.C., 1979.

Albert, M. S. Geriatric neuropsychology. *Journal of Consulting and Clinical Psychology,* 1981, **49**, 835–850.

Beck, A., Rush, D., Shaw, D., & Emery, G. *Cognitive therapy of depression.* New York: Guilford, 1979.

Bedford, P. D. Adverse cerebral effects of anesthesia on old people. *Lancet,* 1955, 2(Part 1), 259–263.

Berger, K. S., & Zarit, S. H. Late life paranoid states: Assessment and treatment. *American Journal of Orthopsychiatry,* 1978, **48**, 528–537.

Birren, J. E. A factorial analysis of the Wechsler-Bellevue Scale given to an elderly population. *Journal of Consulting Psychology,* 1952, **16**, 399–405.

Blenkner, M. Environmental change and the aging individual. *Gerontologist,* 1967, **7**, 101–105.

Blessed, G., Tomlinson, B. E., & Roth, M. The association between quantitative measures of dementia and of senile change in the cerebral gray matter of elderly subjects. *British Journal of Psychiatry,* 1968, **114**, 797–811.

Boll, T. J. Assessment of neuropsychological disorders. In D. H. Barlow (Ed.), *Behavioral assessment of adult disorders.* New York: Guilford, 1981.

Bondareff, W. The neural basis of aging. In J. E. Birren & K. W. Schaie (Eds.), *Handbook of the psychology of aging.* New York: Van Nostrand Reinhold, 1977.

Borup, J. H., Gallego, D., & Hefferman, P. Relocation and its effects on mortality. *Gerontologist,* 1979, **19**, 135–140.

Borup, J. H., Gallego, D. & Hefferman, P. Relocation: Its effects on health functioning and mortality. *Gerontologist,* 1980, **20**, 468–479.

Botwinick, J. Intellectual abilities. In J. E. Birren & K. W. Schaie (Eds), *Handbook of the psychology of aging.* New York: Van Nostrand Reinhold, 1977.

Botwinick, J. *Aging and behavior* (2nd ed.). New York: Springer, 1978.

Botwinick, J., & Birren, J. E. Differential decline in the Wechsler-Bellevue subtest in the senile psychoes. *Journal of Gerontology,* 1951, **6**, 365–368.

Boutselis, M. A. *The use of the Luria-Nebraska memory tests in assessment of senile dementia.* Paper presented at the meetings of the Western Psychological Association, Sacramento, Calif., 1982.

Caird, F. I. Computerized tomography (Emiscan) in brain failure in old age. *Age and Aging,* 1977, 6(Suppl.), 50–51.

Cowan, D. W., Copeland, J. R. M., Kelleher, M. J., Kellett, J. M., Gourlay, A. J., Smith, A., Barron, G., DeGruchy, J. (U.K. team), Kuriansky, J., Gurland, B., Sharpe, L., Stiller, P., & Simon, R. (U.S. team). Cross-national study of diagnosis of the mental disorders: A comparative psychometric assessment of elderly patients admitted to mental hospitals serving Queens County, New York, and the former borough of Camberwell, London. *British Journal of Psychiatry,* 1975, **126**, 560–570.

Eisdorfer, C., Cohen, D., & Veith, R. *The psychopathology of aging: Current concepts.* New York: Scope Publications, 1981.

Epstein, L. J. Depression in the elderly. *Journal of Gerontology,* 1976, **31**, 278–282.

Fink, M., Green, M. A., & Bender, M. B. The face-hand test as a diagnostic sign of organic mental syndrome. *Neurology,* 1952, **2**, 48–56.

Folstein, M. F., Folstein, S. E., & McHugh, P. R. "Mini-mental state": A practical method for grading the cognitive state of patients for the clinician. *Journal of Psychiatric Research*, 1975, **12**, 189–198.

Fox, H. H., Topel, J. L., & Huckman, M. S. Use of computerized tomography in senile dementia. *Journal of Neurology, Neurosurgery and Psychiatry*, 1975, **382**, 948–953.

Funkenstein, H. H., Hicks, R., Dysken, M. W., & Davis, J. M. Drug treatment of cognitive impairment in Alzheimer's Disease and the late life dementias. In N. E. Miller & G. D. Cohen (Eds.), *Clinical aspects of Alzheimer's Disease and senile dementia*. New York: Raven Press, 1981.

Golden, C. J., Hammeke, T. A., & Purisch, A. D. Diagnostic validity of a standardized neuropsychological battery derived from Luria's neuropsychological tests. *Journal of Consulting and Clinical Psychology*, 1978, **46**, 1258–1265.

Golden, C. J., Hammeke, T. A., & Purisch, A. D. *Manual for the Luria-Nebraska neuropsychological battery*. Lincoln: University of Nebraska Press, 1979.

Goldfried, M. R., & Davison, G. C. *Clinical behavior therapy*. New York: Holt, Rinehart & Winston, 1976.

Gurland, B. J. The assessment of the mental status of older adults. In J. E. Birren, & B. B. Sloan (Eds.), *Handbook of mental health and aging*. Englewood Cliffs, N.J.: Prentice-Hall, 1980.

Gurland, B., Dean, L., Craw, P., & Golden, R. The epidemiology of depression and delirium in the elderly: The use of multiple indicators of these conditions. In J. O. Cole & J. E. Barrett (Eds.), *Psychopathology in the aged*. New York: Raven Press, 1980.

Gurland, B. J., Fleiss, J. L., Goldberg, K., Sharpe, L., Copeland, J. R. M., Kelleher, M. J., & Kellett, J. The geriatric mental state schedule: A factor analysis. *International Journal of Aging and Human Development*, 1976, **7**, 303–311.

Hachinski, V., Lassen, N., & Marshall, J. Multi-infarct dementia: A cause of mental deterioration in the elderly. *Lancet*, 1974, **2**, 207–210.

Haley, J. *Problem-solving therapy*. San Francisco: Jossey-Bass, 1976.

Hassinger, M. J., Zarit, J. M., & Zarit, S. H. *A comparison of clinical characteristics of multi-infarct and Alzheimer's dementia patients*. Paper presented at the meetings of the Western Psychological Association, Sacramento, Calif., 1982.

Jacobs, J. W., Bernhard, M. R., Delgado, A., & Strain, J. J. Screening for organic mental syndromes in the medically ill. *Annals of Internal Medicine*, 1977, **86**, 40–46.

Kahn, R. L. The mental health system and the future aged. *Gerontologist*, 1975, **15**, 24–31.

Kahn, R. L., Goldfarb, A. I., Pollack, M., & Peck, R. Brief objective measures for the determination of mental status in the aged. *American Journal of Psychiatry*, 1960, **117**, 326–328.

Kahn, R. L., & Miller, N. E. Assessment of altered brain function in the aged. *IN* M. Storandt, I. C. Siegler, & M. Elias (Eds.), *Clinical psychology of aging*. New York: Plenum, 1978.

Kahn, R. L., Zarit, S. H., Hilbert, N. M., & Niederehe, G. Memory complaint and impairment in the aged. *Archives of General Psychiatry*, 1975, **32**, 1569–1573.

Kapnick, P. L. Organic treatment of the elderly. In M. Storandt, I. C. Siegler, & M. F. Elias (Eds.), *The clinical psychology of aging*. New York: Plenum, 1978.

Kasniak, A. W., Garron, D. C., & Fox, J. H. *Mental status questionnaire scores, short-term memory and cerebral atrophy as measured by computerized tomography*. Paper presented at the meetings of the Gerontological Society, Louisville, Ky., 1975.

Kay, D. W. K. Epidemiological aspects of organic brain disease in the aged. In C. M. Gaitz (Ed.), *Aging and the brain*. New York: Plenum, 1972.

Kay, D. W. K., Beamish, P., & Roth M. Old age mental disorders in Newcastle upon Tyne. Part I. A study of prevalence. *British Journal of Psychiatry*, 1964, **10**, 146–158.

Kiloh, L. G. Pseudo-dementia. *Acta Psychiatria Scandinavia*, 1961, **37**, 336–351.

Kramer, M., Taube, A., & Redide, R. W. Patterns of use of psychiatric facilities by the aged: Past, present and future. In C. Eisdorfer & M. P. Lawton (Eds.), *The psychology of adult development and aging*. Washington, D.C.: American Psychological Association, 1973.

Larsson, T., Sjogren, T., & Jacobson, G. Senile dementia: A clinical sociomedical and genetic study. *Acta Psychiatrica Scandinavica,* 1963, **167**(Suppl.).

Lawton, M. P. The functional assessment of elderly people. *Journal of the American Geriatrics Society,* 1971, **19**, 465–481.

Lewinsohn, P. M., Munoz, R. F., Youngren, M. A., & Zeiss, A. M. *Control your depression.* Englewood-Cliffs, N.J.: Prentice-Hall, 1977.

Libow, L. S. Senile dementia and "pseudosenility": Clinical diagnosis. In C. Eisdorfer & R. O. Friedel (Eds.), *Cognitive and emotional disturbances in the elderly.* Chicago: Year Book Medical Publishers, 1977.

Linn, L., Kahn, R. L., Coles, R., Cohen, J., Marshall, D., & Weinstein, E. A. Patterns of behavior disturbance following cataract extraction. *American Journal of Psychiatry,* 1953, **110**, 281–289.

Lipowski, Z. J. *Delirium.* Springfield, Ill.: Charles C. Thomas, 1980.

Lowenthal, M. F., Berkman, P., & associates. *Aging and mental disorder in San Francisco.* San Francisco: Jossey-Bass, 1967.

Miller, E. Impaired recall and the memory disturbance in presenile dementia. *British Journal of Social and Clinical Psychology,* 1975, **14**, 73–79.

Miller, N. E., & Cohen, G. D. (Eds.), *Clinical aspects of Alzheimer's disease and senile dementia.* New York: Raven, 1981.

Mortimer, J. A., Schuman, L. M., & French, L. R. Epidemiology of dementing illness. In J. A. Mortimer & L. M. Schuman (Eds.), *The epidemiology of dementia.* New York: Oxford University Press, 1981.

National Institute of Aging Task Force. Senility reconsidered. *Journal of the American Medical Association,* 1980, **244**(3), 259–263.

National Nursing Home Survey: United States 1973–1974. Washington, D.C.: U.S. Government Printing Office, 1977.

Norman, D. A., & Bobrow, D. G. On data-limited and resource-limited processes. *Cognitive Psychology,* 1975, **7**, 44–64.

Perry, E. K., Perry, R. H., Blessed, G., & Tomlinson, B. E. Necropsy evidence of central cholinergic deficits in senile dementia. *Lancet,* 1977, **1**, 189.

Pfeiffer, E. A short portable mental status questionnaire for the assessment of organic brain deficit in elderly patients. *Journal of the American Geriatrics Society,* 1975, **23**, 433–439.

Post, F. *The significance of affective symptoms in old age.* London: Oxford University Press, 1962.

Post, F. *Persistent persecutory states in the elderly.* New York: Pergamon, 1966.

Reitan, R. M., & Davison, L. A. *Clinical neuropsychology: Current status and application.* New York: Wiley, 1974.

Rosen, W. G., Terry, R. D., Fuld, P. A., Katzman, R., & Peck, A. Pathological verification of ischemic score in differentiation of dementias. *Annals of Neurology,* 1980, **7**, 486–488.

Roth, M. Natural history of mental health in old age. *Journal of Mental Science,* 1955, **101**, 281–289.

Roth, M. Senile dementia and its borderlands. In J. O. Cole, & J. E. Barrett (Eds.), *Psychopathology in the aged.* New York: Raven Press, 1980.

Sainsbury, P., & Grad, J. Mental illness and the family. *Lancet,* 1963, i, 544–547.

Sainsbury, P., & Grad de Alarcon, J. The psychiatrist and the geriatric patient: The effects of community care on the family of the geriatric patient. *Journal of Geriatric Psychiatry,* 1970, **1**, 23–41.

Schaie, K. W., & Labouvie-Vief, G. Generational versus ontogenetic components of change in adult cognitive behavior: A fourteen-year cross-sequential study. *Developmental Psychology,* 1974, **10**, 305–320.

Schaie, K. W., & Schaie, J. Clinical assessment and aging. In J. E. Birren & K. W. Schaie (Eds.), *Handbook of the psychology of aging.* New York: Van Nostrand Reinhold, 1977.

Schonfield, D. Translations in gerontology—from lab to life: Utilizing information. *American Psychologist,* 1974, **29**, 796–801.

Simard, D., Olesen, J., Paulson, O. B., Lassen, N. A., & Skinhoj, E. Regional cerebral blood flow and its regulation in dementia. *Brain,* 1971, **94**, 273–281.

Simon, A., & Cahan, R. The acute brain syndrome in geriatric patients. In W. M. Mendel & L. J. Epstein (Eds.), *Acute psychotic reaction.* Washington, D.C.: American Psychiatric Association, 1963.

Terry, R. D. Aging, senile dementia and Alzheimer's Disease. In R. Katzman, R. D. Terry, & K. L. Bick (Eds.), *Senile dementia and related disorders.* New York: Raven Press, 1978.

Terry, R. D., & Wisniewski, H. M. Structural aspects of aging of the brain. In C. Eisdorfer & R. O. Friedel (Eds.) *Cognitive and emotional disturbance in the elderly.* Chicago: Year Book Medical Publishers, 1977.

Thompson, L. W., Davis, G. C., Obrist, W. D., & Heyman, A. Effects of hyperbaric oxygen on behavioral and physiological measures in elderly demented patients. *Journal of Gerontology,* 1976, **31**, 23–28.

Wechsler, D. *The measurement and appraisal of adult intelligence* (4th ed.). Baltimore: Williams & Wilkens, 1958.

Weinstein, E. A., & Kahn, R. L. *Denial of Illness.* Springfield, Ill.: Charles C. Thomas, 1955.

Wells, C. E., & Duncan, G. W. Danger of overreliance on computerized cranial tomography. *American Journal of Psychiatry,* 1977, **134**, 811–813.

Zarit, J. *Predictors of burden and distress for caregivers of senile dementia patients.* Unpublished doctoral dissertation. Los Angeles: University of Southern California, 1982.

Zarit, J., Gatz, M., & Zarit, S. H. *Family relationships and burden in long-term care.* Paper presented at the meetings of the Geronotological Society, Toronto, Ontario, 1981.

Zarit, S. H. *Aging and mental disorders: Psychological approaches to assessment and treatment.* New York: Free Press, 1980.

Zarit, S. H., Cole, K. D., & Guider, R. L. Memory training strategies and subjective complaints of memory in the aged. *Gerontologist,* 1981, **21**, 158–164.

Zarit, S. H., & Eiler, J. Clinical assessment. In J. E. Birren & K. W. Schaie (Eds.), *Handbook of the psychology of aging* (2nd ed.). New York: Van Nostrand Reinhold, in press.

Zarit, S. H., Miller, N. E., & Kahn, R. L. Brain function, intellectual impairment and education in the aged. *Journal of the American Geriatrics Society,* 1978, **26**, 58–67.

Zarit, S. H., Reever, K. E., & Bach-Peterson, J. Relatives of the impaired elderly: Correlates of feelings of burden. *Gerontologist,* 1981, **21**, 158–164.

Zarit, S. H., Zarit, J. M., & Reever, K. E. Memory training for severe memory loss: Effects on senile dementia patients and their families. *Gerontologist,* 1982, **22**, 373–377.

Chapter 3

Insomnia

Richard R. Bootzin, Mindy Engle-Friedman, and Lisa Hazelwood

DESCRIPTION OF PROBLEM

Current Definitions and Prevalence

Insomnia refers to a heterogeneous set of problems reflecting a disturbance of the sleep process. Sleep may be disrupted in various ways. These include: difficulty in falling asleep; frequent or prolonged awakenings; premature awakening in the morning; or the subjective impression of an unsatisfactory quantity or quality of overall sleep. Next-day effects on mood and performance are usually also implied. Insomnia is a frequent complaint, and it is particularly prevalent among the elderly (Bixler et al., 1979; Karacan et al., 1976; McGhie & Russell, 1962). For example, in one survey, 23 percent of the respondents over 60 years of age reported experiencing sleep problems either "often" or "all the time," as compared to 13 percent of the population in general (Karacan et al., 1976). It should be noted that these prevalence figures refer to adaptive, healthy, noninstitutionalized elderly individuals. This is the population upon which our research has been focused. It would be expected that sleep problems would be even more prevalent among the frail and institutionalized elderly.

Sleep Architecture. The measure of sleep that has been generally accepted as most reliable and valid is polysomnography. Polysomnography consists of the all-night recording of the electroencephalogram (EEG), electrooculogram (EOG), and the electromyogram (EMG). Other physiological measures such as temperature, respiration, and skin conductance, and heart rate can be measured for special purposes. Through the use of criteria developed by Rechtschaffen and Kales (1968), EEG records, in conjunction with EOG and EMG data, can be scored visually to discriminate sleep from wakefulness and between different stages of sleep. The top half of Figure 3.1 presents a

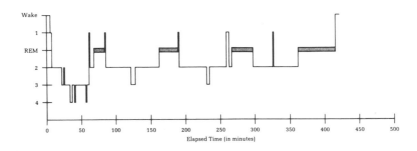

Fig. 3.1.   The stages of sleep and their durations, as measured from midnight on, during a normal night's sleep of a 25-year-old male. The horizontal axis indicates minutes elapsed. The vertical axis indicates types of sleep. Shaded bars represent periods of rapid eye movement (REM) sleep.

normal night's sleep of a 25-year-old male. As can be seen in the figure, deep sleep (Stages 3 and 4) occurs mostly in the first few hours of the night's sleep. Rapid eye movement (REM) sleep periods, from which dreams are typically reported, reoccur every 90 to 100 minutes. The largest proportion of REM sleep occurs in the last half of the night since REM periods tend to increase in duration throughout the night.

The Effects of Aging on Sleep.   The most common sleep problems reported by older adults include increased frequency and duration of nocturnal awakenings, frequent early morning awakenings, increased latency to sleep onset, and increased daytime fatigue (Miles & Dement, 1980). Many of these complaints parallel developmental changes in sleep parameters that occur with advancing age.

The lower half of Figure 3.1 presents a typical night's sleep of a 70-year-old male. Figure 3.1 illustrates one of the most consistent findings associated with the effect of aging on sleep; that is, an increase in the frequency of awakenings, particularly during the last half of the night (Agnew, Webb, & Williams, 1967; Feinberg, Koresko, & Heller, 1967; Kahn & Fisher, 1969; Kales et al., 1967; Williams, Karacan, & Hursch, 1974). Older adults also have more difficulty falling back to sleep than do younger sleepers. For example, Webb and Campbell (1980) found that subjects 50 to 60 years old took longer to fall asleep when awakened after the first 80 minutes of the night than did subjects 21 to 23 years old. This increased difficulty in falling back to sleep later in the night may account for the increased frequency of early morning awakenings among the elderly.

In addition to difficulty falling back to sleep once awakened, many older adults also have difficulty falling asleep initially (Feinberg, Koresko, & Heller, 1967). However, not all studies have indicated that sleep onset latency increases with age. Williams, Karacan, and Hursch (1974) found an increase in sleep latency only for men over 70 years of age. There was little change in sleep latency for males between the ages of 3 and 70 or for females between the ages of 3 and 80 (Hauri, 1977). Since daytime naps increase in frequency with age (Zepelin, 1973), the total sleep of the elderly is about equivalent to that of younger sleepers if the sleep distribution throughout the entire 24-hour day is considered (Webb & Swinburne, 1971; Zepelin, 1973).

A decrease in deep or slow-wave sleep (Stages 3 and 4) is, along with an increase in awakenings, the most widely documented change in sleep associated with aging (Agnew, Webb, & Williams, 1967; Feinberg, Koresko, & Heller, 1967; Kales, 1975; Miles & Dement, 1980; Prinz, Obrist, & Wang, 1975). One-fourth of the population over age 60 may have little or no Stage 4 sleep, although this deficit is much more likely in males than in females (Webb, 1974; Williams, Karacan, & Hursch, 1974). The reduction in slow-wave sleep is due in part to the reduction in amplitude of the EEG waves to the point where they do not meet the amplitude criterion for slow-wave sleep. Thus, slow-wave sleep still occurs in the elderly, but there is a marked loss in EEG amplitude. The relationship between the loss in EEG amplitude and other physiological processes remains to be investigated.

There are also small decreases in REM sleep with aging (Williams, Karacan, & Hursch, 1974). Feinberg, Koresko, and Heller (1967) found that shortened latency to REM sleep, as well as lower absolute and relative amounts of REM, were associated with intellectual decline.

Finally, variability in a number of sleep parameters, including time in bed, total sleep time, sleep latency, number of awakenings, and time awake after sleep onset, increases with age (Williams, Karacan, & Hursch, 1974).

The differences that occur as a consequence of aging are much the same as the differences between nonelderly insomniacs and normal sleepers. Insomniacs show decreased deep sleep (Stages 3 and 4) and total sleep, and increased sleep onset latency and number and duration of awakenings (e.g., Engle-Friedman & Bootzin, 1981; Frankel, Coursey, Buchbinder, & Snyder, 1976; Monroe, 1967). From these data, one might expect that the complaint of insomnia corresponds directly to the degree of psychophysiological deficit. However, the intensity of sleep complaint among nonelderly insomniacs is not always matched by the magnitude of the sleep parameter deficit (e.g., Carskadon et al., 1976; Lewis, 1969; Monroe, 1967). Similarly, although there are clear changes in the psychophysiology of sleep associated with aging, there is little information as to whether those changes are associated with increased sleep complaints.

Two sleep parameters, in particular, seem to be associated with sleep complaints. First, subjective ratings of depth of sleep have been found to be negatively related to total amount of wakefulness and Stage 1 but not positively to the amount of other, "deeper" stages of sleep (Bonnet & Johnson, 1978). Since increased awakenings are characteristic of the sleep of the elderly, it is possible that this accounts for their increased sleep complaints. Second, the sleep of insomniacs shows considerable night-to-night variability (Coates et al., 1979; Engle-Friedman & Bootzin, 1981; Karacan, Williams, Salis, & Hursch, 1971). The complaint of insomnia may be more related to variability than to the magnitude of a sleep-parameter deficit on any one night.

Causes of Insomnia

Besides the changes associated with aging, insomnia may result from a number of factors that include physical pathology, prescription and nonprescription medication, alcohol, caffeine, nicotine, stress and anxiety, psychopathology, inactivity, sleep environment factors, poor sleep habits, and reinforcement for sleeplessness. Since more than one of these factors may contribute to the older adult's sleep problems, the evaluation of each will increase the likelihood of effective intervention.

Physical Disorders. Physical illness can disrupt sleep because of the discomfort of the illness (such as back pain, gastric pain from ulcers, or cardiac pain). The experience of pain, especially that associated with arthritis, constitutes one of the most frequent sleep disruptions among older adults (Prinz & Raskind, 1978). Diabetes may also interfere with sleep through underregulation of blood sugar resulting in glycosuria and nocturia or through overregulation leading to hypoglycemia (Prinz & Raskind, 1978).

Two other physical disorders that disrupt sleep are sleep apnea and nocturnal myoclonus. Sleep apnea is a respiratory disorder in which breathing ceases for at least ten seconds repeatedly throughout the night (Guilleminault & Dement, 1978; Guilleminault, Eldridge, & Dement, 1973). As a result, sleep is repeatedly disrupted. The incidence of sleep apnea increases with age, as do other respiratory problems (Carskadon, Brown, & Dement, 1980). In nocturnal myoclonus, leg twitches occur which may interfere with sleep (Lugaresi, Coccagna, Berti-Ceroni, & Ambrosetto, 1968).

Medication. Both prescription and nonprescription drugs can cause insomnia. All medications, including those used for disorders other than insomnia, should be evaluated. For example, some asthma medication contains adrenaline, which would interfere with sleep if taken at night; and diuretics, which cause increased urination, may awaken the individual more frequently.

The elderly are major consumers of sleep aids. In fact, the use of hypnotics by the elderly has reached crisis proportions. In 1977, 39 percent of prescriptions for hypnotics were for people over the age of 60 who comprised 15 percent of the population (Institute of Medicine, 1979). The figures for the institutionalized elderly are even higher. For example, a U.S. Public Health Service survey of prescribing patterns in skilled nursing facilities found that prescriptions for hypnotics had been written for 94.2 percent of the patients studied (U.S. Public Health Service, 1976).

Despite this heavy reliance on sleeping medication, the use of hypnotics is both ineffective and potentially dangerous for the chronic insomniac. Most hypnotics lose their effectiveness within two weeks of continuous use (Kales, Allen, Scharf, & Kales, 1970). Only one hypnotic, flurazepam (Dalmane), has been found to retain its effectiveness throughout one month of continuous use (Kales, Kales, Bixler, & Scharf, 1975). Tolerance develops rapidly, so larger and larger doses are required to have any effect; and continuous use results in less deep sleep and more light, fragmented sleep. In addition, most hypnotics are REM-sleep depriving and produce a marked REM rebound on subsequent nights. REM-rebound nights are often spent in restless dreaming, nightmares, and fitful sleep. The insomniac may conclude that the hypnotics are needed to avoid the rebound effect; thus hypnotics may lead to drug dependence (Kales et al., 1978). Disrupted sleep caused by taking hypnotics is called *drug-dependent insomnia.*

Besides their effect on sleep, hypnotics have a number of other deleterious side-effects. They produce a drug hangover during awakenings at night and in the morning, can cause deteriorated motor and intellectual functioning (Greenblatt & Allen, 1978), and can increase respiration difficulties (Carskadon, Brown, & Dement, 1980). Many hypnotics have long plasma half-lives. For example, flurazepam has a plasma half-life of from 50 to 100 hours. Thus, side-effects may be observed days, and even weeks, after the individual has stopped taking sleep medication.

The elderly are particularly vulnerable to the dangers of hypnotic use because they are more likely to have disorders aggravated by hypnotics, such as respiratory, hepatic, or renal function (Institute of Medicine, 1979). In addition, the decreases associated with aging in protein-binding ability, circulation time, and kidney and liver metabolism lengthen the time drugs remain in the body, extending the period of potential toxicity (Albert, 1981). The elderly are also likely to have increased risk of toxic interactions from multiple drug use (Miles & Dement, 1980). This is exacerbated by the fact that older persons are more likely to substitute one drug for another, exchange drugs with friends, use a number of physicians, and use drugs beyond their expiration date (Hemminki & Heikkila, 1975).

The same problems of side-effects, multiple drug interactions, and disrupted sleep that are associated with hypnotics also apply to tranquilizers such as diazepam (Valium). There is no evidence that tranquilizers proved an effective treatment for the chronic, severe insomniac.

The active ingredient in most over-the-counter sleep medication is an antihistamine. The rationale appears to be that since drowsiness is a side-effect of antihistamines, if insomniacs can be made drowsy, perhaps they will fall asleep faster and sleep more soundly. There have been few published studies on over-the-counter sleep medication. In no study in which sleep was monitored by means of polysomnography has an over-the-counter sleep medication been more effective than a placebo (e.g., Kales, Tan, Swearingen, & Kales, 1971). Despite their ineffectiveness, there are a number of hazards associated with these drugs. As depressants, they potentiate the effect of alcohol and prescription hypnotics. In addition, they can produce side-effects of confusion, disorientation, and memory disturbance (Institute of Medicine, 1979).

Tryptophan has been proposed as a natural hypnotic since it is an amino acid found in protein. There is no sedative effect from eating foods high in tryptophan. This is because foods that contain tryptophan also contain other amino acids such as tyrosine which compete with tryptophan for transport to the brain (Wurtman, 1982). If tryptophan is ingested as a drug, it does have a mild positive effect on sleep onset and slow-wave sleep (Hartmann, 1978). It has not been shown to be effective for sleep maintenance problems, the primary sleep problem of the elderly. Although tryptophan has few side-effects at low doses, nausea and vomiting have been reported at higher doses. Long-term use may produce an abnormal balance of amino acids that could alter protein synthesis (Institute of Medicine, 1979).

There is now considerable consensus that sleep medication is not the appropriate treatment for the chronic insomniac of any age, but particularly not for the elderly insomniac. If hypnotics are to be replaced as the primary means of treating the elderly insomniac, viable short-term alternatives must be thoroughly evaluated. Possible alternatives will be discussed later in this chapter.

Alcohol. The problems associated with hypnotics and tranquilizers hold for alcohol as well. Like other depressants, alcohol is REM-sleep depriving. Habitual heavy drinking results in fragmented sleep with frequent awakenings. Withdrawal produces REM rebound with fitful sleep and nightmares. Although there is no evidence that an occasional glass of wine or its equivalent should be avoided, habitual heavy drinking before sleep will produce sleep disturbance rather than improved sleep.

An additional problem is that alcohol potentiates the effects of hypnotics and other depressants. Thus, the combination of alcohol and sleeping pills may intensify and prolong deleterious side-effects to produce lethal levels of overdose (Institute of Medicine, 1979).

Caffeine and Nicotine. Both caffeine and nicotine are central-nervous-system stimulants that produce a lighter and more fragmented sleep (Bonnet, Webb, & Barnard, 1979; Soldatos et al., 1980). Caffeine is contained in coffee, tea, chocolate, and soft drinks. Presenting complaints of insomnia and/or anxiety can be due to excessive intake of caffeine and/or heavy smoking. Reducing the intake of caffeine, particularly in the evening, and quitting smoking can lead to substantial improvement in sleep.

Stress. Sleeping difficulties not caused by physical disorder are usually seen as the symptom of some psychological problem. There is considerable intuitive appeal to this assumption since people who ordinarily have no trouble sleeping often develop insomnia during periods of stress. As a person ages, many important life events occur that may be difficult to adjust to and thus may affect sleep. For example, a spouse may die, the person may retire, living arrangements may change, or the individual may become aware of changes in his or her own physical and intellectual functioning. These factors must be assessed since sleep problems may be a short-term reaction to stresses in a person's life.

Psychopathology. There is a large amount of literature on the relationship between psychopathology and sleep disturbance, particularly with regard to anxiety and depression (e.g., Youkilis & Bootzin, 1981). On self-report personality inventories, insomniacs have been found to be more introverted, anxious, neurotic, and depressed than normal sleepers (e.g., Costello & Smith, 1963; Coursey, Buchsbaum, & Frankel, 1975; Haynes, Follingstad, & McGowan, 1974; Kales et al., 1976; Nicassio & Bootzin, 1974). In addition, a number of studies have focused specifically on the sleep of depressed patients. Nearly all studies of depressed patients have found that slow-wave sleep is reduced (Mendelson et al., 1977), and many have suggested that shortened REM latency is symptomatic of severe depression (e.g., Hartmann, 1968; Snyder, 1966).

Kales and Kales (1970) have recommended that antidepressant medication should be prescribed for those patients whose insomnia is diagnosed as *resulting from* depression. It is difficult, if not impossible, however, to determine that depression (or anxiety) is directly causing insomnia since all that is observed is covariation. In cases in which psychological problems accompany sleep disturbance, separate therapeutic attention should be given to each. The therapist should not assume that improvement in one will automatically produce improvement in the other (Bootzin & Nicassio, 1978).

Inactivity. A major problem of the elderly is an inactive life-style. This is particularly true for the institutionalized elderly, but it is also applicable to many healthy, adaptive, noninstitutionalized elderly individuals. In addition to inactivity, the elderly frequently nap during the day. Sleep onset latency is inversely related to the length of time since the individual last slept (Webb, 1975). In addition, the night's sleep following an afternoon or evening nap continues as if the nap was part of the night's sleep. Since afternoon and evening naps contain more deep and less REM sleep, the entire night's sleep is similar to the last half of a typical night's sleep with more light and REM sleep and more frequent awakenings (Webb, 1975). A morning nap, on the other hand, is a continuation of the previous night's sleep and has minimal effect on the subsequent night's sleep architecture.

Hauri (1975) has noted that insomniacs who fall into the habit of sleeping late in the morning or taking naps whenever fatigue overwhelms them are likely to develop circadian rhythm disturbances. This may inadvertently disrupt many bodily cycles, such as those involving temperature regulation and the functioning of the endocrine system, which require 24-hour synchronization. If these circadian cycles become desynchronized, an optimal time for sleeping may never exist.

Sleep Environment.   There are many sleep environment factors, such as the temperature of the room, firmness of the mattress, noise, and whether the bed or bedroom are shared, that may influence the quality of an individual's sleep. There is no ideal room temperature or degree of mattress firmness. People can learn to sleep comfortably in a wide range of temperatures and on many different surfaces. However, individuals may have developed strong preferences to the point where sleep is disrupted if the sleep environment does not correspond to those preferences. This may be a particular problem if the person moves to a new setting. The unfamiliarity of the setting and the lack of familiar sleep paraphernalia, such as bed, pillow, and personal belongings, may cause a prolonged period of disrupted sleep.

The effect of noise on sleep is to decrease the amount of deep sleep and increase the frequency of awakenings. Even people who habitually sleep in noisy environments do not fully adapt to the noise. For example, in a nap study of college students, those who had the music of their choice playing while they fell asleep took longer to fall asleep, had more awakenings and less total sleep than did those who had no music playing (Engle-Friedman, Bootzin, & Hazelwood, 1982). This result held even for students who habitually listened to music while they fell asleep. Since the elderly have more difficulty falling back to sleep once awakened (Webb & Campbell, 1980), the increased frequency of awakenings caused by a noisy environment is likely to be particularly troublesome.

Some sleep problems are caused by incompatibilities between those who share a bedroom. For example, one person may prefer to go to sleep early while the other prefers going to sleep late; or a noisy and restless sleeper may disrupt the sleep of the other person. Note that in the latter example, the noisy and restless sleeper may be urged to seek help even though he or she experiences no subjective sleep problem. It is the sleep of the spouse or roommate that is being disrupted by the noisy and restless sleeper. Under such circumstances, separate beds or bedrooms may be an appropriate solution.

Sleep Habits. Insomniacs may engage in activities at bedtime that are incompatible with falling asleep (Bootzin, 1972; 1976; 1977; Bootzin & Nicassio, 1978). Insomniacs may, for example, use their bedrooms for reading, talking on the telephone, watching television, snacking, listening to music, and probably most disturbing, worrying. The result is that the bed is no longer just a cue for sleeping, it becomes a cue for physiological arousal instead.

Cognitive intrusions may be particularly disruptive. Worries and concerns are often accompanied by emotional upset, yet they may appear in the absence of excessive physiological arousal (Starker & Hasenfeld, 1976). The content of the insomniac's concerns may shift from the general pressures of current and future problems to persevering worries regarding the inability to fall asleep or to get enough sleep during the night (Hauri, 1975).

The bedroom, then, can become a cue for the anxiety and frustration associated with trying to fall asleep. Insomniacs often sleep well any place other than in their own beds. For example, they often sleep better in a sleep laboratory than they do at home (de la Pena, 1978; Engle-Friedman & Bootzin, 1981). In contrast, people who have no difficulty falling asleep in their own beds often have difficulty doing so in strange surroundings.

Poor sleeping habits may help maintain insomnia even if the sleeping difficulties were initially caused by physical illness or situational stress. For the chronic insomniac, sleeping difficulties usually continue long after the initial causes have disappeared.

Reinforcement. Finally, sleep complaints may be reinforced by the attention of sympathetic listeners. Some insomniacs may find that others are more tolerant of their shortcomings when they appear fatigued, groggy, and irritable as a result of sleeping poorly. The inadvertent reinforcement of "sick" behavior has been found to play a prominent role in other disorders as well (e.g., Fordyce, 1976).

ASSESSMENT

Components of Assessment

The assessment of insomnia is a complex task. The nature of the sleep disturbance and its consequences must be accurately described. In addition, each of the possible contributing causes described in the previous section must be assessed. The following is a list of the components of a complete assessment of sleep disturbance.

1. Physical examination and medical history.
2. Detailed personal history.
3. Psychological inventories.

4. Daily sleep diaries.
5. All-night polysomnography.
6. Mood and performance measures.

Measurement of Contributing Variables

Physical Examination. Since insomnia can be caused by physical disorders and drugs, a physical examination and a questionnaire concerning medical history are essential. Before other assessments are undertaken, the individual's physician should be asked to evaluate the extent to which the individual's physical condition and medication regimen could be contributing to the sleep problem.

Physical sleep disorders, such as nocturnal myoclonus, sleep apnea, and narcolepsy should be ruled out. The client with nocturnal myoclonus may report frequent leg twitches throughout the night. Sometimes the client's spouse is more aware of the client's leg movements than is the client. A client with sleep apnea is likely to report excessive snoring, extreme daytime tiredness, frequent movements during sleep, headaches upon awakening, and a dry mouth during sleep or upon awakening. Since the incidence of sleep apnea increases with age, it may be an important determinant of symptoms of insomnia in the elderly.

The primary symptom of narcolepsy is irresistible sleep attacks that may last as long as 20 minutes (Roth, 1978). Associated symptoms include cataplexy (a sudden loss of muscle tone usually lasting for less than two minutes during which consciousness is normal), sleep paralysis (while falling asleep or awakening), and hypnogogic imagery (often emotional or frightening imagery while falling asleep or awakening). The night's sleep of an individual with narcolepsy is unusual in that it typically beings with a REM-sleep period. Other sleepers do not have their first REM-sleep period until about 90 minutes after sleep onset.

If nocturnal myoclonus, sleep apnea, or narcolepsy are suspected, the individual should be referred to a sleep disorders center for all-night polysomnography. Although much can be learned from a detailed history, confirmation from polysomnography may be required for accurate diagnosis and effective treatment.

History. A critically important component of insomnia assessment is a detailed history. It is here that the clinician gets the client's view of the problem, along with information about alcohol, caffeine and nicotine intake, stresses, coping skills, activity level, the nature of the sleep environment, sleep habits, and possible maintaining consequences. There is no set format for obtaining this information. It is usually collected by means of interviews and questionnaires.

Psychological Inventories. Since insomnia frequently accompanies depression and anxiety disorders, it is useful to obtain responses to psychological inventories. Those that we use in our research include the Manifest Anxiety Scale (MAS: Taylor, 1953), the Beck Depression Scale (Beck, 1967), the Cornell Medical Index (Brodman, Erdmann, & Wolff, 1956), the Schedule of Recent Experiences (Rahe et al., 1964), and the Life Satisfaction Questionnaire (Havighurst, 1963). The Schedule of Recent Experiences is particularly useful in identifying those individuals who have experienced a number of recent stressful changes in their lives. Their sleep problems may reflect a short-term adjustment process. The other measures help to identify those who are currently depressed and/or anxious. As will be discussed further in the intervention section, the clinician can use this information to design a more comprehensive treatment plan.

Measurement of Sleep. In addition to assessing the antecedent conditions that may contribute to the individual's insomnia, assessment of the individual's sleep is required. This involves the measurement of many variables (e.g., sleep onset latency, depth of sleep, total sleep, number and duration of wakenings, daytime fatigue). Each variable can be measured using different methods, such as sleep diaries, observers, and polysomnography, each of which has unique advantages and disadvantages. This section is drawn from Bootzin and Engle-Friedman (1981) with a particular focus on the advantages and disadvantages of these methods of assessment for use with older adults.

Daily Sleep Diaries. The use of daily sleep diaries has become a staple of assessment procedures in insomnia treatment research (e.g., Borkovec & Fowles, 1973; Lick & Heffler, 1977; Nicassio & Bootzin, 1974; Turner & Ascher, 1979b). The client fills out the sleep diary each morning upon awakening. As can be seen in Figure 3.2, the sleep diary that we use contains entries for nap taking, sleep latency, number and duration of awakenings, total sleep, quality of sleep, and feeling upon awakening. The client is encouraged to use the comments column to note the occurrence of events that might have affected the night's sleep, such as the use of sleep medication or alcohol, sickness in the family, and emotional distress.

In order to evaluate the nature of the insomniac's problem, it is necessary to have at least one, and preferably two, weeks of completed sleep diaries. Although sleep diary estimates are vulnerable to the same problems of reactivity, reliability, and validity that affect all self-monitoring assessment, daily morning estimates of specific sleep variables are less vulnerable to bias than are retrospective and global sleep complaints. Often as a result of keeping a daily sleep diary, the client learns that the problem is not as severe or as frequent as he or she thought.

SLEEP DIARY

	YESTERDAY:				THIS MORNING:		When I Got Up This Morning, I Felt ___ (circle one)		Overall, My Sleep Last Night Was ___ (circle one)	
	I Napped From ___ To ___ (times)	I Went To Bed At ___ (time)	I Fell Asleep In ___ Mins.	I Awoke ___ Times In The Night	I Stayed Awake ___ Minutes Each Time	I Awoke At ___ (note time)	I Slept A Total Of ___ Hours	EXHAUSTED · · · REFRESHED	VERY RESTLESS · · · VERY SOUND
DAY 1								-2 -1 0 +1 +2	-2 -1 0 +1 +2
DAY 2								-2 -1 0 +1 +2	-2 -1 0 +1 +2
DAY 3								-2 -1 0 +1 +2	-2 -1 0 +1 +2
DAY 4								-2 -1 0 +1 +2	-2 -1 0 +1 +2
DAY 5								-2 -1 0 +1 +2	-2 -1 0 +1 +2
DAY 6								-2 -1 0 +1 +2	-2 -1 0 +1 +2
DAY 7								-2 -1 0 +1 +2	-2 -1 0 +1 +2

Fig. 3.2. The client fills out the sleep diary each morning upon awakening.

It is important that the baseline sleep diary assessment begin after the client has withdrawn from sleep medication. The goal is to learn what the client's sleep is like under unmedicated conditions. Since the chronic use of hypnotics often produces disrupted sleep, withdrawal from sleep medication is usually an effective intervention in improving sleep. However, since there may be after-effects, withdrawal should be done gradually under the supervision of the individual's physician.

Some individuals may be overly concerned about the accuracy of their reports to the point where the desire to be accurate interferes with the person's sleep. It is usually sufficient to reassure such individuals that absolute accuracy is not required.

Clients may find that completing sleep diaries each morning is an unpleasant chore, particularly if the treatment investigation extends over a long period of time. Sometimes clients may forget to fill out the diary. If diaries are collected from clients infrequently, they may not be filled out until immediately before they are collected. This might be several days after the nights of interest. Under these circumstances, sleep diaries would be no more valid than retrospective global sleep complaints. This problem can be reduced by making a discussion of the sleep diary part of the therapy session. If the therapist indicates that the diaries are important, the client is likely to be more conscientious about them. Some investigators have dealt with this problem by having clients mail in their diaries daily (e.g., Lick & Heffler, 1977; Nicassio & Bootzin, 1974).

Despite the many potential sources of bias, daily sleep diaries have fared remarkably well. Diaries provide an inexpensive and, compared to physiological monitoring, nonintrusive means of obtaining daily sleep data from people sleeping at home in their own beds. And, ultimately, the test of an effective treatment is how well the insomniac does at home in his or her own bed.

Test-retest reliability is quite substantial. Coates et al. (1982) found that test-retest reliabilities for sleep diary variables were equivalent to EEG reliabilities, particularly for insomniacs. Measures of validity are encouraging as well. For example, in an evaluation of 122 insomniacs, Carskadon et al. (1976) found that morning-after estimates of sleep latency correlated substantially with EEG estimates ($r = .64$, $p < .01$) and validity of sleep diaries have been reported by Baekeland and Hoy (1971) and Freedman and Papsdorf (1976).

The disadvantages of sleep diaries, including their reactivity and vulnerability to bias, are far outweighed by their advantages of providing daily sleep data, being less intrusive than physiological recording, having high test-retest reliability, and having substantial correlations with other sleep measures. Sleep diaries are a necessary component of insomnia assessment. They are a practical and efficient means of obtaining sleep information, and they provide a measure of the client's view of the disorder.

Observers. Observers have been used to assess sleep onset, total sleep time, sleep maintenance, and sleep quality. Spouses or roommates have been used as observers at home, while nurses are usually used in institutional settings. Typically, observers pay attention to the subject's respiration, movements, and reaction when called by name or when a light is shone (Baekeland & Hoy, 1971). Few investigators have either trained their observers or checked for interrater reliability.

There are practical difficulties in employing a spouse or roommate as an observer. The spouse or roommate of an insomniac may be a good sleeper and fall asleep long before the insomniac does. Coates et al. (1982) found that the spouses of insomniacs were unable to provide consistent data for any sleep variable, even sleep latency estimates from spouses and good sleepers were correlated .99.

Although spouses and roommates may not be able to provide precise data about the client's sleep, they are aware of the severity of the problem and whether there has been any change over time. Thus, spouses and roommates serve as good convergent sources of information about the effectiveness of treatment. In our research (Bootzin, 1975; Nicassio & Bootzin, 1974), we have used spouses and roommates to verify treatment efficacy. Pre- and posttreatment questionnaires were mailed directly to spouses and roommates. Data obtained in this manner confirmed results from the subjects' sleep diaries and global questionnaires. Nevertheless, spouses are potentially susceptible to demand and expectancy effects, as are the insomniacs themselves.

For older adults who live in institutional settings, observation by nurses or staff may be feasible. However, studies of observer reliability and validity done with psychiatric patients have not been encouraging. Nurses' ratings were particularly invalid in assessing sleep onset and sleep duration of depressed patients who had low levels of behavior. They were more accurate in evaluating the sleep of the more animated schizophrenic patients (Kupfer, Wyatt, & Snyder, 1970; Weiss, McPartland, & Kupfer, 1973).

The difficulties associated with observation are substantial. Without reliability checks, observers are likely to drift in their definitions of what constitutes sleep. In addition, observers may be unable to meet their scheduled sleep checks. Erwin and Zung (1970) found that nurses had to delay their checks for as long as four hours on any given night.

Data obtained from observers have not been sufficiently reliable or valid to warrant their use as the sole means of evaluating sleep. Observers may be useful, however, in supplementing information from other sources. They may be particularly useful for institutionalized older adults who are incapable of assessing their own sleep.

Polysomnography. Polysomnography constitutes an excellent process measure of sleep in that it is continuous, it does not interfere with the process being measured, and it can be used across a wide range of subjects and conditions (Webb, 1975). It is generally accepted as the best objective measure of sleep, against which other measures are verified.

Many investigators have reported that insomniacs overestimate sleep latency and underestimate total sleep and number of arousals as compared to EEG assessment (e.g., Borkovec & Weerts, 1976; Carskadon et al., 1976; Lewis, 1969; Monroe, 1967). Since the correlations between sleep diary and EEG estimates are high, the findings of a constant difference need not be of great concern. The same underlying dimension seems to be assessed by both measures.

There are some insomniacs, however, whose sleep complaint is not verified by polysomnography. Consequently, there is a separate classification in the recently published *Diagnostic Classification of Sleep and Arousal Disorders* (Association of Sleep Disorders Centers, 1979) for such insomniacs, that is, subjective DIMS (disorder of initiating and maintaining sleep) complaint without objective finding. If the complaint is corroborated by polysomnography, the diagnostic classification is psychophysiological DIMS. This distinction between subjective and psychophysiological insomnia could have important etiological and treatment implications. As mentioned earlier, the magnitude of the sleep complaint is not always matched by the severity of the psychophysiological deficit.

It should be remembered, however, that polysomnography is not the only "real" measure of sleep. Sleep and sleep onset, like anxiety, are inferred constructs having multiple operational definitions reflecting cognitive, behavioral, and physiological components (Bootzin & Nicassio, 1978). There are times when EEG measures are not valid indicators of sleep, such as after extreme sleep deprivation (Blake, Gerard, & Kleitman, 1939) or with brain-injured subjects (Murray, 1965). Thus, the individual's subjective experience may not always be accurately represented by psychophysiological measures. Evaluation of both the phenomenology and psychophysiology of the sleep disturbance is necessary.

One difficulty with all-night sleep laboratory recordings is that sleep may be under strong stimulus control (Bootzin, 1972; 1976; Bootzin & Nicassio, 1978). A person who has difficulty sleeping at home may sleep quite normally in the sleep laboratory (de la Pena, Flickinger, & Mayfield, 1977; Engle-Friedman & Bootzin, 1981). There are also practical disadvantages to the use of polysomnography. The equipment is costly, trained personnel must maintain all-night vigils, an enormous amount of sleep data is generated making data reduction a chore, and the insomniac must leave the comfort of home to sleep in the laboratory (Lichstein & Kelley, 1979).

Despite these drawbacks, all-night polysomnography has many advantages. First, it is the only way in which detailed, accurate, and continuous information on an extensive number of sleep variables can be obtained.

Second, it is the most accurate means of assessing sleep apnea, nocturnal myoclonus, and narcolepsy. And third, it allows the investigator to distinguish between those with subjective insomnia and those whose insomnia can be verified by polysomnography.

The information obtained from polysomnography is important not only for accurate assessment of the problem, but also for the role it can play in treatment. Many insomniacs are reassured to learn that the sleep they obtain is normal in many important respects; for example, that they have normal REM cycles, or that they are getting more sleep than they thought. The feedback from polysomnography can effectively reinforce the treatment program.

Some of the major disadvantages of polysomnography in a sleep laboratory can be reduced when recordings are taken from people at home in the comfort of their own beds. Under those conditions, subjects do not need to disrupt their schedules to travel to and from a sleep laboratory. This is particularly important for the elderly who may have difficulty traveling. Insomniacs are more likely to participate in extended evaluations, and investigators need not rely on only one or two nights of recording. Most importantly, the cues of the person's sleep environment that might be associated with disrupted sleep would still be present.

A practical method of home recording transmits electrophysiological signals over the telephone lines to a receiving polygraph at a remote laboratory (Coates, Rosekind, & Thoresen, 1978; Rosekind, Coates, & Thoresen, 1978). The electrode leads plug into an eight-channel transmitter that contains a preamplifier and frequency modulator. The equipment includes a two-way intercom so that the subject can be instructed or awakened to follow an experimental protocol. This system duplicates the precision of a sleep laboratory (Coates et al., 1979) but allows the subject to sleep at home. We are currently using this type of equipment in our evaluation of psychological treatments of sleep problems of older adults.

Next-Day Effects. Since the insomniac's complaint often involves the aftereffects of poor sleep, it is important to assess fatigue and performance. Tests of vigilance, reaction time, and arithmetic have been found to be sensitive to sleep loss (Bootzin & Engle-Friedman, 1981). However, these measures have not been used in clinical settings.

In clinical settings, performance, mood, and sleepiness have typically been assessed by means of rating scales or adjective checklists (Gough & Heilbrun, 1965; Pillard, Atkinson, & Fisher, 1967; Zuckerman & Lubin, 1967). For example, Nicassio and Bootzin (1974) asked subjects to rate the following items of 5-point rating scales as part of a general sleep questionnaire: fatigue during the day, ability to function during the day on a task or on the job, and irritability or grouchiness. Another example, the Stanford Sleepiness Scale (Hoddes et al., 1973) is a 7-point rating scale with each of the 7 points labeled with descriptors. Thus, it goes from "1—Feeling active and vital; alert; wide awake" to "7—Almost in reverie; sleep onset soon; lost struggle to remain awake." The authors state that the scale can be readministered as frequently as every 15 minutes to provide useful discriminations.

Currently, we ask clients to fill out a brief four-item rating scale each evening before going to sleep (see Figure 3.3). As a result, we have daily records from the client regarding fatigue, sleepiness, and functioning during the day. This information is useful in determining the extent to which the individual's sleep pattern interferes with daily activities. It plays a role both in initial assessment and in the subsequent evaluation of the effectiveness of treatment.

PRESLEEP QUESTIONNAIRE

Name _____

Date _____

Answer the items by circling the numbers that correspond to your experience today.

1. Feeling upon Awakening in the Morning

1	2	3	4	5
Exhausted				Refreshed

2. Fatigue during the Day

1	2	3	4	5
Very Tired				Not At All Tired

3. Sleepiness during the Day

1	2	3	4	5
Very Sleepy				Not At All Sleepy

4. Ability to Function at Work or at Daily Chores

1	2	3	4	5
Very Poor				Very Good

Fig. 3.3.   The client fills out the presleep questionnaire each evening before going to sleep.

INTERVENTION

Overview

During the past 10 years, a number of short-term psychological interventions for insomnia have been evaluated. For detailed reviews of the short-term psychological treatment literature, the reader is referred to Bootzin and Nicassio (1978) and Youkilis and Bootzin (1981). There is little information in that literature, however, that is directly relevant to the treatment of the sleep problems of the elderly. Despite the high prevalence rate of insomnia among the elderly, none of the studies of nonpharmacological treatments has been focused on the elderly. Although subjects over the age of 60 have been included in some studies, the elderly have not constituted a substantial proportion of any study. In addition, most previous studies have evaluated treatments for sleep onset problems, while the elderly have considerable difficulty with sleep maintenance.

We are in the midst of the first controlled evaluation of alternate psychological interventions for the treatment of insomnia in the elderly. We are evaluating three treatments. Two of them, progressive relaxation training (Bernstein & Borkovec, 1973) and stimulus control instructions (Bootzin, 1972; 1976; 1977), have been thoroughly evaluated with younger adults and therefore are quite promising for use with the elderly. The third treatment, information and support, is also a component of the other two. Thus, in this design, we are evaluating whether specific relaxation or stimulus control instructions add significantly to what can be accomplished by providing support and accurate information about sleep.

After an initial interview, participants fill out questionnaires and personality inventories, agree to abstain from sleep medication (with their physician's permission), keep baseline daily sleep diaries for two weeks, and participate in two home polysomnography recordings. If the individual has either sleep onset or sleep maintenance insomnia, he or she is randomly assigned to one of the three treatments.

The three treatments are provided by advanced graduate students in clinical psychology and counseling who have been trained in each treatment and who receive ongoing supervision. Each insomniac receives four weekly one-hour therapy sessions. Evaluation is provided by means of posttreatment and one-month follow-up questionnaires, daily sleep diaries, and two additional home polysomnography recordings. Sometimes the treatment and evaluation period is lengthened because of bad weather, illness, or other scheduling difficulties. Not all subjects receive polysomnography. Subjects who live too far away to be reached easily by our technicians, and subjects who are unwilling to participate in polysomnography, receive all other aspects of the treatment evaluation.

Intervention Strategies

Information and Support. An important component of effective therapy for a variety of problems is the extent to which the individual stops perceiving himself or herself as a victim of the problem and begins to believe that he or she can cope with it. There are a number of converging lines of evidence that suggest that the individual's cognitive appraisal is important in mediating behavioral change (e.g., Bandura, 1977; 1982; Bootzin & Max, 1980; Lazarus, 1966; Mahoney, 1974: Mischel, 1973; Murray & Jacobson, 1978; Thompson, 1981).

The insomniac's appraisal of the problem may be an important component in its maintenance. Perseverant worry about why one cannot sleep and preoccupation with one's inability to sleep and the consequences of sleeplessness are likely to intensify any existing problem (Youkilis & Bootzin, 1981). It is the goal of the information and support treatment to reverse the cycle by helping the insomniac change his or her appraisal of the problem.

Support and information about sleep are provided in all three treatments. Thus, all subjects are informed about sleep stages and the developmental changes that occur with age as well as the effects on sleep of physical illness, prescription and nonprescription medication, alcohol, caffeine, nicotine, stress, inactivity, naps, sleep environment factors, and reinforcement for sleeplessness. In other words, the type of information that is contained in the first section of this chapter is discussed in the context of each individual's problem.

Two additional points are stressed. First, there are large individual differences in sleep needs. Some people have lived long, productive, satisfying lives getting less than two hours sleep a night for as long as they can remember (Meddis, 1977). In general, the body will get the amount of sleep that it needs. One possibility for clients to consider is that they may not need as much sleep as they believe necessary.

Second, it is not a calamity to go without sleep. While some small performance deficits have been demonstrated after sleep deprivation, other studies have failed to find such effects. There is very little performance deficit following prolonged periods of reduced sleep (Friedmann et al., 1977; Webb & Agnew, 1974) or even following total sleep deprivation for as long as eight days (Pasnau, Naitoh, Stier, & Kollar, 1968). The major effects of sleep deprivation are to produce fatigue and irritability.

Fatigue, however, follows a daily circadian rhythm even if the individual goes entirely without sleep (Kleitman, 1963). A person will be fatigued and have a low body temperature at times when he or she would ordinarily be asleep. On the other hand, the individual will be alert even after sleep deprivation at times when he or she is ordinarily awake. Thus, the day's performance is not as dependent on the previous night's sleep as many clients expect.

To summarize, the goal of the information and support treatment is to help the insomniac put the problem into a coping context. The therapist explores with the client the nature and severity of the problem, possible causes, and alternative solutions.

Although it is too early to report the final results of our study, we can provide some illustrative case histories showing the successful application of each treatment.

CASE ILLUSTRATIONS

Information and Support Treatment

A. is a 69-year-old married male who retired in 1981. He complained that for a number of years his sleep had worsened to the point where it took him one to two hours to fall asleep on three or four nights a week and he awakened five or six times for a total of two to four hours of wakefulness each night. On individual

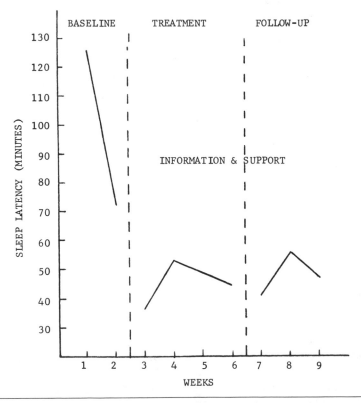

Fig. 3.4.   The effect of information and support on A.'s sleep latency as recorded on his sleep diaries.

difference measures, A. had a Beck Depression score of 6 (not depressed) but a Taylor Manifest Anxiety Score of 40 (highly anxious).

Figures 3.4 and 3.5 present the results of the information and support treatment on A.'s sleep latency and total sleep as recorded on his daily sleep diaries. As can be seen in Figure 3.4, although there was improvement in sleep latency, A. was still averaging about an hour to fall asleep at the end of the follow-up period. However, there was dramatic improvement in total sleep which was maintained during the follow-up.

A.'s responses to posttreatment and follow-up questionnaires confirmed his improvement. He reported that he worried less about sleep, he did not mention sleep difficulties to his friends as often as he did before treatment, and he no longer labled himself an insomniac. Nevertheless, he was not completely satisfied with his improvement. He felt that he could be sleeping even better and he requested an additional treatment.

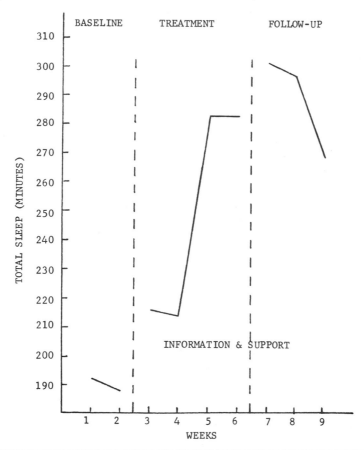

Fig. 3.5.   The effect of information and support on A.'s total sleep as recorded on his sleep diaries.

Relaxation Training

The most frequently recommended psychological treatment for insomnia is some type of relaxation training. This includes a variety of training procedures such as progressive relaxation, autogenic training, transcendental meditation, yoga, hypnosis, and EMG biofeedback. As treatments for insomnia, all of these procedures are based on the same premise: if people can learn to be relaxed at bedtime, they will fall asleep faster.

This premise derives partial support from the sleep research literature. First, there is evidence that many insomniacs are more highly aroused than normal sleepers. A number of studies examining personality characteristics of insomniacs and normal sleepers have found that poor sleepers and insomniacs are much higher than good sleepers on self-report measures of anxiety, depression, and on symptom checklists (Coursey, Buchsbaum, & Frankel, 1975; Engle-Friedman & Bootzin, 1981; Haynes, Follingstad, & McGowan, 1974; Monroe, 1967; Nicassio & Bootzin, 1974).

Some physiological differences between good and poor sleepers also support the proposition that poor sleepers are more aroused than good sleepers. Thus, Monroe (1967) found that poor sleepers had higher rectal temperatures, higher skin resistance, more vasoconstrictions per minute, and more body movements per hour than good sleepers. Johns, Gay, Masterson, and Bruce (1971) found that poor sleepers had higher levels of hormones indicative of heightened adrenocortical activity (and, thus, possibly of stress) than did good sleepers. Whether such heightened arousal in poor sleepers is an instrumental contributor to the sleeping difficulty, a byproduct of it, or a covariate of other causal variables remains open to analysis.

Progressive relaxation, developed by Edmund Jacobson (1938; 1964), has been the most thoroughly evaluated relaxation method for treating insomnia. A number of studies provide evidence for the superior effectiveness of progressive relaxation when compared to placebo control and no-treatment conditions. Progressive relaxation produced substantial improvement for both moderately impaired college student populations (e.g., Borkovec, Kaloupek, & Slama, 1975; Steinmark & Borkovec, 1974) and severe, chronic adult populations (e.g., Carr-Kaffashan & Woolfolk, 1979; Lick & Heffler, 1977; Nicassio & Bootzin, 1974). This improvement has been documented on daily sleep diaries (e.g., Borkovec et al., 1975; Nicassio & Bootzin, 1974) and with convergent polysomnographic laboratory assessments (e.g., Borkovec & Weerts, 1976; Haynes, Sides, & Lockwood, 1977). Progressive relaxation has also produced improvement for both psychophysiological and subjective insomniacs (Borkovec et al., 1979).

Progressive relaxation training is a prime candidate for use with elderly insomniacs. Some caution, however, is appropriate. Although elderly insomniacs have been included in some of these studies, the elderly have not constituted a substantial proportion of any study. Further, relaxation training has not been evaluated as thoroughly with sleep maintenance problems as with sleep onset problems. However, a case study (Coates & Thoresen, 1979) indicates that relaxation training can be effective with sleep maintenance problems and previous studies have reported improvement in total sleep time or number of awakenings as a result of relaxation training (e.g., Borkovec & Fowles, 1973; Lick & Heffler, 1977).

Relaxation training is likely to be an important component of nondrug treatment programs for insomnia of the elderly. As mentioned earlier, many insomniacs are highly aroused and anxious. For them, relaxation training may provide a double benefit—first, as a means of helping to induce sleep, and second, as a general coping skill to be used to deal more effectively with the stresses of the day.

In our program, instruction and guided practice in progressive relaxation follow the procedures outlined by Bernstein and Borkovec (1973). Clients are instructed to practice relaxation twice a day, once in bed before going to sleep. Figure 3.6 is a brief form that the client completes each time he or she

Relaxation Data Form

Name _____   Date _____

When did you practice relaxation today? *Occasion 1* _____
Occasion 2 _____

How relaxed did you feel as a result of practicing relaxation?

Occasion 1:

1	2	3	4	5
Not At All Relaxed		Moderately Relaxed		Completely Relaxed

Occasion 2:

1	2	3	4	5
Not At All Relaxed		Moderately Relaxed		Completely Relaxed

Briefly describe any feelings or sensations that you had while practicing relaxation:

Occasion 1: _____

_____

Occasion 2: _____

_____

Fig. 3.6. The client fills out the relaxation data form each time he or she practices relaxation.

practices relaxation. In this way, the therapist is kept informed about the client's compliance with the homework and with any problems associated with relaxation that may occur.

One common problem in using relaxation with the elderly is that the client may experience arthritic pain as a result of tensing and releasing particular muscle groups. In such instances, we instruct the client not to tense that muscle group, but to just release the tension from whatever level of tension is already present.

We discourage and do not ourselves use tape-recorded relaxation instructions. The goal of relaxation training is for the client to learn a new coping skill that can be available whenever it is needed. We do not want the client's relaxation response to be dependent on the availability of a tape recorder.

At each of the four weekly individual therapy sessions, in addition to practicing and receiving feedback on relaxation, the clients receive support and information about sleep in the context of their personal situations. An illustrative case history of the use of relaxation training is that of B., a 65-year-old married male who retired as a fireman in 1976.

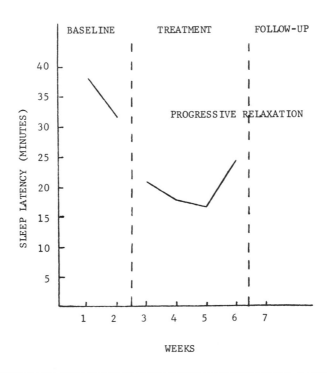

Fig. 3.7.   The effect of progressive relaxation training on B.'s sleep latency as recorded on his sleep diaries.

B. complained primarily of sleep maintenance problems and typically got less than four hours of sleep each night. Before treatment, he took Dalmane and Librium regularly. On the Beck Depression Inventory, he scored 33 (highly depressed); and on the Taylor Manifest Anxiety Scale, he scored 33 (highly anxious).

Figures 3.7 and 3.8 present the results of relaxation training on B.'s sleep latency and total sleep as recorded on his daily sleep diaries. As can be seen in the figures, B.'s sleep improved substantially. Parallel improvement was observed in his daily ratings of fatigue and functioning during the day.

B.'s responses to posttreatment and follow-up questionnaire confirmed this dramatic improvement. Although B. had been losing weight before treatment, he gained 15 pounds during the treatment and follow-up and was now back to his normal weight. His blood pressure also decreased substantially. He reported that he worried much less about sleep, he infrequently mentioned sleeping difficulties to his friends, and he no longer labeled himself an insomniac. He was particularly pleased with the support he received in withdrawing and staying off of Dalmane.

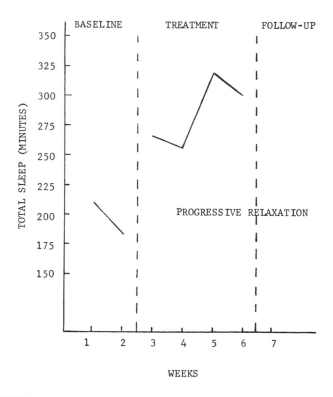

Fig. 3.8. The effect of progressive relaxation training on B.'s total sleep as recorded on his sleep diaries.

It is noteworthy that although B.'s sleep improved considerably, he remained depressed and anxious (Beck of 31, MAS of 35). At least in this case, improvement in sleep did not depend upon improvement in depression, nor did improvement in sleep produce substantial improvement in depression. As mentioned earlier, if psychological problems accompany sleep disturbance, separate therapeutic attention should be given to each. It should not be assumed that improvement in one will produce improvement in the other.

Stimulus Control Instructions

The goals of stimulus control instructions are to help the insomniac acquire a consistent sleep rhythm, to strengthen the bed as a cue for sleep, and to weaken it as a cue for activities that might interfere with sleep. As discussed in the earlier section on causes of insomnia, poor sleep habits can contribute to sleep disturbance. One part of this problem is that the person may never allow himself or herself to acquire a consistent sleep rhythm. This may occur as a result of inconsistent bedtime and/or time of arising in the morning.

Another part of the problem is that insomniacs may engage in activities in the bedroom at bedtime that are incompatible with falling asleep such as reading, watching television, or worrying. In our current research, we have observed that many elderly individuals engaged in many of their daily activities in the bedroom, particularly during the winter months. The result is that the bed and bedtime may become cues for arousal rather than cues for sleep.

From the preceding analysis, a stimulus control treatment for insomnia was developed (Bootzin, 1972; 1976; 1977) to strengthen the cues for falling asleep and separate them from the cues for other activities. The following rules constitute the stimulus control instructions.

1. Lie down intending to go to sleep *only* when you are sleepy.
2. Do not use your bed for anything except sleep; that is, do not read, watch television, eat, or worry in bed. Sexual activity is the only exception to this rule. On such occasions the instructions are to be followed afterward when you intend to go to sleep.
3. If you find yourself unable to fall asleep, get up and go into another room. Stay up as long as you wish and then return to the bedroom to sleep. Although we do not want you to watch the clock, we want you to get out of bed if you do not fall asleep immediately. Remember the goal is to associate your bed with falling asleep *quickly*! If you are in bed more than about 10 minutes without falling asleep and have not gotten up, you are not following this instruction.
4. If you still cannot fall asleep, repeat Step 3. Do this as often as is necessary throughout the night.

5. Set your alarm and get up at the same time every morning irrespective of how much sleep you got during the night. This will help your body acquire a consistent sleep rhythm.
6. Do not nap during the day.

Clients are asked to record the number of times they get out of bed each night in following the instructions. During the four weekly therapy sessions, clients receive support and information about sleep in addition to reviewing the stimulus control instructions and discussing any difficulties they are having. A common problem is the disturbance of the spouse's sleep when the insomniac gets out of bed. Sometimes discussion of the problem directly with the spouse is useful in insuring full cooperation. During the winter, some elderly participants are reluctant to leave the warmth of their beds. Suggestions for keeping warm robes near the bed and keeping an additional room warm through the night along with encouragement to try to follow the instructions were usually effective in promoting compliance.

Stimulus control instructions have been shown to be highly effective in case studies (Bootzin, 1972; Hauri, 1973; Haynes, Price, & Simons, 1975; Turner & Ascher, 1970a) and controlled evaluations (Bootzin, 1975; Lawrence & Tokarz, 1976; Slama, 1975; Tokarz & Lawrence, 1974; Turner & Ascher, 1979b; 1982). The average improvement in sleep onset latency produced by stimulus control instructions from the seven controlled studies is 66 percent as compared to less than 50 percent for relaxation training.

Although the focus of previous evaluations has been on sleep onset latency, improvement in total sleep (e.g., Bootzin, 1975) and number of arousals (Toler, 1978) has also been observed.

Five studies have compared progressive relaxation training and stimulus control instructions. Stimulus control instructions were found to be significantly superior in three studies (Bootzin, 1975; Lawrence & Tokarz, 1976; Slama, 1975), and there was no significant difference between the two treatments in two other studies (Turner & Ascher, 1979b; 1982).

At present, stimulus control instruction appears to be the most effective psychological intervention for insomnia; thus, it holds considerable promise as a treatment for the elderly. However, no evaluation of stimulus control instructions using convergent polysomnography has yet been conducted. This is an important remaining step for documenting the superior effectiveness of stimulus control instructions over other psychological interventions.

Case Illustration

C. is a 58-year-old married woman who is employed full-time doing clerical work. She complained of frequent awakenings and total sleep of four to five hours a night. This was far less than the seven hours of sleep she stated she needed to be refreshed the next day. C. had a Beck Depression score of 2 (not depressed) and a Taylor Manifest Anxiety Score of 12 (not anxious).

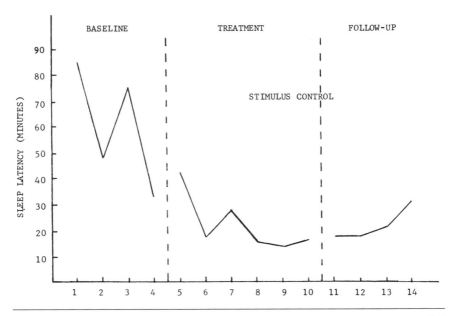

Fig. 3.9.   The effect of stimulus control instructions on C.'s sleep latency as recorded on her sleep diaries.

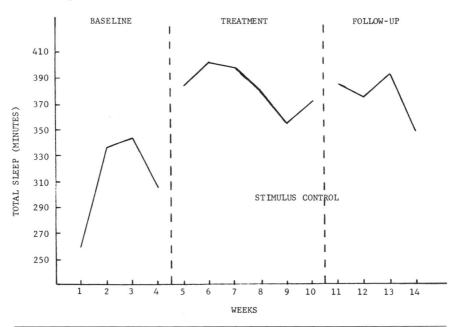

Fig. 3.10.   The effect of stimulus control instructions on C.'s total sleep as recorded on her sleep diaries.

Figures 3.9 and 3.10 present the results of stimulus control instructions on C.'s sleep latency and total sleep as recorded on her daily sleep diaries. As can be seen in the figures, she improved substantially in both sleep latency and total sleep. Although there was a parallel increase in her daily ratings of functioning during the day, there was no relationship between quality of sleep and next-day ratings of fatigue.

On the posttherapy and follow-up questionnaires, C. reported that her sleep problem was "greatly reduced." After treatment, C. stated that her sleep problem no longer affected other areas of her life, she no longer labeled herself an insomniac, and she felt that she had her sleep problem under control. She stated that she particularly benefited from the instruction not to nap and from the reassurance she received that it was permissible to wake up once or twice a night.

In contrast to B., C. was neither depressed nor anxious. It should not be assumed, however, that relaxation training is more appropriate for depressed and anxious patients than stimulus control instructions. In a previous study, stimulus control instructions were found to be more effective than relaxation training even for those subjects who were most anxious (Bootzin, 1975). We will need to wait for the results of the complete evaluation before concluding which treatments are most effective for which individuals.

Compliance with Treatment Procedures

Noncompliance to treatment requirements is a serious problem in treating the elderly. McConatha, McConatha, and Richards (1982) propose a number of factors that contribute to compliance. These include satisfaction with the deliverer of treatment, perceived positive modifying effects of treatment, perceived severity of symptoms, and the intent to comply. In addition, there are enabling factors such as design of the social service delivery system, the acceptance of the condition and regimen by significant others, and availability of time. Factors that prevent or interfere with compliance include interference with roles, cost of treatment and its accessibility, the complexity of the implementation of the treatment plan, and the general declining mental and physical capacity of the participant.

In our program, a number of these factors apply, creating some unique problems in delivering treatment and collecting data from participants. Most of our clients are highly motivated. Their contact with us comes at a time when symptoms of insomnia have become chronic and severe enough to induce them to volunteer for the program. The clients generally project a high degree of intent to comply.

It is an attractive feature of our program that there is no fee for participation. For an elderly population, to whom limited funds are available, this is a sensitive issue. There are, however, hidden costs to the accessibility of the program. The client must travel to campus for two interviews and four treatment sessions. During the winter months in Chicago, appointments are often cancelled and rescheduled. Older individuals fear slipping on the ice and are generally more fearful of illnesses contracted while out in the cold weather. While some subjects were visited at home or chauffeured, others could not participate. It is fortunate that we employed home polysomnography, for it is unlikely that many of our clients would have complied with sleeping in the laboratory during the winter.

Additional hidden costs lie in the complexity of the regimen. It takes time and concentration to complete questionnaires, presleep ratings, and daily sleep diaries. Some participants were stressed by the attention and memory demands of these tasks. Interviewers and therapists repeatedly provided support and reassurance about the participant's performance of these tasks.

Participation in a treatment program, of necessity, involves changing one's behavior. The elderly may be less able to change than younger adults for such reasons as loss of social supports for following new routines, distrust of change, or other cultural and experiential factors (Botwinick, 1973). It is difficult to assess how much lack of compliance was due to age and how much to individual differences. We found, for example, that some spouses were not supportive of their partners' new regimens. Our insomniacs often reported that their families deprecated their sleep problems. In contrast, supportive family members were often very helpful in assisting client compliance.

In treating the elderly, considerable responsibility falls on the therapist. The therapist must be sensitive to perceived setbacks and be especially supportive and encouraging. The therapists must be nonpunishing in attempts to deal with noncompliance, treating it as an opportunity to problem solve with their clients. Often the client was reminded that this was a time-limited evaluation. The client was encouraged to try the procedures as conscientiously as possible for the short time remaining in the evaluation.

Despite all the difficulties mentioned in this section, it is clear that it is possible to treat the sleep difficulties of elderly individuals successfully. The case studies presented indicate that each of the treatments can be successful.

In our present study, we are evaluating the individual contributions of the three treatments. In a clinical setting, there is no need to keep them separate. Information, relaxation training, and stimulus control instructions are not incompatible with one another. They can be effectively combined to meet the clinical needs of the individual.

REFERENCES

Agnew, H., Webb, W., & Williams, R. L. Sleep patterns in late middle-aged males: An EEG study. *Electroencephalography and Clinical Neurophysiology*, 1967, **23**, 168–171.

Albert, M. S. Geriatric neuropsychology. *Journal of Consulting and Clinical Psychology*, 1981, **49**, 835–850.

Association of Sleep Disorders Centers. Diagnostic classification of sleep and arousal disorders

(1st ed.). Prepared by Sleep Disorders Classification Committee. *Sleep*, 1979, **2**, 1-137.

Baekeland, F., & Hoy, P. Reported vs. recorded sleep characteristics. *Archives of General Psychiatry*, 1971, **24**, 548-551.

Bandura, A. Self-efficacy: Toward a unifying theory of behavioral change. *Psychological Review*, 1977, **84**, 191-215.

Bandura, A. Self-efficacy in human agency. *American Psychologist*, 1982, **37**, 122-147.

Beck, A. T. *Depression: Clinical, experimental, and theoretical aspects*. New York: Harper & Row, 1967.

Bernstein, D. S., & Borkovec, T. D. *Progressive relaxation training*. Champaign, Ill.: Research Press, 1973.

Bixler, E., Kales, A., Soldatos, C., Kales, J., & Healey, S. Prevalence of sleep disorders: A survey of the Los Angeles metropolitan area. *American Journal of Psychiatry*, 1979, **136**, 1257-1262.

Blake, H., Gerard, R. W., & Kleitman, N. Factors influencing brain potentials during sleep. *Journal of Neurophysiology*, 1939, **2**, 48-60.

Bonnet, M. H., & Johnson, L. C. Relationship of arousal threshold to sleep stage distribution and subjective estimates of depth and quality of sleep. *Sleep*, 1978, **1**, 161-168.

Bonnet, M. H., Webb, W. B., & Barnard, G. Effect of flurazepam, pentobarbital and caffeine on arousal threshold. *Sleep*, 1979, **1**, 271-279.

Bootzin, R. R. *Stimulus control treatment for insomnia*. Paper presented at the meetings of the American Psychological Association, Honolulu, September 1972.

Bootzin, R. R. *A comparison of stimulus control instructions and progressive relaxation training in the treatments of sleep onset insomnia*. Unpublished manuscript, Northwestern University, Evanston, Ill. 1975.

Bootzin, R. R. Self-help techniques for controlling insomnia. In C. M. Franks (Ed.), *Behavior therapy: Techniques, principles and patient aids*. New York: Biomonitoring Applications, 1976. (Tape)

Bootzin, R. R. Effects of self-control procedures for insomnia. In R. B. Stuart (Ed.), *Behavioral self-management: Strategies, techniques, and outcomes*. New York: Brunner-Mazel, 1977.

Bootzin, R. R., & Engle-Friedman, M. The assessment of insomnia. *Behavioral Assessment*, 1981, **3**, 107-126.

Bootzin, R. R., & Max, D. Learning and behavioral theories. In I. L. Kutash & L. B. Schlesing (Eds.), *Handbook on stress and anxiety*. San Francisco: Jossey-Bass, 1980.

Bootzin, R. R., & Nicassio, P. M. Behavioral treatment for insomnia. In M. Hersen, R. M. Eisler, & P. M. Miller (Eds.), *Progress in Behavior Modification*, Vol. 6. New York: Academic Press, 1978.

Borkovec, T. D. Pseudo (experiential) insomnia and idiopathic (objective) insomnia: Theoretical and therapeutic issues. In H. Eysenck & S. Rachman (Eds.), *Advances in Behavior Research and Therapy* (Pergamon Press), 1979, **2**, 27-55.

Borkovec, T. D., & Fowles, D. Controlled investigation of the effects of progressive relaxation and hypnotic relaxation on insomnia. *Journal of Abnormal Psychology*, 1973, **82**, 153-158.

Borkovec, T. D., Grayson, J. B., O'Brien, G. T. & Weerts, J. C. Relaxation treatment of pseudoinsomnia and idiopathic insomnia: An electroencephalographic evaluation. *Journal of Applied Behavior Analysis*, 1979, **12**, 37-54.

Borkovec, T. D., Kaloupek, G. D., & Slama, K. The facilitative effect of muscle tension release in the relaxation treatment of sleep disturbance. *Behavior Therapy*, 1975, **6**, 301-309.

Borkovec, T. D., & Weerts, T. C. Effects of progressive relaxation on sleep disturbance: An electroencephalographic evaluation. *Psychosomatic Medicine*, 1976, **38**, 173-180.

Botwinick, J. *Aging and behavior*. New York: Springer, 1973.

Brodman, K., Erdmann, A., & Wolff, H. *Cornell Medical Index Health Questionnaire manual*. New York: Cornell University College, 1956.

Carr-Kaffashan, L., & Woolfolk, R. L. Active and placebo effects in the treatment of moderate and severe insomnia. *Journal of Consulting and Clinical Psychology*, 1979, **47**, 1072-1080.

Carskadon, M., Brown, E., & Dement, W. Respiration during sleep in the elderly. *Sleep*

Research, 1980, **9**, 99.

Carskadon, M. A., Dement, W. C., Mitler, M. M., Guilleminault, C., Zarconi, V. P., & Spiegel, R. Self reports vs. sleep laboratory findings in 122 drug-free subjects with complaints of chronic insomnia. *American Journal of Psychology*, 1976, **133**, 1382–1388.

Coates, T. J., Killen, J. D., George, J., Marchini, E., Silverman, S., & Thoresen, C. Estimating sleep parameters: A multitrait-multimethod analysis. *Journal of Consulting and Clinical Psychology*, 1982, **50**, 345–352.

Coates, T. J., Rosekind, M. R., Strossen, R. J., Thoresen, C. E., & Kirmil-Gray, K. Sleep recordings in the laboratory and home: A comparative analysis. *Psychophysiology*, 1979, **16**, 339–346.

Coates, T. J., Rosekind, M. R., & Thoresen, C. E. All night sleep recordings in clients' homes by telephone. *Journal of Behavior Therapy and Experimental Psychiatry*, 1978, **9**, 157–162.

Coates, T. J., & Thoresen, C. E. Treating arousals during sleep using behavioral self management. *Journal of Consulting and Clinical Psychology*, 1979, **47**, 603–605.

Costello, C. G., & Smith, C. M. The relationships between personality, sleep and the effect of sedatives. *British Journal of Psychiatry*, 1963, **109**, 568–571.

Coursey, R. D., Buchsbaum, M., & Frankel, B. C. Personality measures and evoked responses in chronic insomniacs. *Journal of Abnormal Psychology*, 1975, **84**, 239–249.

de la Pena, A. Toward a psychophysiologic conceptualization of insomnia. In R. C. Williams & I. Karacan (Eds.), *Sleep disorders: Diagnosis and treatment*. New York: Wiley, 1978.

de la Pena, A., Flickinger, R., & Mayfield, D. *Reverse first night effect in chronic poor sleepers*. Paper presented at the Association for the Psychophysiological Study of Sleep, Houston, 1977.

Engle-Friedman, M., & Bootzin, R. R. The effect of mood on sleep of insomniac and normal sleepers. *Sleep Research*, 1981, **10** (abstract).

Engle-Friedman, M., Bootzin, R. R., & Hazelwood, L. *The disruptive effects of music on sleep onset and sleep quality*. Unpublished manuscript. Northwestern University, Evanston, Ill. 1982.

Erwin, C. W., & Zung, W. W. Behavioral and EEG criteria of sleep in humans. *Archives of General Psychiatry*, 1970, **23**, 375–377.

Feinberg, I., Koresko, R., & Heller, N. EEG sleep patterns as a function of normal and pathological aging in man. *Journal of Psychiatric Research*, 1967, **5**, 107–144.

Fordyce, W. F. *Behavioral methods for chronic pain and illness*. St. Louis, Mo.: Mosby, 1976.

Frankel, B. L., Coursey, R. D., Buchbinder, R., & Snyder, F. Recorded and reported sleep in chronic primary insomnia. *Archives of General Psychiatry*, 1976, **33**, 615–623.

Freedman, P. R., & Papsdorf, J. D. Biofeedback and progressive relaxation treatment of sleep-onset insomnia: A controlled all-night investigation. *Biofeedback and Self Regulation*, 1976, **1**, 253–271.

Friedmann, J., Globus, G., Huntley, A., Mullaney, D., Naitoh, P., & Johnson, L. Performance and mood during and after gradual sleep reduction. *Psychophysiology*, 1977, **14**, 245–250.

Gough, H. G., & Heilbrun, A. B., Jr. *The adjective checklist manual*. Palo Alto, Calif.: Consulting Psychologists Press, 1965.

Greenblatt, D., & Allen, M. Toxicity of nitrazepam in the elderly: A report from the Boston Collaborative Drug Surveillance Program. *British Journal of Clinical Pharmacology*, 1978, **5**, 407–413.

Guilleminault, C., & Dement, W. C. Sleep apnea syndromes and related sleep disorders. In R. L. Williams & I. Karacan (Eds.), *Sleep disorders: Diagnosis and treatment*. New York: Wiley, 1978.

Guilleminault, C., Eldridge, F. L., & Dement, W. C. Insomnia with sleep apnea: A new syndrome. *Science*, 1973, **181**, 856–858.

Hartmann, E. Longitudinal studies of sleep and dream patterns in manic-depressive patients. *Archives of General Psychiatry*, 1968, **19**, 312–329.

Hartmann, E. *The sleeping pill*. New Haven, Conn.: Yale University Press, 1978.

Hauri, P. *Psychology of sleep disorder: Their diagnosis and treatment*. Paper presented at the

Symposium on Sleep and Dreams, 83rd Annual Convention of the American Psychological Association, Chicago, 1975.

Hauri, P. *The sleep disorders*. Kalamazoo, Mich.: Upjohn Company, 1977.

Havighurst, R. J. Successful aging. In R. J. Williams, C. Tibbitts, & W. Donahue (Eds.), *Process of aging*. New York: Atherton, 1963.

Haynes, S. N., Follingstad, D. K., & McGowan, W. T. Insomnia: Sleep patterns and anxiety level. *Journal of Psychosomatic Research*, 1974, **18**, 69–74.

Haynes, S. N., Price, M. G., & Simons, J. B. Stimulus control treatment of insomnia. *Journal of Behavior Therapy and Experimental Psychiatry*, 1975, **6**, 279–282.

Haynes, S. N., Sides, H., & Lockwood, G. Relaxation instructions and frontalis electromyographic feedback intervention with sleep onset insomnia. *Behavior Therapy*, 1977, **8**, 644–652.

Hemminki, E., & Heikkila, J. Elderly people's compliance with prescriptions and quality of medication. *Scandinavian Journal of Social Medicine*, 1975, **3**, 87–92.

Hoddes, E., Zarcone, V., Smythe, H., Phillips, R., & Dement, W. C. Quantification of sleepiness: A new approach. *Psychophysiology*, 1973, **10**, 431–436.

Institute of Medicine. *Sleeping pills, insomnia, and medical practice*. Washington, D.C.: National Academy of Science, 1979.

Jacobson, E. *Progressive relaxation*. Chicago: University of Chicago Press, 1938.

Jacobson, E. *Anxiety and tension control*. Philadelphia: Lippincott, 1964.

Johns, M. W., Gay, T. J., Masterson, J. P., & Bruce, D. W. Relationships between sleep habits, adrenocortical activity and personality. *Psychosomatic Medicine*, 1971, **33**, 499–508.

Kahn, E., & Fisher, C. The sleep characteristics of the normal aged male. *Journal of Nervous and Mental Disease*, 1969, **148**, 474–494.

Kales, A., Allen, W. C., Scharf, M. B., & Kales, J. D. Hypnotic drugs and their effectiveness: All-night EEG studies of insomniac subjects. *Archives of General Psychiatry*, 1970, **23**, 226–232.

Kales, A., Caldwell, A. B., Preston, T. A., Healey, S., & Kales, J. D. Personality patterns in insomnia. *Archives of General Psychiatry*, 1976, **33**, 1128–1134.

Kales, A., & Kales, J. Evaluation, diagnosis and treatment of clinical conditions related to sleep. *Journal of the American Medical Association*, 1970, **213**, 2229–2334.

Kales, A., Kales, J. D., Bixler, E. O., & Scharf, M. B. Methodology of sleep laboratory drug evaluations: Further considerations. In F. Kagan, T. Harwood, R. Rickels, A. D. Rudzik, & A. Soyer (Eds.), *Hypnotics: Methods of development and evaluation*. New York: Spectrum, 1975.

Kales, A., Scharf, M. B., & Kales, J. D. Rebound insomnia: A new clinical syndrome. *Science*, 1978, **201**, 1039–1040.

Kales, A., Wilson, T., Kales, J., Jacobson, A., Paulson, M., Kollar, E., & Walter, R. O. Measurements of all-night sleep in normal elderly persons: Effects of aging. *Journal of American Geriatric Society*, 1967, **15**, 405–414.

Kales, J. D. Aging and sleep. In R. Goldman & M. Rockstein (Eds.), *Symposium on the physiology and pathology of aging*. New York: Academic Press, 1975.

Kales, J., Tan, T., Swearingen, C., & Kales, A. Are over-the-counter sleep medications effective? All-night EEG studies. *Current Therapeutic Research*, 1971, **13**, 143–151.

Karacan, I., Thornby, J., Anch, M., Holzer, C. E., Warheit, G. J., Schwab, J. J., & Williams, R. L. Prevalence of sleep disturbance in a primarily urban Florida county. *Social Science Medicine*, 1976, **10**, 239–244.

Karacan, I., Williams, R. L., Salis, P. J., & Hursch, C. J. New approaches to the evaluation and treatment of insomnia (preliminary results). *Psychosomatics*, 1971, **12**, 81–88.

Kleitman, N. *Sleep and wakefulness*. Chicago: University of Chicago Press, 1963.

Kupfer, D. J., & Foster, F. G. EEG sleep and depression. In R. L. Williams & I. Karacan (Eds.), *Sleep disorders: Diagnosis and treatment*. New York: Wiley, 1978.

Kupfer, D. J., Wyatt, R. J., & Snyder, F. Comparison between electroencephalographic and systematic nursing observations of sleep in psychiatric patients. *Journal of Nervous and Mental Disease*, 1970, **151**, 361–368.

Lawrence, P. S., & Tokarz, T. *A comparison of relaxation training and stimulus control*. Paper presented at Association for the Advancement of Behavior Therapy, New York, 1976.

Lazarus, R. S. *Psychological stress and the coping process*. New York: McGraw-Hill, 1966.

Lewis, S. A. Subjective estimates of sleep: An EEG evaluation. *British Journal of Psychology*, 1969, **60**, 203–208.

Lichstein, K. L., & Kelley, J. E. Measuring sleep patterns in natural settings. *Behavioral Engineering*, 1979, **5**, 95–100.

Lick, J. P., & Heffler, D. Relaxation training and attention placebo in the treatment of severe insomnia. *Journal of Consulting and Clinical Psychology*, 1977, **45**, 153–161.

Lugaresi, E., Coccagna, G., Berti-Ceroni, G., & Ambrosetto, C. Restless legs syndrome and nocturnal myoclonus. In H. Gastant, E. Lugaresi, G. Berti-Ceroni, & G. Coccagna (Eds.), *The abnormalities of sleep in man*. Bologna, Italy: Aulogaggi, 1968.

Mahoney, M. J. *Cognition and behavior modification*. Cambridge, Mass.: Ballinger, 1974.

McConatha, D., McConatha, J., & Richards, G. Noncompliance to medical regimens in the chronically ill elderly. In R. R. Boyd & D. McConatha (Eds.), *Gerontological practice issues and perspectives*. Washington, D.C.: United Press of America, 1982.

McGhie, A., & Russell, S. The subjective assessment of normal sleep patterns. *Journal of Mental Science*, 1962, **108**, 642–654.

Meddis, R. *The sleep instinct*. London: Routledge & Kegan Paul, 1977.

Mendelson, W. B., Gillin, J. C., & Wyatt, R. J. *Human sleep and its disorders*. New York: Plenum, 1977.

Miles, L. E., & Dement, W. C. Sleep and aging. *Sleep*, 1980, **3**, 119–220.

Miller, N. E., & Cohen, G. D. (Eds.), *Clinical aspects of Alzheimer's Disease and senile dementia*. New York: Raven, 1981.

Mischel, W. Toward a cognitive social learning reconceptualization of personality. *Psychological Review*, 1973, **80**, 252–283.

Monroe, L. J. Psychological and physiological differences between good and poor sleepers. *Journal of Abnormal Psychology*, 1967, **72**, 255–264.

Murray, E. J. *Sleep, dreams and arousal*. New York: Appleton-Century-Crofts, 1965.

Murray, E. J., & Jacobson, L. I. Cognition and learning in traditional and behavioral psychotherapy. In S. L. Garfield & A. E. Bergin (Eds.), *Handbook of psychotherapy and behavior change*. New York: Wiley, 1978.

Nicassio, P., & Bootzin, R. R. A comparison of progressive relaxation training and autogenic training as treatment for insomnia. *Journal of Abnormal Psychology*, 1974, **83**, 253–260.

Pasnau, R. O., Naitoh, P., Stier, S., & Kollar, E. J. The psychological effects of 205 hours of sleep deprivation. *Archives of General Psychiatry*, 1968, **18**, 496–505.

Pillard, R. C., Atkinson, K. W., & Fisher, S. The effect of different preparations on film induced anxiety. *Psychological Record*, 1967, **17**, 35–41.

Prinz, P., Obrist, W., & Wang, H. Sleep patterns in healthy elderly subjects: Individual differences as related to other neurological variables. *Sleep Research*, 1975, **4**, 132.

Prinz, P. N., & Raskind, M. Aging and sleep disorders. In R. Williams & I. Karacan (Eds.), *Sleep disorders: Diagnosis and treatment*. New York: Wiley, 1978.

Rahe, R. H., Meyer, M., Smith, M., Kjar, G., & Holmes, T. H. Social stress and illness onset. *Journal of Psychosomatic Research*, 1964, **8**, 35–44.

Rechtschaffen, A., & Kales, A. (Eds.). *A manual of standardized terminology, techniques and scoring system for sleep stages of human subjects*. Washington, D.C.: Public Health Service, Government Printing Office, 1968.

Rosekind, M. R., Coates, T. J., & Thoresen, C. Telephone transmission of all-night polysomnographic data from subjects' homes. *Journal of Nervous and Mental Disease*, 1978, **166**, 438–441.

Roth, B. Narcolepsy and hypersomnia. In R. L. Williams & I. Karacan (Eds.), *Sleep disorders: Diagnosis and treatment*. New York: Wiley, 1978.

Slama, K. Unpublished master's thesis, University of Iowa, 1975.

Snyder, F. Toward an evolutional theory of dreaming. *American Journal of Psychiatry*, 1966, **123**, 121–136.

Soldatos, C. R., Kales, J. D., Scharf, M. B., Bixler, E. O., & Kales, A. Cigarette smoking associated with sleep difficulty. *Science*, 1980, **207**, 551–553.

Starker, S., & Hasenfeld, R. Daydream styles and sleep disturbance. *Journal of Nervous and Mental Disease*, 1976, **163**, 391–400.

Steinmark, S., & Borkovec, T. Active and placebo treatment effects on moderate insomnia under counterdemand and positive demand instructions. *Journal of Abnormal Psychology*, 1974, **83**, 157–163.

Taylor, J. A. A personality scale of manifest anxiety. *Journal of Abnormal and Social Psychology*, 1953, **48**, 285–290.

Thompson, S. C. Will it hurt less if I control it? A complex answer to a simple question. *Psychological Bulletin*, 1981, **90**, 89–101.

Tokarz, T., & Lawrence, P. *An analysis of temporal and stimulus factors in the treatment of insomnia*. Paper presented at the 8th Annual Meeting of the Association for the Advancement of Behavior Therapy, Chicago, 1974.

Toler, H. C. The treatment of insomnia with relaxation and stimulus-control instructions among incarcerated males. *Criminal Justice and Behavior*, 1978, **5**, 117–130.

Turner, R. M., & Ascher, L. M. Controlled comparison of progressive relaxation stimulus control and paradoxical intention therapies for insomnia. *Journal of Consulting and Clinical Psychology*, 1979, **49**, 500–508.(b)

Turner, R. M., & Ascher, L. M. A within subjects analysis of stimulus control therapy for severe sleep onset insomnia. *Behavior Research and Therapy*, 1979, **17**, 107–112.(a)

Turner, R. M., & Ascher, L. M. Therapist factor in the treatment of insomnia. *Behavior Research and Therapy*, 1982, **20**, 33–40.

United States Public Health Service. *Physician's drug prescribing patterns in skilled nursing facilities*. Washington, D.C.: U.S. Department of Health, Education and Welfare, June 1976.

Webb, W. The rhythms of sleep and waking. In L. Sheving, F. Halberg, & J. Pauly (Eds.), *Anonobiology*. Tokyo: Igaku Shorn, 1974.

Webb, W., & Campbell, S. S. Awakenings and the return to sleep in an older population. *Sleep*, 1980, **3**, 41–46.

Webb, W., & Swinburne, H. An observational study of sleep in the aged. *Perceptual Motor Skills*, 1971, **32**, 895–898.

Webb, W. B. *Sleep: The gentle tyrant*. Englewood Cliffs, N.J.: Spectrum, 1975.

Webb, W. B., & Agnew, H. W., Jr. The effects of a chronic limitation of sleeplength. *Psychophysiology*, 1974, **11**, 265–274.

Weiss, B. L., McPartland, R. J., & Kupfer, D. J. Once more: The inaccuracy of non-EEG estimations of sleep. *American Journal of Psychiatry*, 1973, **130**, 1282–1285.

Williams, R. L., Karacan, I., & Hursch, C. J. *EEG of human sleep. Clinical applications*. New York: Wiley, 1974.

Wurtman, R. J. Nutrients that modify brain function. *Scientific American*, 1982, **4**, 50–59.

Youkilis, H. D., & Bootzin, R. R. A psychophysiological perspective on the etiology and treatment of insomnia. In S. N. Haynes & L. A. Gannon (Eds.), *Psychosomatic disorders: A psychophysiological approach to etiology and treatment*. New York: Praeger, 1981.

Zepelin, H. A survey of age differences in sleep patterns and dream recall among well-educated men and women. *Sleep Research*, 1973, **2**, 81.

Zuckerman, M., & Lubin, B. *The multiple affect adjective checklist*. San Diego, Calif.: Educational and Industrial Testing Service, 1967.

Chapter 4

Social and Daily Living Skills

Roger L. Patterson and David A. Eberly

DESCRIPTION OF PROBLEM

Daily living and social skills are critical for the elderly. Much evidence is available today to indicate that the inability of elderly persons to care for themselves (usually referred to as activities of daily living or ADL) or to function adequately socially is a major problem facing our society. Such deficits, when severe, may result in institutionalization or custodial care by families. Less extreme deficits may also result in isolation and loss of independence. The Health Care Financing Administration (1981) has reported that lack of self-care is the major cause of institutionalization of the elderly.[1] In addition, such deficiencies of self-care skills are recognized among nursing home residents (e.g., Pfeiffer, Johnson, & Chiofolo, 1980) and the loss of adequate social relationships contributes to institutionalization (Lowenthal, 1964). For example, in an early review of studies concerning problems encountered by the elderly, Birren et al. (1963) concluded that:

> As the environment showed qualities of deprivation or displacement of the person (in loss of intimate persons, loss of income, in cultural displacement) the attitudes and behavior of the aged showed more deteriorative qualities. Psychological reactions to the loss of friends and other environmental supports may amplify if not initiate changes in the older nervous system and thereby the rest of the organism. (p. 314.)

More recently, Atchley (1977) stated that breakdown of the social support system was the "primary cause of institutionalization of the elderly" (p. 116).

We hypothesize that the issues of self-care and social supports are strongly interactive in several ways. Most obviously, persons who are not taking good care of themselves and their affairs can survive longer and better in the community if there are others available to care for them. Whether or not others are available may depend on the social skills of the elderly person. Some people may require very little assistance to maintain themselves in the community, but they may lack the ability to relate to others in such a way that even minimal assistance will be provided. Others may require a great deal of assistance but they possess enough desirable social qualities that their needs are readily met. In addition, from behavioral psychology it can be postulated that older people will be more likely to continue adequate self-care and social functions, despite various adversities, to the extent that they have regular and strong relationships with others reinforcing, and thus maintaining, adequate social and self-care behavior. Put simply, if there is no one significant person or persons to care about us, we may stop caring for ourselves. In addition to self-care, desirable emotional states in humans may require an adequate level of social relations.

The other side of this interaction between social supports and self-care is that people become less socially desirable if they fail to practice good hygiene and fail to maintain their residence adequately. One may conceive of a spiral of reciprocal losses of self-care and losses of social supports eventually leading to the need for institutional care. Where the spiral begins may not be as important as the fact that it is occurring.

There are important reasons, both humanitarian and economic, why such issues are of particular concern at this point in history. The economic reason is the huge cost of dealing with the problems of the elderly by institutionalizing them. According to the Health Care Financing Administration's report for the year 1979, 117.8 billion dollars were spent on nursing home care for the elderly: 49 percent of this was paid for by the U.S. government. This cost is expected to grow rapidly because of the projected growth of the elderly population. The number of persons aged 65 and older is expected to double by the year 2030 while the general population increases by only 40 percent. Most importantly, those who need the most care (i.e., those aged 85 and older) are expected to triple in number.

There is also an enormous human cost involved in the loss of a normal existence by large numbers of people. Atchley (1977) reported that the older person fears being placed in a nursing home and that such placement is associated with the loss of independence and rejection by the family. It is also likely that many families feel guilt over institutionalizing a family member.

Prevalence of Self-Care and Social-Skills Problems

There is no question but that the prevalence of social and self-care deficits in the institutionalized elderly is very high. In addition, research data exist that pertain directly to the prevalence of those deficits in community resident elders. One of the best estimates of the prevalence of overall self-care deficits comes from a needs-assessment study of 997 residents of Durham County, North Carolina, aged 65 and over (Blazer & Maddox, 1982). These authors used the Multidimensional Functional Assessment Questionnaire (MFAQ) developed by the Duke University Center for the Study of Aging and Human Development (1978) to assess function in the areas of social resources, economic resources, mental health, physical health, and self-care (ADL). Twenty-two percent of this sample showed impairment on ADL. Further-more, ADL scores were strongly associated with mental-health impairment (r = .61). Significantly, the authors concluded that these data from North Carolina are similar to results of a previous study in Cleveland, Ohio.

Cairl (in press) has recently assembled data revealing the incidence of ADL problems in the elderly population (age 65 +) in the Tampa Bay region of Florida, a favorite retirement area for the United States. Specially con-structed interviews, administered to a scientifically constructed sample, showed that 17.4 percent of this group had problems with one or more basic ADL skills (such as bathing, eating, and toileting), and 13.4 percent had problems with more complex daily living skills (such as cooking, shopping, and transportation).

From these two studies it may be easily concluded that ADL impairment is highly prevalent among people age 65 and older. Furthermore, these ADL deficits are experienced by elderly in the community and not just by those who are institutionalized.

It is difficult, if not impossible, to estimate accurately the prevalence of social-skills deficits among the elderly because previous studies have not directly measured social skills. However, the prevalence of social-skills deficits can be inferred from studies focused on conditions that are known to include social-skills problems. For example, depression and hypochondriasis are common among the elderly (Butler & Lewis, 1977; Zarit, 1980) and have been linked to social-skills deficits (Larson, 1978; Libet & Lewinsohn, 1973; Mad-dox, 1964). Thus, the high prevalence of depression or hypochondriasis among the elderly may be related to high prevalence of social-skills deficits.

The present authors and their colleagues (Eberly, Patterson, Jackson, & O'Sullivan, 1981) conducted a survey of geriatric patients at a state mental hospital. This survey, which included a behavioral assessment, indicated that 76 percent of the patients could not function effectively as members of a group or participate in group activities, and that 66 percent could not initiate social contacts. A survey of all geriatric patients in state mental hospitals conducted by the Florida Department of Health and Rehabilitative Services, Alcohol, Drug Abuse, and Mental Health staff (1981) found that 65 percent could not function as group members; 66 percent could not initiate social contacts; and 42 percent could not respond to overtures.

Social-skills deficits of the elderly may also contribute to numerous problems in living not directly associated with the usual categories of pathology. Thus, Corby (1975) suggests that social-skills deficits are often involved with the elderly person's passivity, problematic and contradictory communication with relatives, and social isolation.

Rationale for the Aging Program of the Florida Mental Health Institute

The basic rationale behind the Aging Program of the Florida Mental Health Institute (FMHI)[2] in Tampa (hereinafter called the Program) was that, in view of the above, it seemed reasonable that improving the social and self-care skills of elderly people might have great humanitarian and economic benefits for society in general and for the affected elderly and their families in particular.

The Program originated from the State Mental Health Agency's concern with the fact that many old people who might benefit from other treatment were being referred to state hospitals primarily for medical and custodial care. The Program sought to develop and to evaluate alternative treatments for two groups of elderly: (1) those already residing in state mental hospitals and local psychiatric wards for whom the realistic goal was to return to noninstitutional community placements; and (2) those currently residing in the local community but who seemed to be in danger of institutionalization without intervention. Thus, the overall purpose of the Program was to promote and maintain community living.

Obviously, there were some conditions and behaviors that required special care and precluded community living as an immediate goal. Criteria were developed to exclude these conditions. To be included in the program, clients had to be: age 55 or older; not in need of acute medical or skilled nursing care; minimally ambulatory by some means; and continent and able to live safely in an unlocked environment without strict supervision. Persons who failed to meet these criteria were felt to require institutional care for medical treatment and safety. There were no diagnostic or financial criteria for admission to the Program.

Other factors also governed the nature of the Program. Given the way the population was defined, treatment approaches that were to be developed had to be effective with a great variety of problems that would have an equally great heterogeneity of etiologies. The Program would also have to be applied by a diversity of personnel, many of whom would not be professionals or very well educated: most of the people who work with the elderly in the state are nonprofessionals, with little formal education.

These factors represent widespread reality: masses of elderly in need of this type of help come from many backgrounds and have a great variety of medical conditions. Doctors, nurses, social workers, and psychologists are not sufficiently available to work directly with the elderly who need their services. Nor are they able to spend the time needed to rehabilitate social and self-care skills deficits.

A review of the relevant literature (Bates, 1975) indicated that a highly structured training environment combined with the availability of medical treatment and good social-work services was a desirable way to approach overcoming social and self-care deficits. Furthermore, behavioral psychology was considered to provide a good general framework for the development of such a structured environment. Although there had been several previous demonstrations of the usefulness of the behavioral model and its concomitant techniques to the problems of the elderly (see Patterson & Jackson, 1980, for a recent review), there were no available comprehensive treatment programs for use with this particular group of elderly based upon the behavioral model. Most of the work with the elderly has been dominated by concepts and by interventions generated by what may be termed the medical and social models.

Both the medical and the social models offer a number of explanations as to why people with advanced age may cease to perform competently within the areas of ADL and social functioning. Probably each is somewhat correct at least some of the time for some of the people. The behavioral model offers many advantages not fully exploited so far in work with the aged. The medical model leads one to look at physiological changes, many of which are not currently reversible. The social model focuses on broad social changes affecting thousands or millions of people which may require many years and heroic interventions. The behavioral approach identifies observable behaviors and interventions that are readily applicable in the present and immediate environment, which will produce relatively quick changes if they are successful.

It is this immediate applicability, with the promise of fast results, that makes the application of behavioral concepts and methods highly desirable. The basic idea underlying our program was that if people displayed problem behaviors or skills deficits that could be defined in observable terms, then structured-learning situations could be created to overcome these problems, if not completely, then at least to some measurable degree.

Overview of the Modular Behavioral Treatment Program

Based upon the above rationale, it was decided that an appropriate approach would be to employ the behavioral model in the form of highly structured treatment components or behavioral modules. Six modules were developed: three taught activities of daily living, and three taught social skills. The three ADL modules taught self-care behaviors that were generally related to three types of placements. ADL I taught those basic self-care and eating behaviors needed for any noncustodial setting. Persons completing ADL I but no higher lever of self-care skills could be placed with families or in foster or boarding homes, which would provide for all other aspects of self-care. ADL II training stressed care of clothing and room, handling small amounts of money, and using the telephone. Persons completing ADL I and II would be prepared for life in the usual boarding home, in most foster homes, and in families, all of whom would be able to provide some assistance with additional needs. ADL III taught skills such as budgeting, meal planning and preparation, and obtaining community resources; it prepared people for independent living.

The social-skills series consisted of three modules and an optional social problem-solving training procedure. Conversation Training taught people to interact socially in a casual way. Communication Training taught people to express basic affects (such as expressing pleasure to someone about something they liked and displeasure about something they disliked). Self-Esteem Training taught people to recognize their own positive characteristics. Interpersonal problem solving was used with those individuals who had specific problems with particular people at this time in their lives; these individuals were taught the specific social behaviors needed to solve these particular problems.

The remainder of this chapter consists of three sections describing the assessments, interventions, and evaluation as used with the modules. The problems dealt with by the modules are very diverse and not specific to diagnostic categories or to particular isolated problems. While, of necessity, the modules are described individually, they should be seen as part of a total program.

ASSESSMENTS

Four major reasons for assessing ADL and social skills of the elderly in treatment settings may be identified: (1) to assess the degree of congruence between the functioning of the person with the requirements of a particular environment; (2) to determine the need for particular types of services in communities or institutions (needs assessment); (3) to prescribe interventions to be used to improve the level of functioning; and (4) to measure change in functioning over time.

With few exceptions, devices for assessing the elderly have been developed to determine readiness for institutional or for community placement, or to determine needs assessment. (See reviews by Bernal, Brannon, Belar, & Cameron, 1977; Curran & Wessberg, 1981; Linn, 1979; Smith, 1979.) Most of the scales used to assess the elderly came out of a psychometric tradition that sought to identify relatively permanent and stable characteristics of individuals. These scales were not concerned with the other two issues listed above: to prescribe interventions and to measure change over time. (Perhaps it is a further indictment of our attitudes toward the elderly that this is the case.)

The Program was interested in assessments that could be used to measure need for intervention and to measure changes occurring as a result of these interventions (Patterson, Penner, Eberly, & Harrell, in press). Two basic classes of instruments were used: (1) behavior rating scales and self-report measures that are general-purpose instruments and have been previously used in other research; and (2) assessments to measure acquisition of the skills taught in the modules.

General-Purpose Instruments

The general-purpose instruments were used to provide indications of relatively global behavioral change. In addition, these instruments could also be used to provide evidence of generalization of modular training since they measured social and ADL skills occurring in places and times other than within any particular intervention procedure.

Two types of behavioral rating scales have been found useful in the Program:

1. The Nurse's Observation Scale for Inpatient Evaluation (NOSIE-30: Honigfeld, Gillis, & Klett, 1966) is a general-purpose, psychiatric behavioral rating scale used for assessing clients in a ward setting. The 30 items on the NOSIE-30 are brief statements describing activities. Clients respond to each item by checking one of five responses indicating the frequency ("never" to "always") of the observed behavior during the most recent three-day period. Examples of items are: "Is sloppy," "Gets angry or annoyed easily," and, "Is messy in his eating habits." Seven different scores are obtained from this instrument. Six of these scores refer to mathematically derived factors. Three of the scores represent "positive factors": Social Competence (COM); Social Interest (INT); and Personal Neatness (NEA). The three negative factors are : Irritability (IRR); Manifest Psychosis (PSY); and Retardation (physical, not intellectual) (REA). The seventh score, Total Assets, is computed from the six factor scores with the use of a mathematical formula. Validity and reliability of the NOSIE-30 has been repeatedly established (Honigfeld et al., 1966; Smith, 1979). Designed to measure change over relatively short periods of time, the population used in the original development of the NOSIE-30 scale was elderly.

2. *The Community Adjustment Potential scale (CAP) portion of the Discharge Readiness Inventory (DRI)* (Hogarty & Ulrich, 1972) was developed to predict discharge readiness and the subsequent community adjustment of hospitalized schizophrenics (Hogarty & Ulrich, 1972). Significantly, the CAP has also been used in a day-care program (Michaux, 1971). The items for the DRI were originally developed by experienced social workers who had been asked to identify the critical components for discharge readiness. The items include social behaviors such as appropriate judgment, affect, and the ability to converse coherently. The 16 items of the CAP are scored in two sets, A and B. Set A (10 items) asks the rater to make judgments based on the client's behavior "during the last week or two" and to provide ratings on a 5-point frequency scale ranging from "never" to "always." Sample items are: "Wants to leave hospital" and "Engages in simple conversations about concrete subjects." Set B (six items) asks the rater, "If the client were to be discharged today, what would be your prognostic judgment about his or her behavior in the community?" Sample items are: "Could get along with his neighbors in his community placement" and "Could move about independently in the community." DRI items generally involve more advanced social and ADL skills than items found in most other scales.

The self-report measures used by the Program were as follows:

1. *Life satisfaction.* Life satisfaction, or subjective well-being, is a subject about which much has been written in the gerontological literature (Larson, 1978). Although several measures of life satisfaction have been created, Larson has noted that all of them measure primarily the same thing, as evidenced by the fact that the correlation between the various scales is high.

The Life Satisfaction Index (LSI) (Neugarten, Havighurst, & Tobin, 1961) was chosen for inclusion because of the great amount of research in which it has been used. It consists of 16 items to which the subject is asked to respond dichotomously (agree or disagree). Sample items are: "As I grow older, things seem better than I thought they would be," and "These are the best years of my life." The original basis for the inclusion of the items was the theoretical assumption that there are five major components of well-being in the elderly: zest rather than apathy; resolution and fortitude; congruence between desired and achieved goals; positive self-concept; and mood tone (Neugarten et al., 1961). The importance given to this type of measure in the gerontological literature would seem to make it highly desirable to include in many clinical and research efforts.

2. *Self-esteem.* Concern with loss of self-esteem by the elderly seems to be very widespread in the literature. The concept of lowered self-esteem is a basic in the theory of Kuypers and Bengston (1973) and in other sociological theories concerned with losses of social functioning in the elderly. The present

author and his colleagues (O'Sullivan, Eberly, Patterson, & Penner, 1979) have used the Self-Esteem scale (RSE) developed by Rosenberg (1965), which has also been used with the elderly by other investigators (Linn, 1979). The RSE is a 10-item Gutman scale created originally for use with adolescents. Examples of items are: "On the whole I am satisfied with myself," and "I certainly feel useless at times." There are four possible responses to each item, ranging from "strongly agree" to "strongly disagree." The scale has high test-retest reliability and has been found to have good convergent, discriminant, and concurrent validity (Rosenberg, 1979). The items themselves appear to have good face validity and are sufficiently general so that they would seem to be usable with many populations.

Assessments Developed for Use with Daily Living

Skills Modules. The subject of daily living skills was the first concern of the developers of assessment methods for use with the disabled elderly. In 1963, Katz et al., developed a scale called the Index of Independence in Activities of Daily Living, or ADL, which measured toileting, bathing, feeding, transferring (as from bed to chair), dressing, and continence. Later, two types of ADL were differentiated by Lawton and Brody (1969): (1) physical maintenance activities (also referred to as physical ADL by Pfeiffer, [1975]); and (2) instrumental activities (IADL). Basic ADL consisted of functions like those measured in the ADL scale of Katz et al. (1977). The term "instrumental ADL," or IADL, was used to refer to activities not essential for self-maintenance, but failure to perform these activities meant that the elderly person required more support from others. Several subcategories of IADL were identified by Lawton and Brody (1969): using the telephone; shopping; food preparation; housekeeping; laundering; obtaining transportation; and taking medication correctly. Although defined some years ago, physical and instrumental ADL continue to be important concepts because of the obvious relationship of such activities to level of care requirements (Health Care Financing Administration, 1981; Pfeiffer et al., 1980).

Assessment devices were developed by the Program for each of the three modules intended to teach daily living skills.[3] These modules were referred to simply as ADL I, II, and III. The nature of the assessments for these modules was such that each specified as completely as possible the target behaviors to be taught in the modules because a major purpose of these assessments was to specify targets for change as well as to measure change. All ADL assessments were administered to determine admission to the module and readministered every fourth week during training to determine progress. A listing of the topics assessed and taught in each of the ADL modules appears in Table 4.1.

Table 4.1.   Topics Covered in Each ADL Module.

ADL I	ADL II	ADL III
1. Oral hygiene	Laundering	Budgeting time and money
2. Bathing	Mending clothing	Meal planning and preparation
3. Hair care	Managing money	Housekeeping
4. Shaving	Meal selection	Obtaining community resources
5. Dressing	Maintaining a room and bathroom	
6. Nail care	Use of the telephone	
7. Personal eating habits		

The division of ADL topics into three levels was related to types of living situations which our clients either had (day treatment) or were expected to have after discharge (residential).

ADL I assessment. As may be seen from Table 4.1, the topics assessed and taught in ADL I consist of basic grooming tasks and eating habits. The grooming is assessed by simply asking clients when they last performed the task and then inspecting them for evidence that the activity was performed recently and correctly. Items are scored either zero or one. A score of zero means that the corresponding activity must be taught.

ADL II assessment. This assessment determines if the client can care for his or her clothing, manage small amounts of money, use a telephone, select proper meals from a cafeteria, and maintain a bedroom and bathroom (see Table 4.1). As with ADL I, the items are administered by asking questions, by inspecting the client, and by arranging performance tests. The two following samples illustrate how this procedure is done.

Cares for own room and bath facilities—Ask client who cleans his or her room and bath facilities. Ask how often he or she dusts, sweeps, makes bed, cleans sink and tub. Ask, are facilities clean now? When possible, observe bedroom and bathroom to see if they are clean and neat. If either answers or observations show lack of performance, score 0.

Dial telephone—Give client practice telephone. Ask client to dial 681-5947. Observe to see if client can dial number correctly.

Items are scored zero and one. Zeroes indicate deficiencies to be corrected.

ADL III assessment. The ADL III assessment is much longer than the other two of the ADL series and relies more on verbal responses, written and oral. For example, under "Budgeting time and money," clients are asked to account for their major expenses and to plan a daily schedule including time for daily tasks, leisure activities, and meals. Under community resources, clients are asked to state where they can get medical help, attend leisure activities, and so forth. A point system is used with these items which pinpoints deficits and provides a numerical score.

Social Skills. As with ADL, initial concern regarding social functioning of the elderly was with rather gross deficiencies of the institutionalized population. Again, the concern was with seriously pathological behavior. Social skills, as the term has come to be used in modern therapies, generally refers to more complex interpersonal behaviors.

In the Program, within the category of basic social skills, we have included both the quality and quantity of interpersonal behaviors. A socially skilled person would be one who exhibits the ability to make casual conversation when appropriate, who is able to control his or her own behavior and to influence that of others by the expression of proper and realistic affect and appropriate interpersonal behavior. Self-esteem (which we define as the ability to recognize and to state positive characteristics of oneself) was also included in the category of social skills because there are indications from the psychological literature that a positive opinion of oneself is correlated with successful social functioning (Rosenberg, 1965, 1979; Wells & Marwell, 1976). People who lack self-esteem are subassertive and are not perceived positively by others. For these reasons, a self-esteem training module and associated assessments were included in the social-skills training.

The assessments for two of the social-skills modules, Communications and Conversation Training, are presented next. The assessments for the self-esteem modules have already been discussed in the section on general-purpose assessments.

Communication Assessment. The assessment was made by trained observers, observing clients in two standard role-play situations (Patterson, Smith, Goodale, & Miller, 1978). As with the ADL modules, the assessment directly measured the skills taught in the module. Training focused on teaching clients to express pleasure and displeasure effectively and appropriately to another person, and this is what was portrayed and measured in the role-play. This assessment device was used during training for each role-play to provide a basis for feedback and reinforcement; it was also used in special, nontraining sessions every four weeks to provide program scores for evaluations and clinical purposes. No coaching, reinforcement, or feedback occurred in these latter sessions.

The actual assessment instrument was a very simple rating scale modeled after that described by Liberman, King, DeRisi and McCann (1975). Although more complex and presumably more precise measures, such as timing eye contact from videotapes (Hersen & Bellack, 1978) and measuring speech volume electronically (Patterson, Teigen, Liberman, & Austin, 1975), have been developed (see Bellack & Hersen, 1979, for a review of this area), these were not deemed appropriate for the Program because they do not provide sufficiently rapid feedback or they require more sophisticated observers and equipment than were available. Previously developed self-report measures were also not considered useful, primarily because almost all of them were developed for use with college students.

Ratings for both pleasure and displeasure situations were made on each of seven items. Each of these items was scored on a 6-point scale ranging from "1" (completely inadequate or inappropriate) to "6" (completely appropriate and strongly emphatic). Of the seven items included, three rated verbal aspects of performance: content, loudness, and voice quality; and three rated nonverbal aspects: hand gestures, body position, and facial expression; the seventh item was a rating of overall performance.

Conversation assessment. Two different assessments were employed in Conversation Testing. One (employed sessional assessment) provided sessional indicators of frequency of conversation during training; the other measured generalization. The sessional assessment consisted of an interval-recording procedure. Clients were all seated in the dayroom so that they could be easily observed. Several observers were each assigned five or six clients. For every other 30-second interval, observers recorded whether or not the client was observed conversing. These data were used as the basis of feedback and reinforcement and also provided sessional indicators of progress.

The generalization measure was administered every fourth week. A time-sampling procedure was employed. Clients were observed wherever they happened to be on the unit at times when no other formal activity was scheduled (such as after dinner for residential clients and during a break after lunch for the day clients.)

INTERVENTIONS

The Aging Program is a total mental-health treatment approach of which the ADL and social-skills modules are a central component. It is true that the entire group of modules, or any of them, could be applied in isolation from the other treatment components. However, this is not recommended. We believe that all of the treatment components should be coordinated with each other and considered as integrated parts of a total approach. It is very poor practice to apply several different uncoordinated approaches to the same individual.

The behavioral model provided the unifying conceptual framework as well as most of the technology of the Program. Medical interventions were used very frequently, but when these were used to address behavioral problems such as delusional talk, every effort was made to define and to measure the problem in behavioral terms. Likewise, social-work services were strong and very valuable to the Program, but again, the focus was on the behavior of the individual in relation to other people and in relation to specific social settings.

The Program employed three facets of behavioral technology in the overall intervention: (1) the modules described in this chapter; (2) a token economy, which is a widely used system of motivating people to perform within treatment programs (Atthowe & Krasner, 1968; Ayllon & Azrin, 1968; Patterson, 1976) in which staff provide clients with objects or points that may be exchanged at later times for rewards or reinforcers (such as soft drinks, toilet items, or extra time with a therapist); and (3) a basic behavioral approach to a variety of difficulties experienced by clients. To provide this unified behavioral orientation to intervention, all staff members were given 30 hours of instruction in behavioral concepts and techniques. In addition, the modules and various other structured activities and individually prescribed behavioral treatments were taught. This training provided the staff with the knowledge and skills needed to implement the Program.

The combination of these basic behavioral approaches was used not only within the formal training sessions but also throughout the entire Program. Thus, idiosyncratic problem behaviors shown by particular individuals that were not part of the content of the training modules could be dealt with outside of the formal training sessions. And skills learned during formal training sessions could be maintained and generalized outside training sessions by reinforcing the behaviors wherever they occurred. In practice, many skills of many clients improved rather rapidly within the training sessions and generalized rather well without much special effort. We assume that this occurred because, in most cases, the clients had learned and generalized many of these skills earlier in life and had stopped performing them relatively recently.

The consistent behavioral approach carried over to our work with families. Rather than deal in generalities, an effort was made to determine quite specifically what the client was or was not doing and/or what the family was or was not doing that made life difficult. For example, in one case it was discovered that a daughter-in-law objected strongly to her husband's mother's "disgusting eating habits and hostile remarks." The mother, in turn, had difficulty eating because of an inability to use one arm. She also had complaints about the home. It was possible to overcome the eating problem by training the client to have more acceptable eating habits, with which, how-ever, she required some assistance. The family was likewise instructed how to assist her with eating. The hostile verbal behavior was decreased by teaching the mother more appropriate ways to express herself by means of social-skills training. Long-term placement back in the home was the outcome.

Structure, Content, and Methodology of the Modules

Each module exists in the form of a manual.[4] The contents of these are described briefly in this section. The format for the manuals follows this outline:

   I. *Introductory Material*

      A. Statement of what is to be taught to whom.

      B. Basics of relevant behavioral techniques.

  II. *Main Body*

      A. Content to be taught.

      B. Specifics regarding technique.

      C. Necessary equipment and aids.

 III. *Assessment and Recording Material*

      A. Assessment instrument and technique

      B. Data-recording forms.

Each manual contains an introduction telling what the module is designed to teach to what type of client. This is followed by a section assessing the user's skills in relevant behavioral techniques, including a discussion of how to explain these techniques to the client. The main body of the module contains a description of the content to be taught, specific target behaviors to be acquired, an explanation of specific teaching techniques to be employed, and a list of equipment and teaching aids to be used. The final section of each manual consists of the assessment methods, materials and instruments, and data-recording forms.

There are several advantages to having predesigned modules. They provide supervisors of treatment programs with a complete set of materials regarding program content and staff activities. They make it relatively simple to check if trainers are indeed teaching specified skills in the specified ways. The assessments and data forms make it possible to determine whether individual clients, or groups of clients, are acquiring the desired skills. The trainers themselves also have an easier job; the manuals inform them: (1) which clients need to achieve better functioning; (2) how to achieve such improved functioning; and (3) how to establish that this has actually been accom-plished.

It is important to realize that the basic techniques used in all six modules were the same, regardless of the content. All modules employed well-established behavioral techniques. The three basic techniques shared by all modules were: (1) instruction or prompting; (2) practice; and (3) reinforcement (see Skinner, 1968). Instruction was accomplished by verbal instructions, modeling, and motor guidance. Verbal instructions were initiated by the trainer, but clients could also instruct each other in some situations. Group discussions were also used. A very important point was that all verbal instruction had to be brief and well circumscribed. Discussions beyond a few minutes were to be avoided. Modeling was accomplished by having either staff or another client demonstrate the desired behavior or some component thereof. Motor guidance, which refers to having a staff person physically guide a client to accomplish some act, was used sometimes but was discontinued as soon as possible. Reinforcement was of two types, social and token. Trainers always immediately recognized and praised correct performance. When tokens were given, the recipients were always reminded exactly how they had earned them and praised for these accomplishments.

These techniques were used to shape and to chain behaviors. Shaping refers to producing correct behaviors by reinforcing a series of increasingly correct approximations to the desired behavior. Chaining refers to learning a complete act by first learning specific components of that act in a correct series. The series may either begin with the first (forward chaining) or last step (backward chaining) required.

ADL I. This training was provided to groups of one to eight people for one hour each day, five days a week. An instructor and an assistant were involved. Where modesty required, men and women were trained separately; and the act of bathing was always performed with only the client and a same-sex trainer present. As with all modules, special assignments of ADL I activities were made to promote generalization and maintenance as needed. The training was divided into seven separate "information units," one of which was presented on a given day, depending upon the deficits and progress of the assigned trainees. These seven units contained outlines of material to be taught which corresponded to the topics presented in Table 4.1. Included were oral hygiene, bathing, hair care, shaving, dressing, nail care, and personal eating habits. A bathroom, hair dryer, manicuring equipment, and other equipment normally needed to perform these tasks were required.

Each session began with a demonstration accompanied by appropriate verbal instruction. Brief group discussion was encouraged. Trainees were first reinforced for responding verbally as to how and why to perform the correct behavior. Then, individuals assessed as requiring practice performed the correct behavior with additional instruction as needed. Reinforcement was always contingent upon correct performance.

ADL II. This module was conducted similarly to ADL I. Training was provided to a group of one to eight people for one hour at a time, two days per week. The material was divided into six information units including doing laundry, mending, managing money, making change, choosing meals, keeping house, and using the telephone. Relevant equipment, including a washer, drier, and telephone, was used for demonstrations and practice. Training began with verbal instruction and demonstrations, followed by group discussions. Clients were questioned regarding the information presented and reinforced for responding correctly. This was followed by actual reinforced practice.

ADL III. ADL III training was similar to standard classroom methods in that the material was largely verbal. Trainers wrote information on a blackboard in addition to speaking about it. Clients were prompted to make verbal responses and reinforced for stating correct answers and engaging in group discussion. Clients were given notebooks in which they were required to write down material for further study and personal reference. The written material was of value to the client in his or her daily life during training and after discharge. For example, the section on meal planning and preparation required a trip to a grocery store and practice in a kitchen in addition to classroom work.

The content of the training was divided into four parts. Part A dealt with the budgeting of time and money, including writing checks and balancing a checkbook. Part B described ways to access and utilize community resources, including social organizations, medical resources, practice bus trips, and other community services. A personal reference book for each trainee was produced in his or her notebook. Part C concerned meal planning and preparation. Meals were developed, from planning and writing the grocery list to actual shopping, cooking, and consuming the meal. Part D taught housekeeping chores, including cleaning ovens, refrigerators, and floors, washing dishes, and taking home-safety precautions. The manual provided standardized content for each of these sections.

Communication Training. Communication training was usually conducted in a group of 4 to 10 clients. They were seated in a semicircle, with two chairs placed in the center for role-plays. A large replica of the assessment rating instrument was posted on one wall.

The basic procedure was to teach all clients the meaning of the verbal and nonverbal target behaviors included in the rating and the meaning of the ratings themselves. Training focused on role-plays of group members who observed each other. A scene, involving either expressing appreciation to someone or expressing dislike combined with a request for new behavior, was explained by the group leader. Examples of these scenes are as follows:

1. Mrs. Jones is your neighbor and she heard you were ill, so she brought you some food she cooked. Express your appreciation to her.

2. Mr. Smith lives in the room next to yours, and he plays his radio very loudly late at night. Tell him you don't like this and ask him to stop doing it.

Two clients then role-played the actor and the recipient of the action. Role-playing was followed by a request from the leader for feedback from the group as to what the actor did well, followed by a request for feedback as to what behaviors needed improvement. Group members were reinforced socially for feedback and reinforced with tokens for giving accurate feedback. The role players were similarly reinforced, but with more tokens, for their participation. After feedback was obtained from the group, the actor was asked to enter the ratings earned on the large rating board on the wall. This procedure was followed by a second role-play of the same scene, either by the original actor or by a model. Models were used at the discretion of the leader when the leader felt that a demonstration of correct performance was required. If a model was used, the second role-play was followed by a feedback session like the first. Whether or not a model was used, the original actor was given a second chance to perform the same scene. This final role-play was always accompanied by a final feedback session that was directed first toward improvements the actor made over the original role-play and then toward additional improvements that could be made in the future.

At the conclusion of the session, all clients were informed of their accomplishments (role playing and/or feedback) and reinforced with tokens. This procedure was continued until clients were able to obtain ratings of four or above on every item during special fourth-week assessment role-plays. In these latter sessions minimal instructions were used, and no reinforcement or feedback was given.

Conversation Training.   This training differed from the others in that it involved very little verbal instruction and no modeling or demonstrations.

Fifteen to 20 clients were assembled in a large dayroom and instructed to spend the next 30 minutes getting to know each other and conversing with each other about anything they chose. They were further informed that someone would come at various times and give them tokens and feedback if they were conversing. Observers were stationed around the room and given the task of observing clients according to an interval-recording procedure. These observers administered social and token reinforcements according to a variable interval schedule averaging one reinforcement every five minutes.

Self-Esteem Training.   This training was provided to clients meeting in groups of 10 or fewer. After a brief explanation of the purpose of this module, the group was told that they were to "accentuate the positive and eliminate the negative" (i.e., that they were to say only good things about themselves and about each other). Since modesty was regarded as a virtue by many, it was necessary to explain to the group that although they may have learned modesty early in life (and it is appropriate at times), it is also important that one be able to be truthful with oneself and with others about what we believe our good characteristics to be. A variety of prompts were used to elicit positive statements. For example, clients were asked what someone should say if they were to write a letter of recommendation for them or to mention the three personal characteristics that they would least like to change. Tokens and social reinforcement were given for appropriate statements. Inappropriate statements, such as "There's really nothing good about me," were put on extinction by being ignored and the leader's attention being directed towards someone else. Attempts were made to elicit at least one positive self-statement from each person in every session. Social reinforcement by group members to each other's positive statements was also actively prompted and reinforced by the leader. Often clients' responses would focus on general traits such as kindness and honesty. These were reinforced, but the leader prompted the client to report recent specific examples illustrating these qualities rather than to leave them as vague generalities. The goal of the group was to increase the number of different, positive attributes rather than merely to repeat the same qualities over and over.

Individually based Interpersonal Skills Training. In addition to the modules described above, additional skills training was provided to many clients as needed. If the staff and client agreed that there was a particular interpersonal problem in the client's life, then the same basic methodology of role playing, feedback, and modeling was used to correct the problem. For example, a client had been placed, against her wishes, in a rather restrictive boarding home in an isolated location "for her own good" because she had at one time exhibited some confusion. As time for discharge from the Program approached, the client and the staff felt that she did not need to return to such a restrictive placement, but that the client would have to convince her relatives that this was the case. The client was a rather meek woman who had difficulty not giving in to her much stronger relatives. After a dozen or so sessions of training, the client stated her case appropriately and effectively and she was able to convince the relatives to help her find a more suitable place to live.

A CASE STUDY

Partial case studies were presented earlier to illustrate specific points. However, a more complete case study will be presented here to illustrate how the assessments, modules, and other activities were used as a treatment package.

A 60-year-old man, Joe, came to the Program after having been in a state hospital continuously for the previous year where he was diagnosed as having chronic schizophrenia, undifferentiated type. He complained currently of "nerves" and arthritis in the right knee. He had a history of several psychiatric hospitalizations during the past eight years, beginning with an arrest for stealing, which he claimed was to get food. The physical examination showed Joe to be in good health. His interview behavior was passive, and he displayed flat affect and depressed mood. He was expressionless, with decreased motor activity and some peculiar posturing. His speech was reduced in amount, slow, and soft. He expressed delusions of reference. There was some impairment of orientation to time. The interviewer estimated his intellectual functioning to be below normal and noted that his insight and judgment were poor.

The social-skills modular assessments, made at time of admission, showed major deficits. In the conversation sessional assessment, he scored zero, then 2 out of 30 on two baseline measures. The generalization measure revealed that he was solitary and failed to interact. In communications, he made the lowest possible overall score; 1 out of 6 on the overall rating for both pleasure and displeasure. Somewhat suprisingly, he failed to show any deficit in ADL I; but deficits were found in ADL II, including mending clothing, handling spending money, and dialing a telephone. The life-satisfaction and self-esteem scores were also moderately low. In addition to the problems dealt with in these six modules, he had trouble recalling the date and the time.

The interventions in this case were all behavioral and social. Joe had been taking antipsychotic medication for several months in the state hospital before admission to the Program, and it was decided to continue the medications. Joe was admitted to all three social-skills modules and ADL II. In addition, he was given training for the problem with dates and with participation in leisure-time activities. He was also assigned to a group for discussing current events.

Four weeks later, Joe had made considerable progress. Conversation sessional assessments showed that he was conversing *22 out of 30 intervals measured in a sample session*. There was also similar improvement on the generalization measure. Ratings on the communication assessment increased to 4 (a good performance, though not very emphatic) on pleasure and to 6 (the maximum rating) on displeasure. Unfortunately, his improvement in self-esteem was not as good, there being very little improvement on the fourth-week assessment. By the fourth week he had learned the skills to overcome his previous deficits in ADL II and he was entered into ADL III. Subsequent to these intial improvements, progress was limited. Joe did not progress well in ADL III, and so he was discontinued from this training. In the social-skills area, he completed Communication Training in about two and one-half months and was offered an opportunity for interpersonal problem solving. He thought that this latter training was silly and he declined. He remained in self-esteem training throughout his stay, but his performance was always sporadic, and little, if any, progress was made in this area.

Joe's scores on the NOSIE-30 and the CAP generally paralleled the module assessments. He improved on all of the scores of the NOSIE and the CAP.

Overall, it seemed that he improved quite a bit in basic social skills and somewhat in ADL skills, but that he did not progress in the more advanced, more highly verbal areas. This information helped to determine that a mildly sheltered placement was needed for Joe. Upon discharge, after four and one-half months in the Program, Joe went to live in a boarding home. Follow-up 12 months after discharge found him still residing in the same home without further need for institutional care.

NOTES

1. Many of these ADL deficiencies were associated with a loss of ambulation and mobility.
2. FMHI is a state-funded organization, having as its mission the development of innovative approaches and the dissemination of useful methodology to the state's mental health system.
3. Originally designed for use with these modules, extensive reliability and validity testing has shown these to be moderately reliable and valid for this population. Further detail regarding this is available in Patterson, Dee-Kelly et al. (in press).
4. For additional information, the reader should see the recent book by Patterson, Dee-Kelly et al. (in press) The reader may also write to the first author of this chapter for additional information.

REFERENCES

Atchley, R. C. *The social forces in later life: An introduction to social gerontology.* Belmont, Calif: Wadsworth, 1977.

Atthowe, J. M., & Krasner, L. Preliminary report on the application of contingent reinforcement procedures (token economy) on a "chronic" psychiatric ward. *Journal of Abnormal Psychology,* 1968, **73**, 37–43.

Ayllon, T., & Azrin, N. *The token economy: A motivational system for therapy and rehabilitation.* New York: Appleton-Century-Crofts, 1968.

Baffa, G. A., & Zarit, S. H. *Age differences in the perception of assertive behavior.* Paper presented at the 30th Annual Meeting of the Gerontological Society, San Francisco, 1977.

Baltes, M. M., & Barton, E. M. New approaches toward aging: A case for the operant model. *Educational Gerontology,* 1977, **2**, 383–405.

Baltes, M. M., Burgess, R. L., & Stewart, R. B. *Independence and dependence in nursing home residents: An operant-ecological study.* Paper presented at the 1st NOVA Behavioral Conference on Aging, Port St. Lucie, Florida, May 21–25, 1978.

Baltes, M. M., & Zerbe, M. B. Independence training in nursing home residents. *The Gerontologist,* 1976, **16**, 428–432.

Bates, H. D. *Gerontology proposal.* Tampa, Fla.: Florida Mental Health Institute, 1975.

Bellack, A. S., & Hersen, M. (Eds.). *Research and practice in social skills training.* New York: Plenum, 1979.

Bernal, G., Brannon, C., Belar, J., & Cameron, R. Psychodiagnostics of the elderly. In W. D. Gentry (Eds.), *Geropsychology: A model of training and clinical service.* Cambridge, Mass.: Ballinger, 1977.

Birren, J. E., Butler, R. N., Greenhouse, S. W., Sokoloff, L., & Yarrow, M. R. (Eds.). *Human aging.* Washington, D.C.: U.S. Government Printing Office, 1963.

Blazer, D. G., & Maddox, G. Using epidemiologic survey data to plan geriatric mental health services. *Hospital and Community Psychiatry,* 1982, **33**, 42–45.

Butler, R. N., & Lewis, M. I. *Aging and mental health.* St. Louis, Mo.: Mosby, 1973.

Butler, R. N., & Lewis, M. I. *Aging and mental health.* St. Louis, Mo.: Mosby, 1977.

Cairl, R. The elderly: Health studies and health utilization patterns. In *Community health policy information study,* Research Triangle Park, N.C.: Research Triangle Institute, in press.

Campbell, D. T., & Fiske, D. W. Convergent and discriminant validation by the multitrait-multimethod matrix. *Psychological Bulletin,* 1959, **56**, 81–105.

Campbell, D. T., & Stanley, J. C. *Experimental and quasi-experimental designs for research.* Chicago, Ill.: Rand-McNally, 1963.

Corby, N. H. Assertion training with elderly populations. *Counseling Psychologist,* 1975, **5**, 69–73.

Curran, J. P., & Wessberg, H. W. Assessment of social inadequacy. In D. Barlow (Ed.), *Behavioral assessment of adult disorders.* New York: Guilford, 1981.

Duke University Center for the Study of Aging and Human Development. *Multidimensional functional assessment: The OARS methodology.* Durham, N.C.: Author, 1978.

Eberly, D. A., Patterson, R. L., Jackson, G. M., & O'Sullivan, M. J. *Survey of residents of G. Pierce Wood Memorial Hospital aged 55 and older.* Tampa, Fla.: Gerontology Program, Florida Mental Health Institute, University of South Florida, 1981.

Eisler, R. M. The behavioral assessment of social skills. In M. Hersen & A. Bellack (Eds.), *Behavioral assessement.* New York: Pergamon, 1976.

Farina, A., Arenberg, D., & Guskin, S. A scale for measuring minimal social behavior. *Journal of Consulting Psychology,* 1957, **21**, 265–268.

Florida Department of Health and Rehabilitative Services, Alcohol, Drug Abuse and Mental Health Program Staff. *Client assessment survey.* Tallahassee: Author, September 1981.

Goldstein, A. P., Sprafkin, R. P., & Gershaw, N. J. *Skill training for community living: Applying structured learning therapy.* New York: Pergamon, 1976.

Gurel, L., Linn, M. W., & Linn, B. S. Physical and mental impairment of function evaluation in the aged: The PAMIE scale. *Journal of Gerontology,* 1972, **27**, 83–90.

Health Care Financing Administration. *Long-term care: Background and future directions.* January 1981.

Hendricks, J., & Hendricks, C. D. *Aging in mass society: Myths and realities.* Cambridge, Mass.: Winthrop, 1977.

Hersen, M., & Bellack, A. S. Assessments of social skills. In A. R. Cimenero, K. S. Calhoun, & H. E. Adams (Eds.), *Handbook for behavioral assessment.* New York: Wiley, 1978.

Hersen, M., Eisler, R., & Miller, P. *Progress in behavior modification.* New York: Academic Press, 1980.

Hogarty, G. E., & Ulrich, R. The discharge readiness inventory. *Archives of General Psychiatry,* 1972, **26**, 414–426.

Honigfeld, G., Gillis, R. D., & Klett, C. J. The nurse's observation scale for inpatient evaluation. *Journal of Consulting Psychology,* 1966, **21**, 69–77.

Katz, S., Downs, T. D., Cash, H. R., & Grotz, R. C. Progress in development of the index of ADL. *The Gerontologist,* 1977, **10**, 20–30.

Katz, S., Ford, A. B., Moskowitz, R. W., Jackson, B. A., & Jaffe, M. W. Studies of illness in the aged. The index of ADL, a standardized measure of biological and psychosocial function. *Journal of the American Medical Association,* 1963, **185**, 914–919.

Kleban, M., Lawton, M. P., Brody, E. M., & Moss, M. Behavioral observations of mentally impaired aged: Those who decline and those who do not. *Journal of Gerontology,* 1976, **31**, 333–339.

Kuypers, J. A., & Bengston, V. L. Social breakdown and competence. *Human Development,* 1973, **16**, 181–201.

Larson, R. Thirty years of research on the subjective well-being of older Americans. *Journal of Gerontology,* 1978, **33,** 109–129.

Lawton, M. P. Assessment, integration, and environments for older people. *The Gerontologist,* 1970, **10,** 38–46.

Lawton, M. P., & Brody, E. M. Assessment of older people: Self-maintaining and instrumental activities of daily living. *The Gerontologist,* 1969, **3,** 179–186.

Lewinsohn, P. M., Biglan, A., & Zeiss, A. M. Behavioral treatment of depression. In P. O. Davison (Ed.), *The behavioral management of anxiety, depression and pain.* New York: Brunner-Mazel, 1976.

Liberman, R. P., King, I. W., DeRisi, W. J., & McCann, M. J. *Personal effectiveness: Guiding people to assert themselves and improve their social skills.* Champaign, Ill.: Research Press, 1975.

Libet, J. M., & Lewinsohn, P. M. Concept of social skills with specific reference to the behavior of depressed persons. *Journal of Consulting and Clinical Psychology,* 1973, **40,** 304–312.

Linn, M. W. Assessing community adjustment in the elderly. In A. Raskin & L. Jarvik (Eds.), *Psychiatric symptoms and cognitive loss in the elderly.* Washington, D.C.: Hemisphere, 1979.

Lowenthal, M. F. Social isolation and mental illness in old age. *American Sociological Review,* 1964, **29,** 54–70.

Maddox, G. L. Self-assessment of health status: A longitudinal study of selected elderly subjects. *Journal of Chronic Diseases,* 1964, **17,** 449–460.

McClannahan, L. E., & Risley, T. R. A store for nusing home residents. *Nursing Homes,* 1973, **7,** 26–31.

Michaux, M. M. *Comparative study of day treatment vs. inpatient treatment.* Sykesville, Md.: Research Department, Springfield State Hospital, 1971.

Miller, L. M. Toward a classification of aging behaviors. *Gerontologist,* 1979, **19,** 283–290.

Neugarten, B., Havighurst, R., & Tobin, S. The measurement of life satisfaction. *Journal of Gerontology,* 1961, **16**(2), 134–143.

O'Sullivan, M. J., Eberly, D. A., Patterson, R. L., & Penner, L. A. *An experimental study of improving life satisfaction of older people by increasing self-esteem through behavioral training.* Paper presented at the 26th Annual Meeting of the Southeastern Psychological Association, New Orleans, 1979.

Patterson, R. L. (Ed.). *Maintaining effective token economies.* Springfield, Ill.: Charles C. Thomas, 1976.

Patterson, R. L., Dee-Kelly, C., Dupree, L. W., Eberly, D. A., O'Sullivan, M. J., & Penner, L. A. *Overcoming deficits of aging: A behavioral treatment approach.* New York: Plenum, 1982.

Patterson, R. L., & Jackson, G. M. Behavior modification with the elderly. In M. Hersen, R. M. Eisler, & P. Miller (Eds.), *Progress in behavior modification,* Vol. 9. New York: Academic Press, 1980.

Patterson, R. L., Penner, L. A., Eberly, D. A., & Harrell, T. L. Behavioral assessments of intellectual competence, communication skills, and personal skills of elderly persons. *Behavioral Assessments,* in press.

Patterson, R. L., Smith, A. G., Goodale, P., & Miller, C. *Improving communication abilities in psychogeriatric clients.* Paper presented at the 29th Annual Meeting of the Southeastern Psychological Association, Atlanta, 1978.

Patterson, R. L., Teigen, J. R., Liberman, R. P., & Austin, N. Increasing speech intensity of chronic patients ("mumblers") by shaping techniques. *The Journal of Nervous and Mental Disease,* 1975, **3,** 182–187.

Pfeiffer, E. *Functional assessment: The OARS multidimensional functional assessment questionnaire.* Durham, N.C.: Duke University Center for the Study of Aging and Human Development, 1975.

Pfeiffer, E. Psychopathology and social psychology. In J. E. Birren & K. W. Schaie (Eds.),

Handbook of the psychology of aging. New York: Van Nostrand Reinhold, 1977.

Pfeiffer, E., Johnson, T. M., & Chiofolo, R. C. *Functional assessment of elderly subjects in four service settings.* Paper presented at the 33rd Annual Meeting of the Gerontological Society, San Diego, Calif.: November 1980.

Phillips, E. L. *The social skills basis of psychpathology: Alternatives to abnormal psychology.* New York: Grune & Stratton, 1978.

Rosenberg, M. *Society and the adolescent self image.* New York: Basic Books, 1965.

Rosenberg, M. *Conceiving the self.* New York: Basic Books, 1979.

Skinner, B. F. *The technology of teaching.* New York: Appleton-Century-Crofts, 1968.

Smith, J. M. Nurse and psychiatric rating scales for assessing psychopathology in the elderly: A critical review. In A. Raskin & L. Jarvik (Eds.), *Psychiatric symptoms and cognitive loss in the elderly.* Washington, D.C.: Hemisphere, 1979.

Ulmer, R., & Lieberman, J. The children's minimal social behavior scale: A short objective measure of personality functioning. *International Journal of Psychology,* 1970, 5, 269–274.

Wells, L., & Marwell, G. *Self-esteem: Its conceptualization and measurement.* Beverly Hills, Calif.: Sage, 1976.

Zarit, S. H. *Aging and mental disorders.* New York: Free Press, 1980.

Chapter 5

Stress Reactions

Boaz Kahana and Eva Kahana

Our aim in this chapter is to develop a conceptual framework for understanding the impact of stress on the elderly. We will discuss definitional issues in studies of stress and explore the mechanisms that mediate the negative impact of life stress on the elderly. Approaches to diagnosing stress-related disorders and therapeutic efforts that help the elderly cope with stressful life events will also be presented.

The study of stress assumes special significance for older adults because of the frequency and intensity of stressful life events that they experience during a life stage when their economic, physical, social, and psychological resources are diminishing (Rosow, 1967). Adaptations required of older persons may range from a new lifestyle posed by retirement, to learning to cope with becoming widowed after a long life of shared existence, to changes in daily living created by relocation to a new housing situation.

LIFE STRESS AND DISEASE

Investigation has been directed at the role of diverse life stresses in the origin and course of physical or mental illness. Hans Selye (1976) has provided a general description of the medical basis of stress and a detailed analysis of its psychosocial implications; he defines stress as the "nonspecific response of the body to any demand." The outcomes of stress will affect the whole of the person, impacting on both physical and psychosocial health.

The relationship of social-psychological stress to illness has been extensively studied and reviews are available (Dohrenwend & Dohrenwend, 1974; Levi, 1971). Social-psychological stress has been implicated in the onset of a wide variety of diseases, including heart disease and mental illness (Friedman et al., 1974; Moos, 1977; Theorell & Rahe, 1971: Thiel, Parker, & Bruce,

139

1973). Studies in psychosomatic medicine also show that mental attitudes can produce bodily changes (Selye, 1976; Hurst, Jenkins, & Rose, 1979).

Hinkle and his co-workers (Hinkle, 1961; Hinkle & Wolff, 1958) were the first to attempt a large-scale study of the relationship between life events and illness. Their studies generally found that illness occurred most often when individuals had life situations they described as unsatisfactory and/or when they experienced difficulty in adapting to their environment following a stressful life event. Rahe, Holmes, and their co-workers (Holmes & Rahe, 1967; Rahe et al., 1972; Holmes et al., 1950) developed the first quantitative measures of life events. The results of their numerous studies indicate that clusters of life events and transitions preceded the onset of illness and that more illness episodes occurred during stressful times.

In sum, there have been consistent suggestions that life stress may be related to the onset of illness. Since many of these studies have been retrospective, one must be cautioned about the danger of attributing causal characteristics to a particular event if a disease process happens to develop sometime in the adjacent time span (Grinker, 1966). Overall, research indicates that a relationship exists between stress and illness; however, the research results suggest a complex interaction of factors, rather than a single or simple causal link.

The above studies suggest that stressful life events cause a decrease in general resistance to all illnesses and thus make a person more vulnerable to disease processes. While these studies indicate some consensus about the relationship between stressful life events and illness, most have utilized younger-aged samples, with very little specific attention to the impact of stressful life events on older adults.

LIFE EVENTS, STRESS, AND THE ELDERLY

The relationship between life events and stress with physical and mental health outcomes in the elderly has been examined on a very limited basis. A review of this research, as well as the conceptual and methodological issues that need to be considered, has been provided by Eisdorfer and Wilkie (1979). It has been hypothesized that the elderly are more susceptible to the effects of stress because they undergo many negative life events and experience many losses during a period when physical decline is concurrent. Thus, they experience special demands for adaptation at a time when their adaptive capacities are diminishing (Rosow, 1974).

In three recent studies, the number and nature of stressful life events occurring among the elderly were studied (Amster & Krauss, 1974; Muhlenkamp, Gress, & Flood, 1975). Two of these studies are based on relatively small samples of elderly ($N = 41$ and 50, respectively) and were conducted with special groups. Muhlenkamp and her associates interviewed members of a senior citizens' club, while Amster and Krauss compared 25 "mentally deteriorated" women with 25 "nondeteriorated" women. The former investigators used the Social Readjustment Rating Scale developed by Holmes and Rahe (1967). The latter developed their own Geriatric Social Readjustment questionnaire based on the work of Holmes and Masuda (1974), using weights assigned by professionals familiar with geriatric populations. Amster and Krauss (1974) obtained a significant association between psychological deterioration of subjects and the degree of adjustment necessitated by life events during the previous five years. The Muhlenkamp et al. (1975) study indicated that older people perceive life events as requiring greater readjustment than do younger people, and reasoned that the elderly may therefore be more severely stressed by the occurrence of life events. Chiriboga and Dean (1978) considered nine dimensions of stress derived from a 138-item life-events questionnaire and asked 182 adult men and women, ranging in age from 21 to 72, to record the incidence of events, how happy or unhappy they were with each event, and current preoccupation with the event. Respondents in this study were comprised of three groups of persons undergoing life transitions. Typically, these subjects fell into the categories of young adulthood, midlife, and the later years (i.e., marriage, empty nest, and retirement). Thus, only about one-third of the sample represented elderly respondents. Younger adults generally reported more events that did older adults, and women reported more life events than men. The sheer frequency of events, however, provided only partial evidence concerning the potentially disruptive effect of life events. When frequency of occurrence was controlled, personal stresses were apparently more intrusive in the lives of the retired and middle-aged respondents; such stresses were least intrusive in the lives of newlyweds. Household stresses did not predict at all for younger men and women, but entered into the predictive equations of both older men and older women. Younger and older men alike shared work stress as a dimension with considerable impact on their lives. The most salient stresses for older women were financial and marital stresses and were associated with negative changes in satisfaction and depression scores.

An important life event, that of moving from one residence to another (a specific instance of which is institutionalization) has been extensively studied in the gerontological literature (Schulz & Brenner, 1977). On the basis of a careful review of this literature, Schulz and Brenner (1977) concluded that the ability of older relocatees to cope with the stresses associated with relocation depended upon (1) the choice the aged individuals had about their relocation, (2) the predictability of the new environment after relocation, and (3) the degree of control the individual had between pre- and postrelocation.

In spite of the fact that there is a sizable body of literature on relocation, previous studies have not focused on the total array of interrelated life changes within which relocation is sufficiently embedded. It is very likely that relocation is often an event that follows a long series of life events and life changes rather than a discrete event that has an impact on the person independent of other events. For example, relocation from one residence to another often follows victimization of older persons in their domicile or neighborhood or through illness or death of a close family member or of a caretaker. Similarly, the influence of being widowed and of retirement from work may have to be studied within the context of changes (e.g., serious physical illness) that may have culminated in the bereavement or need to retire.

The personal salience of life events for community-living aged was considered by Kahana, Fairchild, and Felton (1976). Older persons were found to experience negative life events of illness, bereavement, and diminishing social roles. Hitherto neglected but perhaps equally important were reports of positive life events, such as the addition of a new family member or participation in family celebration. Both negative and neutral events were found to be significant predictors of low morale. This study, based on open-ended questions, also pointed to the absence of life events during the past year in the reports of many respondents. It is important to note that direct questioning yields evidence of frequent life changes during a one-year period among older persons (Kaplan, 1970).

There appears to be conflicting evidence regarding age-related differences in the incidence of stressors. The gerontological literature generally supports the view that as people age, they undergo many and varied losses in social roles, finances, and health (Rosow, 1974). Langner and Michael (1963) report that life stress increased with age in their urban population. In contrast, Markush and Favero (1974) observed a consistent decline in life-changes units when comparing persons under 35 with those aged 35–54 and those in the 55+ age category. It should be noted that their sample focused on "young/old" and did not further break down those over 55 by age. Hough, Fairbank, and Garcia (1976) raise the issue of a possible asymptotic relationship between life events and outcome variables such as illness. They suggest that while an increase in number of life events may lead to increased probability of illness, this relationship may level off at the higher levels.

In the following section we turn to a discussion of the assessment of stressful life events and consider the implications of prevalent approaches to assessment for our understanding the impact of stress on the elderly. Alternative conceptualizations of chronic stress will be presented later.

METHODS AND ISSUES IN STUDIES OF STRESSFUL LIFE EVENTS

Among the diverse approaches taken to measuring stress in the literature, considerations of the frequency and magnitude of the lifestyle changes required by the events has been the most prevalent approach (Rabkin & Struening, 1976). In evaluating the conclusions that can be drawn from studies using this approach, some methodological limitations must be condered.

Life events have thus far been defined in numerous ways. Perhaps the common core in most previous definitions of life events has been Dohrenwend and Dohrenwend's (1974) notion that stressful life events involve change in the usual activities of most individuals who experience them. Life events have typically been operationalized with somewhat different but overlapping lists of events. Differences in these lists reflect cultural, age, and other factors that make some events lists more salient for some groups than for others.

The events lists that have thus emerged do not distinguish between external and internal events (e.g., being fired versus experiencing feelings of sexual inadequacy); nor do they distinguish between discrete events (e.g., death of a close friend) and psychological processes (e.g., feelings of lethargy and inertia). Furthermore, the common use of illness as both a life event and as an outcome results in tautological findings. For example, Hudgens (1974) suggests that 20 out of the 43 events on Holmes and Rahe's (1967) list are in fact symptoms or consequences of illness. The respondents' own views regarding magnitude or importance of a given event are not considered.

In the traditional life-events literature, the change score (or life-change unit weight) for each event is based on the average magnitude of change required by that event as estimated by a panel of judges (Amster & Krauss, 1974). Life stress is assessed by summing the change scores assigned to those events that were experienced by the individual during the past year (or during another designated time period).

Previous research of stressful life events has been criticized in terms of both content and methodology. Major concerns about the content have included the excessively short and incomplete nature of life-events lists and the ambiguity of items. There has also been criticism of the typical distinction between positive and negative life events (Hough, Fairbank, & Garcia, 1976; Mechanic, 1974). An ongoing debate among investigators of life events has surrounded the issue of what kinds of events serve as major determinants of stress and whether positive events are equally stressful as negative or undesirable ones (Holmes & Masuda, 1974). Reflecting one side of this debate, Dohrenwend (1973) has argued that "knowing about the desirability of the events to which the individual has been exposed does not enhance the prediction of psychological distress." Later studies, however, have criticized this emphasis on change without taking the desirability of the events into consideration. Gersten et al. (1974) concluded from their studies of children that nondirectional change scores that disregard the desirability of the events were related to anxiety. That undesirability, however, is the more critical aspect of stress when other dependent variables are considered. In a recent study by Ross and Mirowsky (1979), the undesirability of life events was found to be the best predictor of psychiatric symptomatology.

Holmes and Masuda (1974), using the Social Readjustment Rating Scale (Holmes & Rahe, 1967), report that elderly respondents (60 years of age and older) check only half as many life events as young adults (20–30 years of age). On the other hand, the results of other studies suggest that stress increases with advancing age (Langner & Michael, 1963). Furthermore, Kiyak, Liang, and Kahana (1976) found that elderly respondents, in contrast to college students, assign lower change or readjustment values to many of the normatively designated "negative" life events.

These contradictions and disagreements may be due, in part, to the fact that commonly used life-events lists are limited to events that were judged by the researchers to be salient on *a priori* criteria. Another potential source of confusion is the fact that until recently, life-events inventories were developed and standardized with predominantly younger populations. Thus, they tend to be overloaded with events that are more salient to younger people; the inventories may include items on arrest for criminal activity while overlooking criminal victimization. The fact that life events that are actually experienced by younger persons seldom include catastrophies such as death of spouse or major physical illness, and conversely, the fact that the aged seldom undergo positive life events that necessitate major life changes (e.g., marriage) may make it particularly important to consider event desirability in studies of the aged.

Person-Environment Fit

Much of the research in the area of stress and adaptation has had a crisis orientation, typically focusing on a single, discrete life stress impacting on the elderly individual (Eisdorfer & Wilkie, 1979). Consideration of more chronic and enduring stresses, such as those posed by lack of person-environment congruence, represents a much needed extension in the area of stress research.

The congruence model of person-environment interaction has its historical antecedents in Lewin's (1951) notion that behavior is a function of the relationship between the person and his environment, and in Murray's (1938) need-press model of human behavior. Within both conceptualizations it is assumed that environmental presses represent situational counterparts to internalized needs; environmental presses may either facilitate or hinder the gratification of needs. According to the congruence model, individuals are most likely to seek out, and be found in, environments that are congruent with their needs. Dissonance between press and need is seen as leading either to modification of the press or, in a free-choice situation, to the individual's leaving the field. When such a choice is impossible, the individual must function in a dissonant milieu. Stress and discomfort are assumed to follow (Stern, 1970).

French, Rodgers, and Cobb (1974) define adjustment as the goodness of fit between the characteristics of the person and the properties of his or her environment. These authors underscore the notion, first proposed by Lewin (1951), that quantification of person-environment (P-E) fit requires that characteristics of persons and environments be considered along commensurate dimensions. It should be noted that environments have typically been described interchangeably as providing presses, norms, demands, constraints, or supplies. In turn, persons have been considered as exhibiting commensurate needs, preferences, characteristics, or abilities.

A conceptualization of congruence with special relevance to older populations has been developed by Kahana (1975). In this conceptualization, goodness of fit between person and environment is assumed to be an antecedent of well-being rather than synonymous with it. Whenever there is a lack of congruence between the individual's needs and his or her life situation, either due to a change in environment (e.g., new housing or institutionalization) or due to a change in needs or capacities, various adaptive strategies are evoked to increase the degree of fit between the person and the environment (Kahana & Kahana, 1982).

In an initial empirical study designed to test the proposed congruence model (Kahana, Liang, & Felton, 1980), the effect upon morale of personal and environmental variables, as well as the degree of congruence between them, was examined. "Person" variables were operationalized as expressed preferences and environmental features were represented as normative expectations perceived by the staff. Seven commensurate dimensions of person and environment were included: (1) segregation; (2) congregation; (3) institutional control; (4) structure; (5) stimulation; (6) affect; and (7) impulse control.

These dimensions were selected, in part, because of their value in differentiating among environments and people and because they had individual and environmental analogs, respectively. Thus, these dimensions were deemed suitable for testing the need-press model of fit, as they were likely arenas in which incongruence could result in adaptive problems for the individual. In areas where an older individual has experienced changes in need and preferences, he or she may be especially vulnerable to environmental incongruence. Thus, a person who can no longer delay gratification may find it especially problematic to be placed in an environment where a great deal of delay is expected of him or her.

The relationshp between personal, environmental, and person-environment fit characteristics and the morale of the elderly were investigated in a study of 124 residents of homes for the aged (Kahana, Liang, & Felton, 1980).

The results of this study suggest that fit scores derived from independent measures of persons and environments along the dimensions of impulse control, congregation, and segregation make a substantial contribution to our understanding of the morale of older people in homes of the aged.

This study also points to the importance of P-E fit in the arenas of congregation, impulse control, and segregation. In contrast, personal and/or environmental characteristics rather than fit were more important along the dimensions of affective expression and institutional control in explaining morale.

This study's findings regarding the direction of P, E, or P-E influences on morale along specific dimensions also provide some important data relevant to practice and policy. With regard to impulse control, our findings validate the notion that environmental press for impulse control needs to be matched with residents' capacity for control, with either lesser or greater press than that needed by residents being detrimental to morale. With regard to the congregate and segregate dimensions of environments, our findings reveal that fit in terms of needs for sociability appear to be more important than needs for privacy and needs for homogeneity. It is also useful to note that environmental stimulation facilitates morale regardless of degree of personal preference for stimulation. Consequently, programs that add stimulation to the institutional milieu should be helpful to all residents. With regard to affect, on the other hand, individual differences in affective expression directly relate to morale with environmental press for affective expression having little impact on the morale of residents.

FACTORS RELATED TO AMELIORATING THE IMPACT OF STRESS ON OLDER PERSONS

Social Supports and Stress

In considering the factors that ameliorate the negative consequences of stressful life situations on the elderly, social supports as well as personal resources play an important role.

Though there are a variety of definition of support system, the common core generally coincides with Hogue's (1976) definition of social-supports "as a set of persons consisting of a focal or anchor person, and the linkages of relationships among these people." George (1980) distinguishes between "social networks" and "social-support systems." The former are seen as reflecting patterns of social involvement, the latter as comprised of those individuals who may provide support at times of stress. Social-support networks are based either on a sense of obligation (formal service providers), or on a sense of affection (family and friends), or both. The maintenance of meaningful social ties is likely to promote the development of social-support systems. Conversely, the individual who has isolated himself or herself from social interaction and who has seldom provided help to others is unlikely to have access to a social-support system that can provide him or her with assistance during times of need. Social supports are seen as critical to the functioning and adaptation of the individual in general but especially in times of crises when the existence of supportive relationships can attenuate the harmful effects of stress (Caplan, 1974).

Using an interactionist model of adjustment, Berghorn and Shafer (1979) found that in frail elderly, social and environmental resources mitigated the effects of personal impairments on adjustment in later life. These investigations also found that informal assistance, socializing, and the use of formal supports modified the impact of the older persons' impairments.

A perusal of the literature points to the value of a broad view of social-support networks for the study of stress-adaptational outcomes. Such an approach calls for considering types of support systems (formal and informal), structural aspects of support networks (i.e., individuals comprising the support networks), and functioning of the network in terms of amounts and types of assistance provided. Additional factors such as awareness of services and accessibility are likely to determine the utilization of formal services.

Personal Coping Strategies

The variables of adaptation and coping have been recognized as valuable conceptual tools in understanding how persons deal with stresses and daily problems by both psychologists and sociologists. In fact, Pearlin and Schooler (1978) have suggested that the study of adaptation may represent a potentially useful point of convergence in sociological and psychological approaches for understanding the functioning and well-being of the older person.

Although the importance of adaptive strategies for psychosocial well-being is implicit in all theories of personality (Hall & Lindsey, 1970), there has been relatively little specific research focused on adaptive strategies of older people. Until recently, conceptualizations of adaptation have lacked cohesiveness. Styles of coping have sometimes been equated with personality traits (Lieberman & Cohler, 1976). There has been little concern with the success of a particular style of coping for the individual. The specific environmental demands for, or constraints on, coping have rarely been considered.

Within the psychological literature, coping has been regarded as a form of defense against threats aroused in individualized situations by some (Lazarus, Averill, & Opton, 1974). On a more positive note, other approaches have emerged from developments in personality theory (Moos, 1974) that emphasize personal strivings toward environmental mastery and competence and that focus on adaptive ego process (Erikson, 1950; Hartman, Kris, & Lowenstein, 1949; White, 1959).

Psychologists studying adaptation have focused on processes for handling everyday life stresses as well as major life crises and transitions (Alker, 1968). Haan (1963) distinguished between adaptive strategies characterized by a quality of positive problem solving and strategies that are essentially maladaptive. Both kinds of strategies are assumed to be elicited by conflicts. Alker (1968), elaborating on Haan's model, suggests that adaptive strategies are "flexible, differentiated, reality oriented, purposive, effective and permissive of open, ordered impulsive satisfaction." In contrast, defensive behavior is seen as rigid, distorting, and permissive of impulse gratification by subterfuge.

In considering these conceptualizations, a perhaps questionable assumption is that appropriate need gratification is typically within the individual's control. When environmental or personal options are limited, such as in the case of older persons experiencing major life stresses, instrumental approaches to modify one's situation may not be possible. Similarly, in the case of persons undergoing extreme stress, such as the victims of the Holocaust, whose personal and environmental options may be severely limited, the demarcation between coping and defensive behavior may be blurred.

Gerontological research on the adaptation patterns of the aged has made use of theoretical perspectives of activity and disengagement theories (Stephens, 1973). Some studies have suggested that personality types provide information on the basis of which predictions about various patterns of adaptation may be made (Neugarten, 1964; Reichard, Livson, & Peterson, 1962). Thus, Reichard, Livson, and Peterson have found three personality types that adjust well to retirement: (1) the mature type—individuals who view themselves realistically, are free of emotional conflicts, and are basically satisfied with their lives; (2) the rocking-chair type—passive individuals who are happy to be retired and relieved of the responsibilities of work; and (3) the armored type—individuals who defend themselves against passivity and feelings of dependency and helplessness; who "counteract" the aging process by keeping active and involved. They also found two types that adjust poorly to aging: (1) the angry type—individuals who have been unable to achieve their goals in life and hence cannot accept their growing old, which means these goals will remain unfulfilled; and (2) self-haters—individuals who react to feelings of failure by intropunitive means and self-blame and depression.

The Reichard, Livson, and Peterson study can be readily explained by the person-environment fit model. The mature type of retiree is at peace with himself and the environment. He is satisfied with his accomplishments and with his contribution to society and with what society contributed to him. Thus, there is a good fit between him or her and the environment. The rocking-chair type is also pleased with his new fit with the environment; it suits him better now, with its reduced demands compared with before retirement. The armored type was originally in a poor fit with his surroundings but has used intrapsychic and behavioral means to accommodate to the environment. The poor adjusters, the angry type and the self-haters, were unable to establish an adequate fit. Various styles of coping with stresses of aging were also analyzed in terms of their adaptive value in the cross-cultural work of Gutmann (1969) and Goldstein and Gutmann (1972).

Having reviewed a number of conceptual approaches to the study of adaptation, we have yet to answer the question: How can the older person handle the disruption of his previous lifestyle and the frustration inherent in the reduced options that result from aging?

Consistent with their above-mentioned congruence models, Kahana and Kahana (1982) suggest five basic coping styles for dealing with noncongruence. In a longitudinal study of institutionalized elderly, their coping strategies have been considered in terms of instrumental, intrapsychic, affective, and escape approaches to problem solving and in terms of resigned helplessness, which is reported inability to cope with stress.

1. Instrumental Strategies. Persons adapting this style of coping seek to do something about the situation that is not congruent to their needs. They might employ strategies reflecting varying activity levels or engagement with the specific problem situation. Yet all would have in common an overt recognition of the problem and exhibition of specific behaviors to deal with the problem. Finding a lack of sufficient privacy, our hypothetical resident may go in his room and shut the door, assertively tell people to leave him alone, or complain to those in charge. He might seek assistance from others, such as having his children arrange for a private room, or may actively try to change the environment by himself by, for example, working out an arrangement with his roommate whereby each of them would be alone in the room on specified days.

2. Intrapsychic Strategies. Another strategy the individual may take is an intrapsychic or psychological solution. Rather than dealing with the conflict in the environment by engaging the world, he or she avoids the conflict by making accommodations within himself or herself or by cognitive restructuring (Lazarus, 1966: Pearlin & Schooler, 1978). Such persons may deny or repress the existence of conflict. They may recognize that conflict exists but accept the situation as a necessary evil. They may diminish the saliency of the problem by focusing away from it or might actually change their needs and preferences to fit in with the new environment. They may turn to religion, think that things will eventually work themselves out, or refuse to accept the situation as problematic.

Behaviorally, these individuals may appear to accept or do nothing about the situation and the existence of conflict may not be outwardly observable. The older person would portray strongly expressed needs for privacy before entry to the home, show concern with privacy at interview one after institutionalization, and deemphasize the importance of privacy at later interviews.

3. Affective Strategies. Given the existence of incongruence, a third general set of strategies for dealing with the situation is reflected in an affective or expressive orientation. Affective expression or display is not used as part of an instrumental resolution but becomes an end in itself.

Using expressive resolutions, these older residents may tell everyone that one cannot find privacy in the institution, they may be generally belligerent or cry about the lack of privacy. While these resolutions may not serve to change the noncongruent situation, they may be effective in releasing tension or dealing with a reality that cannot readily be altered.

4. Escapist Resolutions. A fourth set of coping strategies involves action that is not directed at solving the problem situation, but a turning to alternative activities, avoiding the problem or denying it. The hypothetical resident may "leave the field," engage in displacement activities such as excessive sleeping, tension-reduction activities, such as excessive drinking or overeating, or he/she may withdraw and stick to himself/herself.

5. Resigned Helplessness. A fifth category refers to an impotence or inability to cope with the problem situation. A response to the problem of lack of privacy may be, "I would not know what to do," or "I would go to pieces." A physiological response such as becoming nervous or developing physical problems such as ulcers is also included here.

In the above conceptualization, the adaptive strategies marshalled by the older person are assumed to be related (1) to the individual's earlier types of adaptation and coping; and (2) to the responsive modes to the changing demands of the environment. Thus, coping styles are viewed as having both *traitlike*, as well as *situation-specific*, determinants.

Although adaptive strategies are often presented as if they reflect distinct, mutually exclusive styles, it should be recognized that they overlap. Thus, in any given problem situation, individuals may use a combination of coping responses. They may try to change the situation (instrumental), they may learn to view the situation from a new perspective (cognitive restructuring), or they may express feelings (affective).

Gal and Lazarus (1975) stress the importance of the availability and utilization of active behaviors in coping with stress and, based on, review of a series of studies, suggest that active coping results in more desirable psychological and social outcomes. This positive role of activity is especially pronounced when the behavior is functionally related to the situation. This focus on active coping styles is also reflected in the work of Shanan (1978) and that of Kahana and Kahana (1978) in considering instrumental coping styles among the elderly. In studies of institutionalized aged, the latter investigators found that the different coping styles are not all equally efficacious and that affective strategies resulted in more negative outcomes than did instrumental or intrapsychic cognitive appraisal responses.

CLINICAL ASSESSMENT OF STRESS AND COPING

The use of life-events inventories for the assessment of stress has thus far been largely confined to research and has not generally been part of clinical assessment. Nevertheless, there appear to be promising developments in the area of measurement for both stress and coping that may have utility for future clinical use. (A detailed review of such measures is provided in Kahana, Fairchild, & Kahana, 1982.) Particularly promising for future clinical use are Antonovsky's (1979) Life Crisis Inventory and a recent modification of the Holmes and Rahe Social Readjustment Rating Scale (1967), both of which include subjective evaluations of the perceived stressfulness of specific life events as rated by older people (Kahana, Kahana, & Kiyak, 1979).

In spite of these promising developments, at this point the best determination of stress reactions for clinical purposes is still based on a careful history obtained convergently from both the patients and family members. Such a history should be complemented by a traditional psychodiagnostic evaluation of the elderly patient aimed, in part, at ruling out diagnoses of organic brain syndrome or a psychotic reaction. It is nevertheless important to recognize that at times stress reactions are superimposed on other forms of psychiatric symptomatology. Consideration of recent life events, environmental stresses, and life-crisis history provides important background for clinicians in establishing a diagnosis of stress reaction. Certain stressful situations such as widowhood or retirement are commonly considered by mental-health professionals in diagnosing elderly patients. However, many other important but somewhat more subtle stressors (such as intergenerational conflict or relocation of close friends) may be overlooked in considering mental-health problems of late life.

In making a determination of stress-related disorders, it is very important for the clinician to determine the subjective stressfulness of given events. It is often tempting to assume problems that arose subsequent to presumed stressors to be consequences of those stressors, yet this may not in fact be the case in individual situations.

For a long time, gerontologists believed that relocation invariably had a deleterious effect on old people (Schulz & Brenner, 1977). Recent research (Kahana & Kahana, 1982), however, indicates that relocation and environmental change may in fact be helpful to many older people and may result in positive psychosocial outcomes. In our study of relocation to Florida and Israel, the majority of the subjects reported improved health and improved morale subsequent to relocation (Kahana & Kahana, 1982). For many, this relocation served to reduce the stress of constant fear of being the victims of crime and of being cooped up in an apartment for fear of being attacked in the neighborhood. Relocation also often reduced the stress of crowded living situations and of troublesome winter weather. The results suggest that, from a therapist's perspective, it may indeed be useful to consider the potential benefits of environmental intervention or change in helping the older person cope with certain stressful life situations.

The careful assessment of person-environment congruence, or fit, represents another important aspect of detecting stress reactions among the elderly. The needs and preferences of the client must be elicited and articulated. The clinician needs to recognize that different aspects of person-environment fit may be more important at different periods in the older person's life. Thus, for example, environmental constraints preventing impulse gratification (e.g., sexual expression) may be more problematic during the younger years while older persons may have more difficulty coping with physical features of the environment that lead to discomfort (e.g., not enough heat in the apartment). Environmental and situational changes presumed to increase fit must then be considered. In making a determination of the degree of person-environment fit, the older person's own assessment of his or her personal preferences should be obtained in addition to information about his or her characteristics and needs, based on test data or information from family members or other informants. Studies indicate that even impaired elderly are able to articulate their preferences about salient aspects of their living environments (Kahana, Liang, & Felton, 1980).

Evaluation of the specific life stresses impacting a particular individual should be comprehensive and include information about early trauma, cumulative and repeated life crises, as well as data about recent life events. The assessment, of course, needs to include a careful delineation of the demands of the environment. In addition, information about the patient's characteristic and recent modes of coping with stress should be obtained. All of this material provides diagnostic information that should be integrated with data from psychological test batteries.

Case History of Assessment

Mr. Jones was referred for assessment during the spring of 1982. At the time Mr. Jones was 68 years old. Since the death of his wife two years before, he had been living by himself, managing his household and personal affairs reasonably well. During the six months prior to the referral, however, he had several minor accidents at home and had developed increasing somatic symptoms followed by periods of depression. Hopsital tests did not reveal any serious organic basis for his varied symptoms. When Mr. Jones's children arrived from out of town following his hospitalization, he was not eager to see or talk to them.

It was at this point that a psychologist was consulted. Psychological testing revealed that Mr. Jones was a man of bright-normal intelligence with no signs of cognitive impairment. (He did well on WAIS subtests of Block Design, Digit Symbol, and Digit Span, consistent with his other subtest scores.) There were intermittent themes depicting depressive ideation as well as anger and hostility on the Rorschach. Nevertheless, classical signs considered diagnostic of depression were absent in the Rorschach (e.g., low M, constricted Experience Balance, etc.).

On the Thematic Apperception Test, Mr. Jones provided some important clues to the presence of feelings of abandonment by friends who have died and abandonment by his children who live far away. A careful life-history interview was also conducted. The interview revealed that Mr. Jones's best friend and confidant of many years, Mr. Morgan, had suffered a stroke during the previous summer and had been placed in a nursing home where he was making reasonable progress. Mr. Jones tried to get to see his friend at least two or three times a week, taking two buses to get to the nursing home. Because of changes in public transportation routes (apparently caused by cutbacks in funding), Mr. Jones found it increasingly difficult to visit Mr. Morgan.

Just before Thanksgiving, Mr. Morgan's condition worsened and Mr. Jones asked his children who were then visiting him to drive him to the nursing home to visit his friend. His daughter did not find time for what she considered an unimportant chore. The day after Thanksgiving, Mr. Morgan died. On the way to the funeral, Mr. Jones slipped and had his first accident.

In the above case, important information about a highly stressful life event was revealed by a combination of an in-depth interview and psychological test data. An understanding of the nature of the stress, the patient's ways of attempting to cope with it, as well as other dynamic factors was necessary in order to initiate appropriate therapeutic intervention. In the case of Mr. Jones, the diagnostic phase was followed by brief insight-oriented psychotherapy aimed at helping Mr. Jones learn to understand and to accept his grief over the loss of his friend, as well as his anger against his children, and to stop directing his anger against himself. By resolving his grief, Mr. Jones was able to separate his own fate from that of his friend. As therapy progressed, he showed a marked decline in his somatic preoccupations.

INTERVENTION IN STRESS REACTIONS OF THE ELDERLY

Therapists often speak of treating a "stress reaction" when they have not been able to discern either an underlying organic etiology or a neurosis with a long history to account for the patient's current symptoms. Rather, the problem is felt to be directly attributable to the effects of stress and trauma upon the psychic organization.

Reactions to stress are widely recognized as one of the most frequent reasons for emotional disturbances that have an onset late in life (Butler & Lewis, 1977). It is also generally acknowledged that such problems are more amenable to psychotherapy than are organic brain syndromes, psychoses, or psychotic depression. Yet when one reviews actual approaches to psychotherapy with the aged, surprisingly few specific guidelines are given to mental-health professionals for the management of such stress reactions. It is interesting to note, for example, that among the 21 articles of the otherwise very useful NIMH-produced volume entitled *Readings in Psychotherapy with Older Persons* (Steury & Blank, 1977), not one specifically addresses the treatment of stress reactions in late life.

Therapists working with elderly patients suffering from stress reactions receive little help from the literature on this topic because the topic is either ignored or the therapist is told only what not to use with this population.

Even though systematic guidelines for treatment of stress reactions among the elderly are largely absent, clinicians have available a variety of potentially useful approaches. Critical treatment-outcome studies have not been conducted in this area but clinical experience does provide some guidelines.

There is considerable disagreement regarding the use of insight-oriented or psychoanalytically based therapies for the elderly in general and for the treatment of stress reactions in particular. On the one hand, it has been suggested (Sobel, 1981) that older persons are unable to benefit from insight-oriented therapies, viewed as treatments of choice with younger people. Insight-oriented dynamic therapies imply the extension of ego control over previously repressed impulses that are allowed to emerge in the course of therapy. Such approaches are not seen as advisable where the ego has been weakened or battered by a stressful life situation or the ravages of aging. On the other hand, there have been some recent indications that psychoanalytically oriented psychotherapy may have a place in the treatment of stress reactions among older persons (Sifeos, 1982).

Strategies for dealing with stress-related responses regardless of age, in the framework of psychoanalytic therapy, have been reviewed by Horowitz (1980). Special modification of traditional therapeutic approaches are suggested based on special needs of persons with hysterical, obsessional, or narcissistic personality dispositions. Butler and Lewis (1977) recommend the use of short-term insight-oriented therapy consisting of a series of 15-minute sessions to resolve certain stress or grief reactions. Butler and Lewis (1977) have also reported success with age-integrated life-crisis groups with members ranging in age from 16 to over 80. The elderly were helped to overcome their feelings of rejection by the younger generation by participating in groups in which the three-generational family was symbolically reconstituted.

A number of other innovative therapeutic approaches appear to hold promise for treatment of stress reactions in older persons. Recent research in the area of locus of control and therapeutic intervention (Rodin & Langer, 1980) suggests that therapy may result in increased feelings of self-worth to the extent that more options for control and responsibility are included in the treatment. Several programs (Beck, 1982; Langer & Rodin, 1976) have based themselves on this conceptualization, stressing the importance of enhanced control, perception of control, and environmental mastery for older persons experiencing stressful life situations, including institutional living. On a more general level, these therapeutic efforts are based on Seligman's (1975) model of learned helplessness. Older persons whose opportunities to engage in useful social roles are diminished often experience feelings of lessened competence and helplessness. The latter has been attributed (Seligman, 1975) to experiencing uncontrollable situations, that is, those in which outcomes are independent of an individual's behavior.

Helping behaviors, and especially those forms of helping that do not include expectations for reciprocity of exchange, provide opportunities for maximal environmental control for aged persons and may have important therapeutic value. Since the helper is not awaiting indications of reciprocity from the recipient of his or her aid, an element of uncertainty and lack of control is removed. In this situation, reinforcement for one's helping behavior is directly within the giver's control (Kahana & Midlarsky, in press). The therapeutic value of reciprocity is illustrated in the following case:

Mrs. Smith is a widowed elderly woman who was becoming increasingly incapacitated by arthritis. With her children living thousands of miles away, she felt very little personal control over her situation and was becoming helpless and despondent. However, after she became involved as a volunteer in a telephone reassurance program to help other isolated elderly, her sense of self-worth was greatly restored. She felt that while there was little she could do to improve her own health or social interactions with her family her newfound sense of being needed by others helped provide meaning to her life or as she said: "added life to my years."

Therapeutic Approaches Aimed at Enhancing Person-Environment Fit

One of the shortcomings of traditional therapy perhaps is that it often assumes that the environment cannot be changed, rather than encouraging individuals to find or create new environments that will suit their needs better. In contrast, therapeutic efforts within a person-environment fit conceptualization explicitly focus on both the person and the environment as potentially modifiable. Within this approach, the therapist feels more freedom to explore changes in the environment as a means of providing the patient with increased comfort, better adjustment, and improved functioning. The person-environment-fit conceptualization of stress presents some important, but as yet insufficiently recognized, guidelines for intervention and for enhancing the mental health of older persons. Similar environmentally based approaches have recently been advocated in approaching the treatment of mentally impaired older persons (Lawton, 1980).

People working in the field of ecological psychology distinguish alpha press from beta press as sources of poor person-environment fit; that is, the older person's needs may be mismatched with objective environmental features (alpha press). Carp (1976) cites the example of an older person who is homebound because of fears of victimization. If, in fact, the individual's fears are founded in the reality of an objectively high-crime neighborhood, stress may be best reduced by trying to relocate the person to a safer area. If, on the other hand, the perception (in this case, misconception or exaggerated fear) is the problem, then psychotherapy for reducing anxiety may be the approach of choice to alleviate the behavioral manifestations of stress reaction.

The person-environment-fit model also provides some fairly clear-cut action guidelines for staff working with residents in institutional settings. For example, let us consider an individual who has difficulty in handling unstructured or ambiguous situations. Lack of clear rules and lack of clarity regarding what to expect in different situations are very upsetting to this type of individual and leave him or her at a loss as to what to do. If the institution has few norms for behavior and the role of this new resident is ambiguous, he or she may expect further difficulties in coping with the new situation and in adjustment. Unsuccessful attempts to cope with such incongruent environments may lead to further withdrawal and psychological deterioration of the older patient. It should also be noted that many of the observed psychological decrements of aging may in themselves be a function of lack of person-environment fit experienced by the older person. An example of this is the often-cited "flattened affect" of the aged (Botwinick, 1978). This may in part be a defense adopted by those aged whose emotional needs are not being met.

Similarly, avoidance of stimuli may result from consistent experience of noxious stimuli.

In institutional settings, specifications of salient dimensions of person-environment fit may serve as a useful tool for sensitizing staff not only to personal needs of the elderly but also to those environmental features and characteristics that are most likely to pose potential sources of incongruence for the elderly. Lawton's (1980) ecological model has suggested that excessive environmental demands in relation to the older person's abilities result in negative outcomes. The person-environment-fit model would further sensitize staff who work with the aged to individual differences in amounts of activities or stimulation desired by residents.

The person-environment-fit model has special value in the management of the relocation process as older people enter new environments. The success of actual (Bourestom & Pastelan, 1975) and of simulated (Hunt, 1980) site visits in minimizing negative effects or relocation stress may be the result of a closer fit between personal anticipation and environmental realities. A detailed description of environmental features serves to orient relocatees (Bourestom & Pastelan, 1975). It also enables them to anticipate lack of person-environment fit in salient areas, to articulate their expectations, and possibly take action to maximize person-environment fit. The therapeutic use of the person-environment-fit model also includes provision of some choices among environmental alternatives along dimensions salient to the older person. Thus, in residential settings, new tenants who have great privacy needs or low needs for stimulation may be provided with rooms or apartments that maximize private space and are relatively distant from noise and activity.

Analyzing and delineating both the larger environment and immediate personal life space of the older person (Felton & Kahana, 1975) may be accomplished by developing environmental checklists to be used by staff along with personal-preference inventories provided to residents. Intake interviews may be designed to allow for the best person-environment fit. Even where it is not possible to establish congruent macroenvironments, personal space may be organized so as to meet the elderly's environmental preferences. Accordingly, appropriate placement of even standard furnishings may enhance congruence.

A striking example of specific matching of environments to the needs of the elderly has been presented in the work of Cosin (1958) in Britain where circular corridors were adapted to accommodate the wandering needs of mentally impaired residents. The prevalent approach in the United States is to restrain or medicate patients who have a great need for motor expression as well as those with some mental impairment. The approach described by Cosin of matching environments to patient needs reportedly resulted in improvement of both physical and mental function in these aged.

Lawton (1978; 1980) has consistently sensitized gerontologists to the need for designing environments that take into account the special characteristics of older populations. Thus, it may be argued that the person-environment-fit congruence model has direct relevance and potential value for the development of ecologically oriented intervention programs and treatment strategies designed to enhance the mental health of the elderly. The underlying assumptions of the person-environment-fit model alert therapists to look beyond the confines of traditional approaches to treatment. It is particularly well suited to the functions of the mental-health consultant who may recommend psychotherapeutic interventions to help older persons cope better or environmental changes to reduce or change the demands of the environment. The overall goal is environment fit and concomitant reduction in stress.

Stressful reactions by the elderly often involve responses to a complex set of stressors that may be attendant to a major life event such as widowhood. The person-environment-fit model provides a framework for handling a complex constellation of stressors. Stressful life events often come because of environmental change or result in environmental change. In addition, personal needs may also change subsequent to stress, and the delicate fit equilibrium between person and milieu is likely to be upset. Widowhood represents a stressful life event that frequently brings about both personal and environmental changes. Changes in the person's social environment often arise as married friends reduce interactions with the widowed individual. On the other hand, changes may also take place as the family-support network set into motion cares for bereaved persons, resulting in intensive attempts to help them care for their affairs. Families may not accurately assess personal needs and preferences of older members who have undergone stressful life experiences. The role of the therapist in such situations involves identification of the older client's needs and assisting the family as well as the client to accept and attempt to meet those needs.

Mrs. Parton, age 73, presented for consultation accompanied by her anxious but well-meaning daughter. Mrs. Parton appeared shy, obedient, and sadfaced. She had been widowed almost a year earlier and had become increasingly unable to cope with the demands of her life situation. Although initially she handled her changed life situation with reasonable ease, as time went on she became increasingly withdrawn. She also began to experience sleep difficulties and she was losing weight. Her physician uncovered no medical problems. Her daughter and other family members had made valient efforts to "make up for her loneliness" or took turns taking her to various meetings, luncheons, and visits with friends. Unfortunately, these attempts to help and support Mrs. Parton did not improve her clinical condition. She appeared to go through the motions of socializing but often excused herself early and went home to cry.

The therapist proceeded to question Mrs. Parton carefully about her bereavement, her interactions with family and friends, and most of all her own needs and preferences in handling her grief. Mrs. Parton spoke with tenderness and sadness about the loss of her husband and apologetically explained that she can't help but want to sit home and think about her past. She tried her best not to offend her well-meaning and solicitous family and tried to run with them from one "empty activity to another." Yet, being confronted by groups of people was becoming increasingly burdensome to her. She felt anger toward herself for being ungrateful and not sufficiently appreciating her daughter's efforts on her behalf. Upon being questioned whether she ever felt angry toward her family for intruding in her grief, she began to cry. "Yes," she said and it was this "unfair" feeling that upset her terribly.

Mrs. Parton felt relieved upon being able to discuss her needs for privacy and shared her need and comfort at being able to grieve. She enjoyed working around the house and being a homebody. The therapist gave her support in expressing her wishes and needs to others and acknowledging that she finds too much socializing upsetting. A greater person-environment fit could be achieved by enabling Mrs. Parton to voice her need for working through her grief alone and expressing her preference for privacy as opposed to extensive interpersonal interactions, which she found oppressive rather than enhancing.

The issues of family involvement that is incongruent with personal definitions of needs are also illustrated in the case of Mr. Sales:

Mr. Sales experienced severe grief after the death of his wife of 45 years. His functioning declined markedly and he gave the impression of being unable to care for his needs and to maintain an independent household for himself. His children noted with dismay that laundry accumulated, that Mr. Sales had no food in the house, and the house was dirty. Mr. Sales spent his days just moping around the house. The "family council" of four children and spouses sought to find the best acceptable solution. The direction appeared clear: Mr. Sales needed a good home for the aged where his needs could be cared for. The family reached this decision and presented Mr. Sales with a choice of two fine homes in the area. This is where the real problem began. Mr. Sales appeared "unreasonable and intransigent." Considering the care and effort that had gone into their deliberations, the family disagreed when Mr. Sales came up with a different solution: he planned to look for a wife instead. To the dismay and embarrassment of his children he joined the local senior citizens' club with the explicit hope of finding a life companion. This is when the children sought the help of a therapist hoping that their father could be brought "to his senses" and to accept the only "logical" alternative, that is, institutionalization. Meanwhile Mr. Sales was making progress on his plan. He started to date a 75-year-old lady who had been a widow for several years and who was still running her own business on a part-time basis.

The therapist met Mr. Sales 10 months after his wife passed away and 5 months after he met his new wife to be. Mr. Sales came to therapy confused and guilty over disobeying his children and feeling shameful over his desire to remarry. After several sessions of discussion regarding Mr. Sales's past and current situation, his feelings of guilt diminished. He remembered the many occasions when his own children "disobeyed" him and saw that they are "individuals with their own autonomy and needs." Mr. Sales was able to articulate his own needs and to apply the same argument to his current situation.

He remarried 12 months after his wife passed away (marking the end of the official mourning period in his religion). Mr. and Mrs. Sales were very happy together and led rather active lives, participating in many recreational and social events and family get-togethers. Both were basically healthy older people who needed reassurance in asserting and articulating their own needs. Their families also needed help in recognizing that their parents' well-being would be best served by life situations consistent with their self-perceived needs and preferences.

Having overcome his grief and settled into a satisfactory and happy marriage, Mr. Sales had no trouble returning to his former independent life style. The couple led an active social life and eventually gained the acceptance of both families.

Therapeutic Efforts Aimed at Improved Coping

It has been argued that adaptive capacities of older people are diminished (Rosow, 1967). Yet there are frequent and major readaptations required of older people through discontinuities posed by retirement, bereavement, impaired health, and loss of social roles. Many older people are unable to cope, and succumb to these stresses. Yet others make successful adjustments and display great resourcefulness in coping with change.

Stressful situations often require flexible coping styles. Yet, it is this flexibility and adaptability that older persons may often lack. Clinical observation suggests that the greater the stress, the more rigid the older client (or patient) may become.

Therapeutic strategy may profitably include explicit attempts aimed at helping the older person utilize alternative coping strategies. Kahana (1975b) has developed a group-therapy program that aims to assist elderly people consider and utilize alternative coping strategies.

This group therapeutic approach is based on the assumption that awareness of a wide array of coping strategies and recognition of situation-appropriate coping styles may be useful in enabling older people to deal with life stresses. The group approach focuses on shared problem-solving strategies and experiences among group members and on sensitizing group members to labeling and identifying problems correctly and developing appropriate solutions for them. The technique also focuses on overcoming resistances to tackling problem-solving situations and on marshalling the resources of the participants based on successful previous problem-solving strategies. Groups generally consist of six to eight members and have been conducted in institutional settings and in community-center senior adults programs. In the institutional groups, members ranged from those on self care to those with mild impairments. Severely confused residents were excluded from participation. Groups met for five to twelve sessions at weekly or twice-weekly intervals.

The most common concerns of the institutionalized elderly involved the stress of coping with institutional living. In the senior center, groups were recruited from among those volunteering to participate and through group worker referrals. There were special groups focusing on widowhood and retirement. No exclusions were made, even if the participants did not undergo the stress that was the group's specific focus. In the case of the widowed crisis group, additional problem areas discussed included intergenerational tensions and establishment of new social ties.

In the competent-coping therapy approach, the past is heavily relied upon in attempting solutions of problematic situations. Thus, the patients are made to utilize past experiences and already learned solutions that did not clash with the patient's defenses. The therapist acts as a group leader, encouraging participants to share problem situations they have experienced and discussing their efforts in dealing with them as well as eventual problem resolutions. Group members are also encouraged to express their feelings and associations from their life experiences. A listing is made of the types of concerns voiced by each of the participants, their attempts to cope with them, and their resolutions. During the initial two sessions, participants raise issues as well as potential solutions.

During the following several sessions, residents also discuss methods for resolving a common set of hypothetical problems, for example, Mr. Green is told by his ophthalmologist that he needs a cataract operation but is given no details regarding why or about the course of recovery. The following several sessions are open-ended, allowing the group to develop its own discussion format and focusing primarily on the ability of group members to serve as resources to one another. In general, there was broad participation among the group members. Participation of institutional aged in such a program is more variable, with isolates appearing in such groups and with a somewhat differing agenda of coping problems. In these situations there are clear advantages for combining group and individual therapy.

Prevalent approaches to successful problem solving noted by group members included such instrumental behaviors as seeking more information, asking for assitance, finding appropriate resources, and organizing action groups. In addition, expressive and escapist coping strategies were identified and discussed. Thus, given a situation where an aged person has to share living quarters with others and has insufficient stimulation in his environment, he may employ varied coping strategies. Thus, he may leave the field (e.g., go to the public library or visit his children as often as he can). He may change his location in the environment (e.g., stay out of his room and sit in the backyard). He might attempt to change the environment by moving to a residence in the center of town or in a room closer to the hub of activity. Or using expressive resolutions, an older individual may complain to everyone that life has lost meaning because there is little to do or even cry about the boredom he is experiencing. The relative value of each of the above coping strategies would be discussed by group members under different circumstances. Group members would then be assisted by the therapist in overcoming personal obstacles to coping competently.

Direct therapeutic consequences of competent-coping approaches and intervention aimed at enhancing person-environment fit lie primarily in resulting in an enhanced sense of environmental and personal satisfaction (Kiyak, 1978), in a greater sense of control and mastery over one's environment, and in diminished symptoms of depression and anxiety. Although these approaches have not been extensively used with older persons whose primary symptoms were cognitive impairment, it may be anticipated that better mastery and greater control would also yield some improvements in cognitive functioning. The following case illustrates the therapeutic advances possible.

Mr. Jenkins, aged 66, had been looking for part-time work ever since his retirement. He found the idleness of his days at home upsetting and anxiety provoking. After many months of searching, he was getting increasingly discouraged. At home he would initiate fights with his wife and refused to socialize with friends and neighbors. Periods of agitation were followed by depression and a sense of aimlessness. Mrs. Jenkins found the ad for a "competent-coping" group at the senior center and encouraged her husband to attend, largely as a means of getting him out of the house. Mr. Jenkins became quite a resource-person to the group, even during the first three weeks of his therapy, after which time he began to talk about his own problems. He recognized that after unsuccessful attempts at instrumental coping, he had turned toward complaining and other subjective ways of resolving his problems. After discussion of his futile attempts to find work, he became aware of the variety of coping strategies that were open to him. He recognized the value of cognitive restructuring and the options of redirecting his goals toward a more active leisure participation, seeking more gratification in his marriage, including working toward a more active and gratifying sex life, and toward involvement in meaningful volunteer activities. Having restructured his goals, he was able to engage successfully in instrumental problem solving. He "interviewed" several agency representatives in his efforts to find the best environment for making meaningful contributions. He settled on the volunteer program of the local hospital where he worked in the emergency room assisting families of patients. The sense of satisfaction and excitement conveyed by Mr. Jenkins became a positive factor in assisting other group members to explore better coping strategies in dealing with the stressful situations they encountered.

Competent coping approaches to help elderly persons deal with stressful situations may be usefully employed either alone or in conjunction with other therapeutic efforts. Although the examples outlined above did not involve group-therapy situations, similar approaches can also be incorporated in individual therapy or counseling programs. A major distinguishing feature of this approach is the use of more direct cognitive problem-solving approaches as compared to the more passive role that therapists usually assume in dynamically oriented therapies. The active participation of the therapist is also complemented by the active problem solving that clients are encouraged to do. Competent-coping approaches can enhance their success when family members or staff working with the client are also involved in the therapeutic process and help reinforce the client's attempts to utilize new adaptive strategies.

CONCLUSIONS: INTERVENTION-RELEVANT DEFINITION OF STRESS AND COPING

In arriving at an overall orientation to stress, we have reviewed what are currently accepted guidelines from the literature. In addition, several important qualifications have also been proposed. First of all, we would like to suggest that a definition of stress should not be limited to "objective" life events or stressors; instead, it should include the respondent's own judgments about type and degree of stress that he or she experiences as a result of, or in conjunction with, the event. This emphasis is consistent with classic sociological theory, as well as a cumulative body of research, and with research that has demonstrted the importance of the "definition of the situation" (Thomas, 1923) for predicting the impact of given situational factors on the individual.

Definitions of stress should also go beyond the currently prevalent discrete, single event. Recognition of the cumulative and ongoing effects of life crises represents one important facet of such an expanded definition. Clinically and theoretically useful definitions of stress should also focus on the multitude of situations that can be sources of stress for the older person by upsetting the previously existing degree of fit between the person and his or her environment. This conceptualization clearly includes stressors that affect the elderly on an ongoing basis as well as major or sudden events. Thus, our position is that a comprehensive analysis of stress must focus not only on major life events and crises but also on the degree of person-environment fit (Kahana, 1979) because the latter is seen as a source of stress.

The process variables customarily included in stress research include cognitive strategies and behavioral interventions as described by respondents to be their typical mode of coping when confronting a hypothetically stressful situation (Sidle et al., 1969). Assessment of coping, strategies should also include consideration of actual coping behaviors (past and present) using self-reports and/or behavioral observations. The existence and utilization of supports, resources, and services also comprise an important factor in determining the success of the older person's coping with stress. The development of suitable therapeutic and service programs for older persons who experience life stresses represents an important challenge to policy planners and service providers (Ehrlich & Kahana, 1970). Our orientation to understanding the impact of stress on the elderly underscores the importance of both formal and informal service supports to allow us to consider intervention-relevant aspects of coping with stressful life events among the elderly. Most of society's ameliorative efforts in aiding the elderly are provided in the form of some type of service or support. Programs to assist aged who are experiencing stress may range from efforts at reducing stress to improving coping skills and providing support.

In conclusion, then, the authors would like to point to the usefulness for clinicians, as well as for researchers, of considering the conceptual and empirical strides that have been made by researchers in formulating the relationship between stress, coping, and psychosocial outcomes, including psychopathology. We must go beyond citing a diagnostic label, such as stress reaction, and examine the complex dynamics of stress to allow us to formulate a greater range of therapeutically effective interventions to help older clients who have had, or who are undergoing, stressful experiences. We must carefully examine temporal aspects of the stresses as well as qualitative aspects of the type of stresses faced by older clients in order to make the best use of the available resources for the problems of the aged individual. Furthermore, outreach is necessary to encourage the elderly to avail themselves of such services.

REFERENCES

Alker, H. A. Coping, defense and socially desirable responses. *Psychological Reports,* 1968, **22,** 985–988.

Amster, L. E., & Krauss, H. H. The relationship between life crises and mental deterioration. *Old Age, International Journal of Aging and Human Development,* 1974, **5,** 51–55.

Antonovsky, A. *Health, stress, and coping: New perspectives on mental and physical well-being.* San Francisco: Jossey-Bass, 1979.

Barnes, J. Class and community in a Norwegian island parish. *Human Relations,* 1954, 39–58.

Beck, P. Two successful interventions in nursing homes. *The Gerontologist,* 1982, **22,** 378–383.

Berghorn, F. J., & Shafer, D. E. *Support networks and the frail elderly.* Paper presented at the 32nd Annual Meeting of the Gerontological Society, Washington, D.C., 1979.

Botwinick, J. *Aging and behavior.* New York: Springer, 1978.

Bourestom, N. D., & Pastelan, L. A. *Forced relocation: Setting, staff, and patient effects. Final report to NIMH.* Institute of Gerontology, University of Michigan, Ann Arbor, Michigan, 1975.

Butler, R. N. Myths and realities of clinical geriatrics. In S. Steury & M. L. Blank (Eds.), *Readings in psychotherapy with older people.* Rockville, Md.: U.S. Department of Health and Human Services, National Institutes of Mental Health, 1977.

Butler, R. N., & Lewis, M. I. *Aging and mental health* (2nd ed.). St. Louis, Mo.: Mosby, 1977.

Caplan, G. *Support systems and community mental health.* New York: Behavioral Publications, 1974.

Carp, F. M. Short-term and long-term prediction of adjustment to a new environment. *Journal of Gerontology,* 1974, **29**, 444–453.

Carp, F. M. Housing and living environments of older people. In R. H. Binstock & E. Shanas (Eds.), *Handbook of aging and the social sciences.* New York: Van Nostrand Reinhold, 1976.

Carp, F. M., & Carp, A. *P-E congruence and well-being.* Unpublished manuscript, Wright Institute, Berkeley, Ca.,1979.

Chiriboga, D. A., & Dean, H. Dimensions of stress: Perspectives from a longitudinal study. *Journal of Psychosomatic Research,* 1978, **22**, 47–55.

Cohen, J., & Cohen, P. Applied multiple regression/correlation analysis for the behavior sciences. Hillside, N.J.: Erlbaum, 1975.

Cosin, L. *The active treatment of the elderly sick based on a dynamic fourfold assessment.* 1958. (Mimeo)

Dohrenwend, B. S. Life events as stressors: A methodological inquiry. *Journal of Health and Social Behavior,* 1973, **14**, 167–175.

Dohrenwend, B. P., & Dohrenwend, B. S. *Stressful life events: Their nature and effects.* New York: Wiley, 1974.

Ehrlich, P., & Kahana, E. *Door to door survey of elderly population in a transitional neighborhood.* Paper presented at Gerontological Society Meetings, Toronto, October 1970.

Eisdorfer, C., & Wilkie, F. L. Stress and behavior in aging. Issues in mental health and aging. *Proceedings of the Conference on Research in Mental Health and Aging,* 1979, **1**, 60–66.

Erikson, E. *Childhood and society.* New York: Norton, 1950.

Felton, B., & Kahana, E. *Personal lifespace and person-environment fit in institutions for the aged.* Paper presented at the 10th International Congress of Gerontology, Jerusalem, Israel, June 1975.

French, J., Rodgers, W., & Cobb, S. Adjustment as person-environment fit. In G. V. Coelho, D. A. Hamburg, & J. E. Adams (Eds.), *Coping and adaptation.* New York: Basic Books, 1974.

Friedman, G. D., Urey, H. K., Klatsky, A. L., & Siegelaub, U. S. A psychological questionnaire predictive of myocardial infarction. *Psychosomatic Medicine,* 1974, **36**, 327–343.

Gal, R., & Lazarus, R. The role of activity in anticipating and confronting stressful situations. *Journal of Human Stress,* 1975, **12**, 4–20.

George, L. K. *Role transition in later life.* Monterey, Calif.: Brooks/Cole, 1980.

Gersten, J. C., Langner, T. S., Eisenberg, J. G., & Orzek, L. Child behavior and life events: Undesirable change or change per se? In B. S. Dohrenwend & B. P. Dohrenwend (Eds.), *Stressful life events: Their nature and effects.* New York: Wiley, 1974.

Goldstein, T., & Gutmann, D. A T.A.T. study of Navajo aging. *Psychiatry,* 1972, **35**, 373–384.

Grinker, R. R. Psychosomatic aspects of the cancer problems. *Annals of New York Academy of Science,* 1966, 876–882.

Gutmann, D. *The country of old men: Crossnational studies in the psychology of later life.* Occasional paper in Gerontology series. Ann Arbor, Mich.: Institute of Gerontology, 1969.

Haan, N. Proposed model of ego functioning: Coping and defense mechanisms in relationship in IQ change. *Psychological Monographs,* 1963, **77**(8), 1–23.

Hall, C., & Lindsey, G. *Theories of personality.* New York: Wiley, 1970.

Hamburg, D., Coelho, G. V., & Adams, J. E. Coping and adaptation: Steps toward synthesis of biological and social perspectives. In G. V. Coelho, D. A. Hamburg, & J. E. Adams (Eds.),

Coping and adaptation. New York: Basic Books, 1974.

Hartman, H., Kris, E., & Lowenstein, R. Notes on the theory of aggression. *Psychoanalytic Study of the Child,* 1949, **4**, 9–36.

Hinkle, L. E. Ecological observations of the relation of physical illness, mental illness and social environment. *Psychosomatic Medicine,* 1961, **23**, 289–296.

Hinkle, L. E., & Wolff, H. G. Ecologic investigations of the relationship between illness, life experience and the social environment. *Annals of Internal Medicine,* 1958, **49**, 1373–1388.

Hogue, C. C. *Support systems: A model for research and services to older Americans.* Unpublished paper presented at the National Gerontological Society Meeting, New York, October 15, 1976.

Holmes, T. H., Goodell, H., Wolf, S., & Wolff, H. G. *The nose. An experimental study of reactions within the nose in human subjects during varying life experiences.* Springfield, Ill.: Charles C. Thomas, 1950.

Holmes, T. H., & Masuda, M. Life change and illness susceptibility. In B. S. Dohrenwend & B. P. Dohrenwend (Eds.), *Stressful life events.* New York: Wiley, 1974.

Holmes, T., & Rahe, R. The social readjustment rating scale. *Journal of Psychosomatic Research,* 1967, **11**, 219–225.

Horowitz, M. J. Psychoanalytic therapy. In E. L. Kutash & L. B. Schlesinger (Eds.), *Handbook on stress and anxiety: Contemporary knowledge, theory, and treatment.* San Francisco: Jossey-Bass, 1980.

Hough, R. L., Fairbank, D. T., & Garcia, A. M. Problems in the ratio measurement of life stress. *Journal of Health and Social Behavior,* 1976, **17**, 70–82.

Hudgens, R. W. Personal catastrophe and depression: A consideration of the subject with respect to medically ill adolescents and a requiem for retrospective life-event studies. In B. S. Dohrenwend & B. P. Dohrenwend (Eds.), *Stressful life events.* New York: Wiley, 1974.

Hunt, M. *The effectiveness of a simulated site visit to familiarize the elderly with a new environment.* Unpublished manuscript, Institute of Gerontology, University of Michigan, Ann Arbor, 1980.

Hurst, M., Jenkins, C. D., & Rose, R. M. The relation of psychological stress to onset of medical illness. In C. A. Garfield (Ed.), *Stress and survival: The emotional realities of life-threatening illness.* St. Louis, Mo.: Mosby, 1979.

Kahana, B. *Advances in group therapy with the aged.* Paper presented at American Psychological Association, Chicago, 1975.(a)

Kahana, B. *Competent coping—A psychotherapeutic strategy.* Paper presented at International Gerontological Association, Jerusalem, Israel, June 1975.(b)

Kahana, B., Kahana, E., & Hasegawa, K. Adaptive strategies and institutionalization of the aged: U.S. and Japanese perspectives. *Proceedings of the 11th International Congress of Gerontology,* Tokyo, 1978.

Kahana, B., Kahana, E., & Kiyak, A. Changing attitudes toward the aged. *National Journal,* November 10, 1979, 1913–1919.

Kahana, E. *Theoretical approaches to the study of environment-person interaction.* Paper presented at Conference on Person-Environment Interaction, Manhattan, Kansas, April 1974.

Kahana, E. A congruence model of person-environment interaction. In P. G. Windley & G. Ernst (Eds.), *Theory development in environment & aging.* Washington, D.C.: Gerontological Society, 1975.

Kahana, E., Fairchild, T., & Felton, B. *Positive and negative life events: Relationship to vulnerability and well-being of the aged.* Paper presented at the American Psychological Association Meetings, Washington, D.C., August 1976.

Kahana, E., Fairchild, T., & Kahana, B. Measurement of adaptation to changes in health and environmental changes among the aged. In R. Mangen & W. Peterson (Eds.), *Handbook to research instruments in social gerontology.* University of Minnesota Press, 1982.

Kahana, E., & Kahana, B. *Strategies of coping in institutional environments.* Progress report submitted to NIMH, 1979.(a)

Kahana, E., & Kahana, B. *Voluntary relocation, adaptation and mental health of the aged.* Progress report submitted to NIMH, 1979.(b)

Kahana, E., & Kahana, B. Environmental continuity, discontinuity, futurity and adaptation of the aged. In G. Rowles & R. Ohta (Eds.), *Aging and milieu: Environmental perspectives on growing old.* New York: Academic Press, 1982.

Kahana, E., Liang, J., & Felton, B. Alternative models of person-environment fit: Prediction of morale in three homes for the aged. *Journal of Gerontology,* 1980, 584–595.

Kahana, E., & Midlarsky, E. Is there help beyond exchange? Contributory options in late life adaptation. *Academic Psychology Bulletin,* in press.

Kaplan, H. B. Self-derogation and adjustment to recent life experiences. *Archives of General Psychiatry,* 1970, **22**, 324–331.

Kiyak, A., Liang, J., & Kahana, E. *A methodological inquiry into the schedule of recent life events.* Paper presented at Symposium on Life Events, American Psychological Association, New York, August 1976.

Kiyak, H. A. Person-environment congruence models as determinants of environmental satisfaction and well-being in institutions for the elderly. *Doctoral Dissertations,* Wayne State University, Detroit, Michigan, 1978.

Kleemeier, R. W. The use and meaning of time in special setting. In R. W. Kleemeier (Ed.), *Aging and leisure.* New York: Oxford University Press, 1961.

Korchin, S. S., & Bosawitz, H. The judgment of ambiguous stimuli as an index of cognitive functioning in aging. *Journal of Personality,* 1956, **25**, 81–95.

Kutash, E. L., & Schlesinger, L. B. (Eds.). *Handbook on stress and anxiety: Contemporary knowledge, theory, and treatment.* San Francisco: Jossey-Bass, 1980.

Langer E., & Rodin, J. The effects of choice and enhanced personal responsibility: A field experiment in an institutional setting. *Journal of Personality and Social Psychology,* 1976, **34**, 191–198.

Langner, T., & Michael, S. *Life stress and mental health.* London: Collier-Macmillan, 1963.

Lawton, M. P. Institutions and alternatives for older people. *Health and Social Work,* 1978, **3**, 109–134.(a)

Lawton, M. P. *Sensory deprivation and the effects of the environment on management of the senile dementia patient.* Paper presented at the National Institute of Mental Health Conference on Clinical Aspects of Alzheimer's Disease and Senile Dementia, Bethesda, Md., December 1978.(b)

Lawton, M. P. *Environment and aging.* Monterey, Calif.: Brooks/Cole, 1980.

Lawton, M. P., & Nahemow, L. Ecology and the aging process. In C. Eisdorfer & M. P. Lawton (Eds.), *Psychology of adult development and aging.* Washington, D.C.: APA Publications, 1973.

Lazarus, R. S. *Psychological stress and the coping process.* New York: McGraw-Hill, 1966.

Lazarus, R., Averill, J., & Opton, E. The psychology of coping: Issues of research and assessment. In G. V. Coelho et al. (Eds.), *Coping and adaptation.* New York: Basic Books, 1974.

Levi, L. *Society, stress and disease, Vol. 1: The psychosocial environment and psychosomatic diseases.* London: Oxford University Press, 1971.

Lewin, K. *A dynamic theory of personality.* New York: McGraw-Hill, 1935.

Lewin, K. *Field theory in social science.* New York: Harper, 1951.

Lieberman, M., & Cohler, B. *Constructing personality measures for older people.* Unpublished manuscript, Department of Health, City of Chicago: University of Chicago, 1976.

Lowenthal, M. F., Turnher, M., & Chiriboga, D. *Four stages of life.* San Francisco: Jossey-Bass, 1975.

Markush, R. E., & Favero, R. V. Epidemiologic assessment of stressful life events, depressed mood and psychophysiological symptoms—A preliminary report. In B. S. Dohrenwend & B. P. Dohrenwend (Eds.), *Stressful life events: Their nature and effects.* New York: Wiley, 1974.

Mechanic, D. Discussion of research programs on relations between stressful life and episodes of physical illness. In B. S. Dohrenwend & B. P. Dohrenwend (Eds.), *Stressful life events: Their nature and effects.* New York: Wiley, 1974.

Mitchell, J. C. *Social networks and urban situations.* Manchester, England: University of Manchester Press, 1969.

Moos, R. Psychological techniques in the assessment of adaptive behavior. In G. V. Coelho, D. A. Hamburg, R. Moos, & P. Randolph (Eds.), *Coping and adaptation.* New York: Basic Books, 1974.

Moos, R. *Coping with physical illness.* New York: Plenum, 1977.

Muhlenkamp, A., Gress, L. D., & Flood, M. A. Perception of life change events by the elderly. *Nursing Research,* 1975, **2**, 109–113.

Murray, H. A. *Exploration in personality.* New York: Oxford University Press, 1938.

Neugarten, B. A developmental view of adult personality. In J. E. Birren (Ed.), *Relations of development and aging.* Springfield, Ill.: Charles C. Thomas, 1964.

Neugarten, B. L. Personality and aging. In J. E. Birren & K. W. Schaie (Eds.), *Handbook of the psychology of aging.* New York: Van Nostrand Reinhold, 1977.

Pearlin, L. E., & Schooler, C. The structure of coping. *Journal of Health and Social Behavior,* 1978, **19**, 2–21.

Peck, R. F. Psychological developments in the second half of life. In B. Neugarten (Ed.), *Middle age and aging.* Chicago: University of Chicago Press, 1968.

Pincus, A. *Toward a conceptual framework for studying environments.* Unpublished doctoral dissertation, University of Wisconsin, Madison, 1968.

Pollack, K., & Kastenbaum, R. Delay of gratification in later life. In R. Kastenbaum (Ed.), *New thoughts on old age.* New York: Springer, 1964.

Quayhage, M. P., & Chiriboga, D. *Geriatric coping schedule: Potential and problems.* Paper presented to the 29th Annual Meeting of the Gerontological Society, New York, October 13–17, 1976.

Rabkin, J. G., & Struening, E. L. Life events, stress, and illness. *Science,* 1976, **194**, 1013–1020.

Rahe, R. H., Biersner, R. J., Ryman, D. H., & Arthur, R. J. Psychosical predictors of illness behavior and failure in stressful training. *Journal of Health and Social Behavior,* 1972, **13**, 393–397.

Reichard, S., Livson, F., & Peterson, P. C. *Aging and personality: A study of eighty-seven older men.* New York: Wiley, 1962.

Rodin, J., & Langer, E. Aging labels: The decline of control and the fall of self-esteem. *Journal of Social Issues,* 1980, **36**, 2, 12–29.

Rosow, I. *Socialization to old age.* Berkeley: University of California Press, 1974.

Rosow, J. *Social integration of the aged.* Glencoe, Ill.: Free Press, 1967.

Ross, C. E., & Mirowsky, J. A comparison of life event weighting schemes: Change, undesirability and effect-proportional indices. *Journal of Health and Social Behavior,* 1979, **20**, 166–177.

Schulz, R., & Brenner G. Relocation of the aged: Review and theoretical analysis. *Journal of Gerontology,* 1977, **32**, 323–333.

Seligman, M. E. P. *Helplessness: On depression, development, and death.* San Francisco: Freeman, 1975.

Selye, H. *The stress of life.* New York: McGraw-Hill, 1956.

Selye, H. *The stress of life* (2nd ed.). New York: McGraw-Hill, 1976.

Shanan, J. *Active and passive coping styles among the aged.* Unpublished manuscript, Hebrew University, Jerusalem, Israel, 1978.

Sidle, A., Moos, R. H., Adams, J., & Cady, P. Development of a coping scale: A preliminary study. *Archives of General Psychiatry,* 1969, **20**, 226–232.

Sifeos, P. *Psychoanalytic therapy with the aged.* Paper presented at National Institute of Mental Health Conference on Psychodynamic Research Perspectives on Development, Psychotherapy and Treatment in Later Life, Md., November 5-8, 1982.

Sobel, E. F. Anxiety and stress in later life. In I. Kutash, L. B. Schlesinger, & associates (Eds.), *Handbook on stress and anxiety—Contemporary knowledge, theory and treatment.* San Francisco: Jossey-Bass, 1981.

Stephens, B. J. *Loners, losers and lovers: A sociological study of the aged tenants of a slum hotel.* Unpublished doctoral dissertation, Wayne State University, Detroit, Mich., 1973.

Stern, G. *People in a context.* New York: Wiley, 1970.

Steury, S., & Blank, M. L. (Eds.), *Readings in psychotherapy with older people.* Rockville, Md.: NIMH, 1977.

Theorell, T., & Rahe, R. H. Psychosocial factors and myocardial infarction. An inpatient study in Sweden. *Journal of Psychosomatic Research,* 1971, **15**, 25-31.

Thiel, H. G., Parker, D., & Bruce, T. A. Stress factors and the risk of myocardial infarction. *Journal of Psychosomatic Research,* 1973, **17**, 43-57.

Thomas, W. I. *The unadjusted girl.* Boston: Little Brown, 1923.

Wetzel, J. W. *Person-environment interventions with aging depressed women in institutions.* Paper presented at the 31st Annual Scientific Meeting of the Gerontological Society, Clinical Medicine Section, Dallas, November 16-20, 1978.

White, R. Motivation reconsidered: The concept of competence. *Psychological Review,* 1959, **66**, 293-333.

AFTERWORD

Linda Teri and Peter M. Lewinsohn

OVERVIEW: INTRODUCTION

The chapters of this book present an array of problems that were selected because of their prevalence among the elderly. Each chapter provides guidelines for the assessment and treatment of these problems. Each problem, however, is vast enough to merit much more discussion and analysis. We hope now to stimulate an appreciation for the answers these chapters provide as well as a curiosity for the unanswered questions that remain. Thus, we will conclude this book by addressing some of the issues addressed by these chapters, discussing the issues relevant across chapters, and directing the reader to other resources for further information.

DEPRESSION: DOLORES GALLAGHER AND LARRY THOMPSON

Depression has often been considered a normal, if unfortunate, condition of aging. Gallagher and Thompson are to be commended for entering this area, using the vast information available on depression in younger age groups, and systematically investigating the utility of this knowledge with the elderly.

Avenues of future clinical and empirical investigation stimulated by this chapter are many. Three seem most appealing and pressing: (1) the clarification of decision rules for determining a diagnosis of depression in an older adult; (2) the identification and sound justification for modifications in treatment procedures that are necessary for the elderly; and (3) the extension of Gallagher and Thompson's techniques to the frail elderly.

Gallagher and Thompson's chapter indicates the complexity of assessing depression in the elderly. A basic knowledge of how to assess depression and an understanding of the interweaving roles of age-appropriate behaviors and attitudes, physical health and illness, and client-clinician rapport become crucial in successfully identifying and treating the depressed elderly. While

Gallagher and Thompson offer general guidelines for ferreting out these overlapping issues, clinical judgment is still very much required to evaluate and assess adequately the impact of these issues on the client's depression.

At this time, the treatment of depression in the elderly also requires considerable innovation. Gallagher and Thompson discuss the types of modifications they have employed and provide support for the idea that treatment of depressed elderly can follow treatment protocols designed for younger age groups. They also indicate, however, the importance of age-related and individually tailored modifications. Questions remain regarding what modifications should be undertaken, when, and for what reasons.

Gallagher and Thompson provide a format for clinicians working with depressed elderly in an outpatient setting. An exciting avenue of investigation would be to apply their approach to a more frail population, possibly those in long-term care facilities and those suffering some degree of cognitive impairment. Recent research indicates that the presence of depressive symptoms among these groups is "often overwhelming, sometimes reaching levels of 80%" (Hyer & Blazer, 1982, p. 34). This research has also demonstrated a clear and compelling relationship between depressive symptoms, perceived quality of life, and other problems. One cannot help but envision the beneficial impact an effective intervention could have with these elderly.

Because the assessment and treatment of depresssion still relies heavily upon clinical judgment, it would be helpful if clear-cut rules could be hypothesized and then empirically and clinically investigated, so that the clinician can have specific guidelines for diagnosis and intervention. Although no such guidelines exist at present, readers interested in more information on assessment and treatment of depression are encouraged to look for a forthcoming book by Gallagher and Thompson (in preparation). In the interim, readers are referred to *Depression in Late Life* by Dan Blazer (1982). Intended for professionals, this book is based upon Blazer's many years of clinical experience and research with depressed elderly. His book provides chapters on "late life bereavement and depressive neurosis," and "depressive disorders associated with physical illness and alcohol use," among others. In order to be prepared for the many problems posed by depressed patients, the reader is urged to acquire as much information and sensitivity to these issues as possible.

DEMENTIA: STEVEN ZARIT AND JUDY ZARIT

Anyone who has ever worked with a dementia patient knows full well the range of despair and frustration the family suffers. (Readers without first-hand experience of dementia and the drain it can place on family and health-care providers are referred to *The 36 Hour Day,* by Mace & Rabins [1981].

This excellent publication is easy to read and provides a poignant "we've been there" intimacy that will help the reader understand what it is like to live and work with a dementia patient.) Frequently, the patient is not aware of the decrements in functioning he or she is experiencing. The family, however, is all too aware. Zarit and Zarit's chapter provides a model for intervention with the families of dementia patients. The model offers hope by helping families cope with a difficult and trying situation and offers a clear and structured path for the professional helping these families.

Two questions stimulated by this chapter involve aspects of working with dementia that the Zarits did not address: (1) treating the dementia patient directly, and (2) treating the institutionalized, or about-to-be institutionalized, patient.

Comparable to depression, dementia is a complex disorder. The accurate diagnosis of dementia may save the family, client, and society the extraordinary expenditure of energy and resources engendered by fruitless intervention attempts (for example, costly medical treatments for organically suspected problems when no such problems exist or time-consuming and frustrating psychosocial interventions when the problem is organic). When questions of dementia arise, a complete assessment to rule out other diseases and difficulties is essential. As the Zarits indicate, however, much controversy exists over the utility of different assessments and the types of assessment required among this patient population. Readers interested in more information on this controversy and on the assessment and treatment of dementia are referred to Zarit's (1980) own work and to Lezak (1983) for further information on the role of neuropsychological assessment.

Not all patients are unaware of the difficulties they are experiencig. Particularly in the early stages of the dementing illness, their memory and concentration problems can be very frustrating for them. It is not uncommon for dementia patients also to exhibit depression, withdrawal, and paranoia. The clinician must be knowledgeable in handling the emotional and cognitive components of the dementing illness. Regarding the cognitive component, there is some controversy about the utility of providing specialized training to enable dementia patients to use their remaining mental facilities so as to assure maximum efficiency and functioning. While this deserves further systematic study, at this time the judgment of the clinician is paramount. The drawbacks of continually exposing patients to frustrating tasks cannot be overlooked.

There are certainly times when the older adult can no longer be sustained in the home: the emotional, financial, and physical toll is too great to be maintained. How families handle this decision and the transition, if necessary, from personal home care to professional care is an extremely sensitive issue. Clinicians working with the elderly must confront this issue at various times and are advised to be adequately aware of the full range of services available in the community—from those offering home respite care to those offering professional inpatient care. In addition, clinicians should be aware of the levels of independent living the elderly person might be able to achieve with some minimal support or intervention.

In addition to facilitating the transition from personal to professional care, the clinician may be called upon to work with the problems of dementia within an institutionalized setting. Indeed, Pfeiffer (1980) estimates that over 50 percent of nursing home residents have impairments associated with dementia. An exciting avenue of investigation would be the extension of the Zarits' approach to nursing home residents and personnel. Many of the difficulties nursing home staff encounter are comparable to the difficulties families encounter, and the potential amelioration of these difficulties would certainly enhance life in institutions for resident and staff alike.

INSOMNIA: RICHARD BOOTZIN, MINDY ENGLE-FRIEDMAN, AND LISA HAZELWOOD

Insomnia can be an insidious and deleterious disorder. As time goes by, the associated changes in mood and increase in fatigue can turn insomnia into a major disruption and concern. In addition to upsetting the life of the affected individual, insomnia can also affect the lives of those around the insomniac. At the extreme, families unable to cope with the older adult's disruption of his or her sleep patterns and the subsequent disruption of their own sleep pattern may consider institutionalization when before they had not. The repeated loss of "a good night's sleep" might well be the final straw in the family's attempt to deal with an aged adult in the home.

While the negative consequences of continued insomnia can be complex, insomnia itself is a much more clearly defined problem than the other problems discussed in this book. Drawing upon many of the procedures Bootzin has employed with younger clients and using information about elderly sleep patterns, the chapter by Bootzin, Engle-Friedman, and Hazelwood provides a structure within which to assess and treat the elderly insomniac.

The primary question stimulated by their chapter is one raised by the authors themselves: How useful will this procedure be with "real" clinical populations?

The subjects/patients discussed in this chapter were all individuals who volunteered to participate in a study on the treatment of insomnia. They were described as a highly motivated group and may or may not have resembled the patient typically seen in clinical settings. Those seen in clinics may be more likely to have multiple problems, more difficult to work with, and less likely to comply with instructions. The reader should be aware of these potential important differences and use the treatment procedures described with an awareness of the issues pertinent to clinical case management. Some of these issues include: (1) What is the role of other problems in addition to insomnia? If multiple problems exist, how should insomnia intervention complement the total treatment plan? If other problems exist, how will they complicate the intervention for insomnia? (2) How will patients comply with the requirements of the insomnia procedures? How can the procedures be modified to assure compliance, if problems develop? Which individuals or aspects of the patient's environment may facilitate or hinder compliance? (3) How can maintenance and generalization be programmed into the treatment package to assure that patients maintain their gains independent of the clinician? Again, which individuals or aspects of the patient's environment may facilitate or hinder maintenance?

The extension of the work reported in this chapter to actual clinical cases is a very exciting avenue to anticipate. Readers interested in more information about stimulus-control procedures for insomnia are referred to Youkilis and Bootzin (1981) and Bootzin and Nicassio (1978). The potential utility of these procedures with individuals suffering from insomnia alone or insomnia coupled with another problem (such as the arthritic patient who cannot sleep because of muscle tension or pain or the depressed patient whose insomnia is part of a constellation of depression symptoms) is clear. Equally clear is how the remediation of insomnia could improve the quality of one's life considerably.

SOCIAL AND DAILY LIVING SKILLS: ROGER PATTERSON AND DAVID EBERLY

The need for the clinician working with elderly patients to be aware of techniques to employ with the elderly in residential or inpatient care facilites cannot be overstated. While the elderly are underrepresented in outpatient mental-health facilities, they are grossly overrepresented among inpatient mental-health facilities; the number of elderly consigned to nursing homes is increasing as well (Lawton, 1978). Thus, the practicing clinician needs to be familiar with techniques required to help the frail, severely impaired, institutionalized elderly.

Patterson and Eberly provide a clearly structured, systematic procedure for assessment of, and training in, social and daily living skills. Their approach to assessment and intervention is a direct one, rather than an indirect one that has been prevalent in the past (e.g., recreation therapy, arts and crafts) (see Sherwood & Moor, 1980). Their chapter is based on their own empirical research which is discussed in greater detail elsewhere (Patterson et al., 1982). The practicing clinician should be aware of this empirical support for Patterson's work and should avail himself or herself of the additional clinical information and structure available there.

Two sets of questions are stimulated by this chapter: one concerns the adaptability of this approach to other residential or inpatient facilities; the other concerns the adaptability of this approach to outpatients, such as those seen in community mental-health settings or by private practitioners.

Institutions usually have their own structure and accepted models of assessment and intervention. It is unlikely that they will accept a program that requires major reorganization of existing procedures. More likely, they will try new programs hesitantly, accepting some aspects and declining others. The advantage of Patterson's program is that it can be divided into smaller modules and introduced gradually into an already existing facility. According to Patterson and Eberly, the modules were designed to function independently as well as to be part of the overall package. The package, taken as a whole, is comprehensive. Thus, the practicing clinician may adopt some or all of the assessment and intervention aspects described, depending on the needs of the institution and its residents. The program described by Patterson and Eberly also represents the combined effort of many individuals, working on similar objectives in a supportive environment. It will be exciting to investigate Patterson's approach in less structured environments, with different levels of staff working with different populations.

Patterson and Eberly make an excellent case for the importance of social and daily living skills in the elderly: they suggest that these skills are logically tied to the ability to function within the community and maintain an adequate lifestyle. It would be interesting to investigate if training in social and daily living skills would have a positive impact upon a person seen in a traditional outpatient setting say, once or twice a week. Would his or her skill and ability to cope with the environment improve? It is easy to see how many aspects of the assessment and intervention procedures discussed here can be extended to this outpatient population. One would expect certain modifications to be necessary (e.g., the involvement of family or community resources), but this potential extension provides an exciting avenue for further inquiry.

STRESS: BOAZ KAHANA AND EVA KAHANA

Stress, more than the other topics included in this book, represents an amorphous entity whose boundaries are never completely clear. The term "stress" could refer to a single, discrete traumatic event (such as rape or death of a spouse) and/or to a slow accumulation of multiple small but chronic irritants (such as marital problems or financial difficulties). Paralleling the amorphousness of the problem, the chapter by Kahana and Kahana presents a general approach to assessment and intervention. Their chapter provides the reader with a framework within which to organize his or her thoughts on this topic while also providing some direction and guidelines for the clinical management of stress reactions as they occur in institutionalized and community-residing elderly.

The very nature of this framework stimulates numerous questions. Two broad issues seem most pressing: (1) the specification of techniques for the assessment and intervention of stress reactions, and (2) the systematic application and empirical validation of these techniques to the elderly experiencing different types of stress.

A general framework serves a number of important functions. It enables the clinician faced with an elderly patient exhibiting multiple and varied problems to conceptualize these problems coherently and begin to determine priorities for assessment and intervention; it also enables the clinician faced with a patient exhibiting a stress reaction to which the clinician has not previously been exposed to understand what this particular reaction has in common with reactions with which he or she is familiar. But a general framework does not provide clearly delineated and carefully pinpointed definitions, assessment procedures, and treatment techniques. All of these are crucial and exciting steps for future clinical and empirical work. Clinical procedures may most easily be specified with stress reactions that have been caused by discrete stressful events; the less discrete, more pervasive stresses may generate reactions for which specific formulations are more difficult but certainly no less possible or necessary. The latter reactions may, in fact, be more problematic for the elderly (see Pfeiffer & Busse, 1973).

As approaches to stress reactions are being carefully developed and specified, their effectiveness with elderly patients must be seriously assessed. The utility of the person-environment fit with the elderly in determining how the environment facilitates or hinders therapeutic progress can be great. While this is not unique to the elderly with stress, it may be even more critical for the elderly faced with dramatically new and different environments within which they have to cope (e.g., moving into a child's home or into a nursing home).

Although conceptualized together, one would realistically expect different stress reactions to require different procedures for assessment and treatment. Further, the effectiveness of techniques originally developed for younger age groups (with similar problems) with elderly patients may vary depending on the nature of the specific problem. For example, one would hypothesize that certain stresses are more relevant to the elderly (e.g., relocation versus pregnancy) and have different importance to them (e.g., death of a spouse after 50 years of marriage). As a consequence, intervention techniques will probably need to be varied and adaptable. Programmatic and individualized approaches to elderly persons experiencing stress reactions are a fruitful area for future investigations.

INTEGRATION

Each of the chapters in this book has focused on the assessment and intervention of one particular problem. The focus has been on applied clinical knowledge that has gained empirical support. As noted earlier, each of these problems is too broad to be covered exhaustively in one chapter and the interested reader is heartily referred to the references cited in this and in each chapter for further information.

For the practicing clinician, the problems covered in these chapters are rarely seen in isolation. It would be more common to encounter an elderly patient who exhibits depression, insomnia, social-skill deficits, and cognitive impairment, who is also experiencing a number of stressful life events. It is the role of the practicing clinician to recognize these difficulties as well as to prioritize the symptomatic manifestations for adequate treatment planning. In addition, it is the role of the practicing clinician to remain cognizant of the role of the great individual variation present in individuals experiencing similarly classified disorders. For example, two 84-year-old men with insomnia may present very different clinical pictures: one may live alone, function well independently, have little experience with sleep medications, and have few additional physical or psychosocial difficulties; the other may live with his family, be able to function only with considerable caretaking and support, have relied heavily on prescription and nonprescription sleep medication, and be experiencing multiple additional physical and psychosocial difficulties. The need for integrative and inclusive information on the multiplicity of causal and resultant problems in the elderly is critical. (We have provided some recommendations and references for this in the introduction.)

Neugarten (1982) argues for a continuum based not upon chronology but upon levels of biopsychosocial functioning. While we have chosen here to address the aspects of assessment and intervention techniques as they apply to the elderly, it is important to recognize that much individual variability does exist. Idiographic evaluation of the individual in terms of his or her current level of adjustment is critical at any age level and perhaps all the more critical with the elderly, where our lack of knowledge and presence of bias may make generalizations too tempting—and too inaccurate.

The field of clinical geropsychology is a new and rapidly expanding field. It will be of empirical and clinical interest in years to come, to determine which ideas and findings discussed here are relevant to other generational cohorts as they age, and which are unique to the cohort considered "elderly" in the 1980s. While we may safely assume that modifications, improvements, and innovations will continue, we may also anticipate the very real need for continuing education and ongoing evaluation of our techniques by clinicians and researchers alike.

There are, of course, still many other topics relevant to the aging adult not included here that are important to the practicing (or about-to-practice) clinician. These areas include: bereavement and widowhood, chronic and acute pain, incontinence, sexual dysfunction, long-term care, consultation, pharmacotherapy, and comprehensive and neuropsychological assessment. While the urge to expand this book and be all-inclusive was great, the very real need to make available to professionals a volume that begins to address common problems of the elderly was paramount. In 1978, M. Powell Lawton delivered a master lecture at the American Psychological Association Convention in which he commented that: "One looks in vain through the literature for empirical evaluations, with replication, of older people treated (individually) by differing approaches. . . . the experience of the clinicians who now treat older people needs to be mobilized into the production of a therapeutic state-of-the-art-plus cookbook" (Lawton, 1978, p. 26). It is our hope that this book moves clinical geropsychology one step closer to achieving that goal and that future empirical and clinical work will continue this progress.

REFERENCES

Blazer, D. G. *Depression in late life*. St. Louis, Mo.: Mosby, 1982.

Bootzin, R. R., & Nicassio, P. Behavioral treatment of insomnia. In M. Hersen, R. Eisler, & P. Miller (Eds.), *Progress in Behavior Modification*. New York: Academic Press, 1978.

Hyer, L., & Blazer, D. G. Depressive symptoms: Impact and problems in long term care facilities. *International Journal of Behavioral Geriatrics,* 1982, 1, 33–44.

Lawton, M. P. *Clinical geropsychology: Problems and prospects*. Master lecture delivered at American Psychological Association Convention, 1978.

Lezak, M. *Neuropsychological assessment*. New York: Oxford University Press, 1983.

Mace, N. L., & Rabins, P. V. *The 36 hour day*. Baltimore, Md.: Johns Hopkins University Press, 1981.

Neugarten, B. L. *Successful aging*. Public lecture delivered at American Psychological Association Convention, 1982.

Patterson, R. L., Dupre, L. W., Eberly, D. A., Jackson, G. M., O'Sullivan, M. J., Penner, L. A., & Kelly, C. D. *Overcoming deficits of aging: A behavioral approach*. New York: Plenum, 1982.

Pfeiffer, E. The psychosocial evaluation of the elderly patient. In E. W. Busse & D. G. Blazer (Eds.), *Handbook of geriatric psychiatry*. New York: Van Nostrand, 1980.

Pfeiffer, E., & Busse, E. W. Mental disorders in later life—Affective disorders; Paranoid, neurotic, and situational reactions. In E. Busse & E. Pfeiffer (Eds.), *Mental illness in later life*. Baltimore, Md.: Garamond/Pridemark Press, 1973.

Sherwood, S., & Moor, V. Mental health institutions and the elderly. In J. E. Birren & R. B. Sloan (Eds.), *Handbook of mental health and aging*. Englewood Cliffs, N.J.: Prentice-Hall, 1980.

Youkilis, H. D., & Bootzin, R. R. A psychophysiological perspective on the etiology and treatment of insomnia. In S. N. Haynes & L. A. Gannon (Eds.), *Psychosomatic disorders: A psychophysiological approach to etiology and treatment*. New York: Praeger Press, 1981.

Zarit, S. H. *Aging and mental disorders: Psychological approaches to assessment and treatment*. New York: Free Press, 1980.

Author Index

Subject Index

About the Editors and Contributors

THE EDITORS

Peter M. Lewinsohn, Ph.D., is a Professor of Psychology, co-director of the doctoral program in clinical/community psychology and Director of the Geropsychological Services Program at the University of Oregon in Eugene. He is well known for his work on the behavioral assessment and treatment of clinical depression. He has published over 100 articles and book chapters and is senior author of *Control Your Depression* (with R. Murphy, M. Youngren, and A. Zeiss, Englewood Cliffs, N.J.: Prentice-Hall, 1978) and of *The Coping with Depression Course: A Psychoeducational Intervention for Unipolar Depression* (with D. Antonuccio, J. Steinmetz, and L. Teri, Eugene, Oregon: Castalia Press, 1983).

Linda Teri, Ph.D., is a Research Associate/Clinical Instructor in the Department of Psychology and with the Geropsychological Services Program at the University of Oregon in Eugene. She received her doctorate in psychology from the University of Vermont in 1980. Since that time she has been actively engaged in teaching, conducting research, and clinical work and supervision in the areas of depression and geropsychology. She is the author of numerous professional papers and presentations and co-author of *The Coping with Depression Course: A Psychoeducational Approach to Unipolar Depression* (with P. Lewinsohn, D. Antonuccio, and J. Steinmetz, Eugene, Oregon: Castalia Press, 1983).

THE CONTRIBUTORS

Richard R. Bootzin, Ph.D., is Chairperson of, and a Professor in the Department of Psychology at Northwestern University in Evanston, Illinois. Dr. Bootzin is well known for his work in behavior therapy and insomnia.

David Eberly, M.S., is currently Associate Institute Director of the Florida Mental Health Institute. His special interests are the evaluation of mental-health service-delivery programs and training practitioners in innovative programs.

Mindy Engle-Friedman is a clinical graduate student in the Department of Psychology at Northwestern University in Evanston, Illinois. Her major area of interest is disorders across the age span.

Dolores Gallagher, Ph.D., is Education and Evaluation Coordinator of Geriatric Research, Education and Clinical Services at the V.A. Medical Center in Palo Alto, California. Dr. Gallagher is well known for her clinical and empirical work on depression in the elderly. She is currently working on a book with Larry Thompson in that area.

Lisa Hazelwood is a clinical graduate student in the Department of Psychology at Northwestern University in Evanston, Illinois. Her major area of interest is psychosomatic disorders in the elderly.

Boaz Kahana, Ph.D., is a Professor of Psychology at Oakland University in Rochester, Michigan. Dr. Kahana is the author of numerous papers on stress and relocation trauma.

Eva Kahana, Ph.D., is a Professor of Psychology at Wayne State University in Detroit, Michigan. Dr. Kahana is the author of a variety of papers on stress and relocation trauma.

Roger L. Patterson, Ph.D., is Director of the Gerontology Program at the Florida Mental Health Institute in Tampa, Florida. Dr. Patterson is the author of numerous publications in the area of behavioral therapy with the elderly and senior author of *Oncoming Deficits of Aging: A Behavioral Approach* (New York: Plenum, 1982).

Larry W. Thompson, Ph.D., is currently Director of the Gerontology Research Program at the V.A. Medical Center in Palo Alto, California. Dr. Thompson is well known for his work in cognitive deficits in aging and depression among the elderly. He is currently collaborating with Dolores Gallagher on a book on depression in the elderly.

Judy M. Zarit, Ph.D., is a geriatric mental-health specialist and psychologist at the Didi Hirsch Community Mental Health Center in Culver City, California. She has authored numerous articles and professional presentations on family intervention for dementia.

Steven H. Zarit, Ph.D., is an Associate Professor of Gerontology and Psychology at the Andrus Gerontology Center at the University of Southern California in Los Angeles. Dr. Zarit is well known for his work on assessment and treatment of dementia and is the author of *Mental Disorders among the Elderly* (New York: Free Press, 1980).

Pergamon General Psychology Series

Editors: Arnold P. Goldstein, Syracuse University
Leonard Krasner, SUNY at Stony Brook